TEACHING CONTENT AREA READING SKILLS

A Modular Preservice and Inservice Program

FOURTH EDITION

Harry W. Forgan
University of Miami

Charles T. Mangrum II
University of Miami

WITHDRAWN

Merrill, an imprint of
Macmillan Publishing Company
New York
Collier Macmillan Canada, Inc.
Toronto
Maxwell Macmillan International Publishing Group
New York   Oxford   Singapore   Sydney

Cover Photo: Paul Conklin

This book was set in Aster.

Administrative Editor: Jeff Johnston
Production Coordinator: Victoria M. Althoff
Art Coordinator: Vincent A. Smith
Cover Designer: Brian Deep
Photo Editor: Gail Meese

Photo Credits: pp. 1, 37, 87 by Lloyd Lemmerman/Merrill; pp. 69,
235 by Jean Greenwald/Merrill; p. 115 by Charles Quinlan; p. 147
by Merrill; p. 179 by Alan Cliburn; p. 209 by David Strickler.

Library of Congress Catalog Card Number: 88-62630
International Standard Book Number: 0-675-21072-0
Printed in the United States of America
3   4   5   6   7   8   9—92   91

To
Ruth Ann and Jane

Whose encouragement, help, and loyalty make every undertaking—and all of life—a joyous pursuit.

PREFACE

You may find this book different from textbooks you have used in college courses or inservice programs. It is not a research textbook, with summaries of knowledge organized by chapter and subsections. Although there is a definite need for the research textbook, there is also a need for an alternative text—the *applied textbook*. An applied textbook combines experience with information from research to supply the reader with a way of performing. This applied textbook helps content area teachers develop the basic competencies for helping students read the written materials that are used in subject areas.

We think the competencies that content area teachers need for helping students read materials are best developed through the use of a *modular* format such as the one in this book. A module is a self-instructional package designed to help the user accomplish certain objectives. An objective consists of those things you will be able to do, know, and/or feel after instruction that you may not have done, known, and/or felt before instruction. The nine modules in this book will help you enable your students to read the materials you use in your content area classes.

In this fourth edition, we have made changes to make this modular program more readable and useful to students. The changes were suggested by the many university and college professors and inservice directors who have used the textbook since it was first published. Despite our changes, we have maintained the basic theme and format of the original textbook. This fourth edition will help content area teachers acquire the competencies they need to effectively and efficiently help students read their textual materials.

We extend a special note of appreciation to Edward Fry for developing the Graph for Estimating Readability (extended form), to Alton Raygor for developing The Raygor Readability Estimate, and to Natividad Santos for developing the Classification Scheme for Reading Questions—all three of these devices should prove valuable to content area teachers. We appreciate the opportunity to share with our readers the devices and the suggestions for their effective use. The following reviewers provided valuable comments and suggestions: Omer Bonenberger, Cedarville College; Michael Jessup, Towson State University; Edwin Prettyman, Ball State University; and Robert White, University of New Mexico. We also acknowledge our present and past University of Miami students and inservice teachers who gave us many excellent suggestions for this edition. Their comments and suggestions keep us thinking about the practical aspects of reading instruction.

Finally, we continue to receive and appreciate the necessary encouragement and support of our wives, Ruth Ann and Jane, and our children, Jennifer, Jim, Mykel, and Mark as we proceed with our writing projects.

Harry Forgan
Charles Mangrum

CONTENTS

OVERVIEW

THE NINE RESPONSIBILITIES OF CONTENT AREA TEACHERS

Before you begin to complete the modules in this textbook you should become aware of your basic responsibilities as a teacher for helping students read content area materials. Read each of the following responsibilities to learn about the competencies you will be developing.

Responsibility 1. Selecting materials
Teachers must know how to select textual materials which are appropriate for their students in terms of content, textual aids, and readability. Teachers select textbooks for large groups of students when they serve on school system textbook selection committees. They select textbooks for small groups of students when they choose a textbook from the school book depository to use with their classes.

Responsibility 2. Matching materials to students
Today's teacher makes assignments from a variety of reading material to help students acquire the basic concepts in his or her content area courses. Many of these materials are obtained by students from the school library or media center. As a teacher you must know how to use an informal suitability survey so you can help students select materials that are appropriate for their reading levels.

Responsibility 3. Differentiating Reading Assignments
Effective teachers use a variety of print and nonprint materials to help students acquire the information and important concepts about their content area. Content area teachers need to know how to prepare reading assignments that are differentiated according to the students' achievement in processing printed material.

Responsibility 4. Teaching Specialized Vocabulary
Every content area has its own specialized vocabulary. Teachers are expected to help students expand their vocabularies as they grow in

subject area knowledge. To do so, you will need guidelines and activities for teaching the specialized vocabulary of your area.

Responsibility 5. Helping Students Comprehend Printed Text

Reading is an active process that requires comprehension. Students often need help in comprehending subject area materials. You must be able to help students develop comprehension strategies for reading the specialized reading materials in your content area.

Responsibility 6. Teaching Study Strategies

Different types of study strategies are appropriate for different content areas. Since content area teachers have themselves employed study strategies, they are the most qualified persons to help students develop appropriate strategies for their specific areas. You must teach your students the most appropriate study strategies for your content area.

Responsibility 7. Helping Students Pronounce Difficult Words

Students often encounter long and difficult words in content area materials. You are not expected to teach beginning word-recognition skills, but you should be able to help students develop a strategy for pronouncing multisyllable words that may at first appear unfamiliar to your students.

Responsibility 8. Motivating Reluctant Readers

Many students know how to read, but are reluctant to read. You should be able to use a strategy to increase motivation for reading assignments. Teachers can motivate students to read by providing purposes, projecting a positive attitude, providing students with feedback, and ensuring success.

Responsibility 9. Helping Problem Readers

Just because students are reluctant to read does not mean they are reluctant to learn. Some students are far behind in reading achievement and need assistance to read their assignments. Every content teacher is responsible for identifying and referring problem readers and for adapting instruction so problem readers can succeed. You are expected to help problem readers survive—and learn—in your classroom while they are overcoming their reading problems.

As you can see from the descriptions of these responsibilities, you are not asked to forget your content area and teach beginning reading.

Rather you are expected to assume the responsibilities of an effective teacher. All teachers must select appropriate materials, match the materials to the students, give students information and suggestions for reading, motivate students, and help students who are behind. Once you develop these competencies you will naturally provide more effective instruction.

THE ORGANIZATION OF THIS BOOK

The format of this book is different from most textbooks. Each unit is organized into a module. A module is like a chapter, but it differs in an important way. Modules have specified objectives which are followed by information and activities designed to develop competencies in the user. Chapters typically provide information but do not develop competencies.

In examining the modules you will notice that each includes the following:

1. Overview
This section provides an introduction to the module and explains why content area teachers need to acquire the competency developed by the module.

2. Enabling Elements
The major sections of each module are the enabling elements. Each enabling element restates the specific objective and provides information and activities to help you accomplish the specific objective. One of the activities in every enabling element suggests that you read a study guide. Study guides include the background information you need to accomplish the objectives. In addition to the background information, many of the study guides include practicum exercises to help you put your new skills to work. The study guides make the modules relatively self-contained, since you need not refer to other resources to accomplish the objectives.

3. Posttest
A *Posttest* is included for each of the nine modules. The posttest items are based on the objectives and are used to determine whether or not you have accomplished the objectives. Posttest items vary in format. Some of the items require you to list or describe, and others are simulation-type activities requiring you to apply your newly developed skills.

4. Posttest Answers

Answers are provided in each module, so you can check your responses as a method of self-evaluation. The results of your self-evaluation determine if you have accomplished the objectives. If so, you can go on to the next module. If not, you may want to return through some of the enabling elements, as directed.

5. References

In some cases you may want more information or may wish to consult other sources for different ideas. The references have been selected because we think they are the most helpful and readily available to content area teachers.

INSTRUCTIONS FOR COMPLETING THE NINE MODULES

Your instructor may have specific suggestions for completing the modules in this book. If not, we suggest beginning with Module 1. The following instructions explain the recommended procedure for completing each module. After completing Module 1, complete the remaining modules in any sequence, according to your needs as a content area teacher.

Instructions

1. Read the Overview to determine if the module meets your specific professional needs. If the module meets your specific needs, continue reading.
2. Complete the Enabling Elements in sequence. Use the study guides and activities as appropriate.
3. When you have completed all activities for your selected objectives, take the Posttest to determine if you have met the evaluative criteria.
4. If performance was not satisfactory, return to previous Enabling Activities as needed, or consult your instructor. Retake the appropriate Posttest items.
5. When the module has been completed, you may wish to examine the References for additional information or study.

We hope you enjoy using the modules to develop the nine responsibilities of content area teachers.

MODULE
ONE

Selecting Textual Materials

CHAPTER OUTLINE

Overview
  Rationale
  Objectives
Enabling Element 1
  Factors to Consider When Selecting Textual Materials
Enabling Element 2
  How to Use Graphs for Estimating Readability
Enabling Element 3
  How to Use the SMOG Grading System to Estimate
  Readability
Posttest
Posttest Answers
References

OVERVIEW

Rationale

As a teacher you will need to select materials for your students to read in conjunction with course assignments. These materials may include textbooks, newspapers, magazines, and pamphlets. When selecting textual materials, you should be concerned about (1) the content, (2) aids available for students, and (3) the readability. You want to be sure the content is appropriate for the goals of instruction in light of the students' backgrounds. Textual aids such as side headings and illustrations may make the materials easier for students to use. Finally, you want to obtain materials that are appropriate in terms of readability, or the difficulty of materials to be read. This module will help you provide appropriate reading materials for your students.

OBJECTIVES

General Objective

You will select textual materials that are appropriate for students in your content area.

Specific Objectives

1. You will list and describe the three major factors you should consider when selecting textual materials.
2. You will use readability graphs to estimate the readability levels of textual materials.
3. You will use the SMOG grading system to estimate readability.

ENABLING ELEMENT 1
Factors to Consider When Selecting Textual Materials

Specific Objective 1

You will list and describe the three major factors you should consider when selecting textual materials.

Enabling Activities

1. Read Study Guide 1, "Selecting Textual Materials." Identify the factors that you should consider when selecting textual materials.
2. Make a list of the criteria you consider to be important when selecting textual materials for students.
3. Use the checklist to select books, magazines, or other textual materials.
4. Reflect upon your own reading and ask, "What makes some materials easier to use?"
5. Ask your students, "Why are some materials easier to read than others?" Have you identified other factors that may make some material more difficult than others?
6. Why should you learn about the factors that influence readability? How can this information help you as a teacher? Discuss these questions with your colleagues.

STUDY GUIDE 1
Selecting Textual Materials

If you were going to buy a car today, you would not go to the nearest car dealer and say, "I want to buy a car. Anything that is about ten thousand dollars will be fine." There are certain factors you want to consider. Does the car fit your needs? Do you like its looks? How does it ride? You should similarly be concerned when you are selecting textual materials for your students.

The first factor you want to consider is the *content*. As you consider this factor, several questions may come to your mind.

1. "Does the content match my instructional goals?"
2. "Do my students have the background experience necessary to understand the content?"
3. "Are there a sufficient number of examples to help my students learn the major concepts?"
4. "Is the content sequenced appropriately?"

These are just a few of the questions you may have regarding the content of the textual material. Can you think of a few more? Write them here.

5. _____
6. _____
7. _____

The second factor to consider is the number and types of learning *aids* available in the textual material. For example, well-designed textual materials frequently contain such useful aids as: chapter outlines and overviews, illustrations, side headings stated as questions to provide the reader with purposes for reading, time lines to show temporal relationships, highlighted key concepts, in-text definitions of technical terms, as well as the standard aids such as a table of contents, index, and glossary of terms.

The number of learning aids available in the textual materials will depend somewhat on the type of printed material you are using. A valuable pamphlet for use in your content area may have only side headings, illustrations, and boldface print to highlight key words and concepts. A textbook should have these plus a table of contents, index, summaries, activities, a glossary, and other learning aids. Keep in mind that the number of learning aids provided is dependent upon the nature of the printed material. List the learning aids you believe should be found in textual material appropriate for your students.

1. _____
2. _____
3. _____
4. _____
5. _____

The third factor to consider when selecting textual material is *readability*. Readability is the objective measure of the difficulty of a book or article. Readability levels are generally reported in terms of grade level. Therefore, one might find a textbook written at the ninth-grade level, fourth-grade level, and so forth. The readability of texts and supplementary reading materials should be of great concern to teachers, because students are expected to gather information and develop new skills through reading. Teachers thus need to know what factors influence readability and how to determine readability.

Even though readability formulas are useful, there are some limitations. First, most readability formulas do not take into consideration the concepts presented in the materials. Some materials that are within the students' reading level according to the readability formulas may be more difficult to read than other materials because they deal with concepts that are beyond the students' understanding.

Another limitation of readability formulas is that they do not consider the use of slang, satire, multiple meanings, or the interest of the reader. Likewise, readability formulas cannot be used with certain types of material such as poetry in which the sentence structure is different. These limitations must be kept in mind when applying the formulas to reading materials.

USING A CHECKLIST

A single criterion such as readability level should not be used to select textual materials. When selecting textual material you should evaluate the content, learning aids, and readability. The following checklist contains some of the important criteria you should use. You should add others to personalize the checklist for your specific needs.

Checklist for Selecting Textual Material

Directions: Read each question under the headings Content, Aids for Learning, and Readability. Examine the textual material and write an answer for each question.

Content

1. Does the content match the course objectives? _____
2. Is the information up-to-date? _____
3. Do my students have sufficient background to understand the ideas introduced in the text? _____
4. Are new concepts introduced one at a time and are sufficient examples provided to help my students understand the concepts? _____
5. Are abstract concepts carefully and fully explained? _____
6. Are the sentences and paragraphs organized and written in a style so the content is clear? _____
7. Does the author help students apply their newly acquired information? _____
8. Does the author highlight information that may be particularly appealing to my students? _____

Aids for Learning

1. Is there a preface or similar section that overviews the textual material? _____
2. Do the table of contents and index enable students to locate information quickly? _____
3. Do the headings and subheadings help students establish purposes for reading? _____
4. Does the glossary obtain clearly stated definitions for the specialized vocabulary words presented in the textual material? _____
5. Are the appropriate type and number of illustrations provided? _____

6. Are graphs, tables, and charts clearly explained? _____
7. Are boldface print, italics, and/or other aids used to highlight important information? _____
8. Are the activities suggested by the authors appropriate and appealing to students? _____
9. Are questions provided for guiding students' reading and thinking? _____
10. Are summaries provided to help students synthesize the information they are learning? _____

Readability

1. Is the reading level appropriate? _____
2. Is the vocabulary appropriate? _____
3. Is the size of the print appropriate? _____
4. Do the authors use an organizational structure that is easy for students to follow and understand? _____
5. Is the writing style appealing? _____
6. Is the sentence and/or paragraph structure unnecessarily complex? _____
7. Does the material look as if it would be interesting to read? _____

As you evaluate textual materials for use in your class, think of the analogy to purchasing a car. You do not want to buy just any car. You want to buy a car that meets your needs. Your needs are turned into criteria you use to select and eventually buy the best car for you. It is the same when selecting textual materials for your students. You must first establish the criteria you will use for selecting the textual material. We believe you should use at least three criteria: content, aids for learning, and readability. Perhaps you will remember these three major criteria by remembering the mnemonic device—CAR—which will help you recall content, learning aids, and readability when selecting textual materials.

Like many teachers you will find it easy to evaluate the content and learning aids in textual materials. However, you may not have the competencies necessary to determine readability. If you need to learn how to use procedures for determining readability, go on to Enabling Element 2 where you will learn how to use graphs to estimate the readability of printed materials. If you know how to use the Fry graph and/or Raygor graph to estimate readability, go directly to Enabling Element 3 where a different procedure for determining readability is explained.

ENABLING ELEMENT 2
How to Use Graphs for Estimating Readability

Specific Objective 2

You will use readability graphs to estimate the readability levels of textual materials.

Enabling Activities

1. Read Study Guide 2, "How to Use Graphs for Estimating Readability," and familiarize yourself with the procedures for estimating readability using the Fry and Raygor graphs.
2. Most readability formulas are for the English language; however, applications are growing. Locate the Klare article, "Assessing Readability," in the References for this module if you want to learn about formulas available to measure materials in any of these foreign languages: French, Dutch, Spanish, Hebrew, German, Hindi, Russian, and Chinese.
3. Do you need more practice in counting syllables? If so, read these words aloud and count the number of sound units you hear. Check your responses with those listed on page 23 of this Enabling Element.

a. very	i. matches
b. telephone	j. Washington
c. ¢	k. seventeenth
d. environment	l. 1961
e. drenched	m. any
f. basketball	n. $4.98
g. hopeful	o. let's
h. ERA	

4. When counting the number of sentences in a 100-word passage, the hundredth word is often not the last word in a sentence. The proportion of the last sentence must be determined if this is the case. What proportion (in a decimal) is each of the following sentences?

   a. The last sentence contains 8 words, 4 of which are in the 100-word count.
   b. The last sentence is 15 words, and 4 of the words are part of the 100-word selection.
   c. The last sentence includes 32 words, and 9 of these are in your 100-word passage.

   Check your responses with those listed on page 23 of this Enabling Element.

5. Let us suppose you find that the readability estimate of a selection is tenth grade. What is the range of the true estimate of readability? Check your response with the answer on page 24.

6. According to Fry's graph, what are the readability levels of selections with the following counts?
   a. 128 syllables in five sentences
   b. 156 syllables in seven sentences
   c. 160 syllables in ten sentences
   Check your responses with the answers on page 24 of this Enabling Element.
7. Do the Practicum Exercises to see if you can follow the directions for using Fry's graph.

STUDY GUIDE 2
How To Use Graphs For Estimating Readability

Fry's Graph

Edward Fry (1968, 1977) developed a quick, easy, usable technique for estimating the reading difficulty of written material for grade one through graduate school.

Fry's Graph for Estimating Readability is an outgrowth of the need for a simple and efficient technique for estimating reading difficulty. Fry's graph uses the traditional factors of sentence length and word difficulty to determine readability; however, word difficulty is estimated by counting syllables rather than by the cumbersome and lengthy technique of comparing every word to a list of words to determine its difficulty. Fry (1969, pp. 534–38) reports that the Fry Graph for Estimating Readability correlates 0.90 with the Spache Readability Formula and 0.94 with the Dale-Chall Readability Formula. These high correlations indicate considerable consistency between formulas and support the wide acceptance and use of Fry's graph.

The graph requires two factors be used to estimate reading level: average sentence length and total number of syllables. (See Figure 1.1.) The top heading in Fry's graph is "average number of syllables per 100 words." The numerals at the top of the graph, then, refer to the number of syllables contained in a 100-word selection. A 100-word selection with short words may contain as few as 108 syllables; thus, each word is only about one syllable long. A 100-word selection with long words may contain more than 182 syllables. If a 100-word selection contains 182 syllables, many of the words are more than one syllable long.

Now look at the left side of the graph and notice the statement, "average number of sentences per 100 words." As you examine the left side of the graph, you will notice that the number of sentences ranges from two (long sentences) to twenty-five sentences (short sentences). If there are only two sentences in 100 words, each sentence is about 50 words long. Likewise, if there are twenty-five sentences in 100 words, each sentence is about 4 words long. If a 100-word selection has fewer than two sentences or more than twenty-five sentences, Fry's graph cannot be used.

Average number of syllables per 100 words

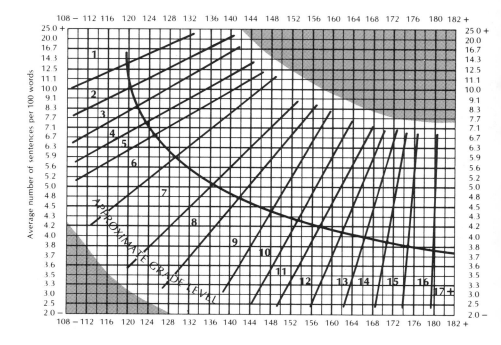

Expanded Directions for Working Readability Graph

1. Randomly select three (3) sample passages and count out exactly 100 words each, beginning with the beginning of a sentence. Do count proper nouns, initializations, and numerals.
2. Count the number of sentences in the hundred words, estimating length of the fraction of the last sentence to the nearest one-tenth.
3. Count the total number of syllables in the 100-word passage. If you don't have a hand counter available, an easy way is to simply put a mark above every syllable over one in each word: then when you get to the end of the passage, count the number of marks and add 100. Small calculators can also be used as counters by pushing numeral 1, then push the + sign for each word or syllable when counting.
4. Enter graph with *average* sentence length and *average* number of syllables: plot dot where the two lines intersect. Area where dot is plotted will give you the approximate grade level.
5. If a great deal of variability is found in syllable count or sentence count, putting more samples into the average is desirable.
6. A word is defined as a group of symbols with a space on either side: thus, *Joe, IRA, 1945,* and & are each one word.
7. A syllable is defined as a phonetic syllable. Generally, there are as many syllables as vowel sounds. For example, *stopped* is one syllable and *wanted* is two syllables. When counting syllables for numerals and initializations, count one syllable for each symbol. For example, *1945* is four syllables, *IRA* is three syllables, and & is one syllable.

Figure 1–1
Graph for Estimating Readability—Extended
Note: This "extended graph" does not outmode or render the earlier (1968) version inoperative or inaccurate; it is an extension.
(*Source:* By Edward Fry. Reprinted from *The Journal of Reading,* December 1977. Reproduction permitted. No copyright.)

As you look at the center of the graph, you will notice that grade-level bands range from first grade to seventeenth grade. Thirteenth grade is the freshman year of college; the fourteenth year is the sophomore; the fifteenth is the junior year of college; and the sixteenth is the senior year of college. The seventeenth + grade level indicates the readability would be at a level appropriate for a graduate student.

You will notice that some areas of the graph are gray. Grade-level scores in these areas are invalid because the lines converge or diverge. Readability estimates are most valid when they are near the center line on Fry's graph.

Now that you have carefully examined Fry's Graph for Estimating Readability, you are ready for directions on how to use the graph. Refer to the graph as you read these directions.

Directions for Using Fry's Graph

Fry (1977, pp. 242–52) gives the following directions (which we have partially adapted) for obtaining reading level estimates:

1. *Select a representative passage from written material for which you wish to know the reading level.* Since you use only a sample from the printed material for which you want to determine readability, it is essential that the material you select is representative of the entire article or book. After you find a representative selection, count 100 words in the sample, beginning with the first word of a sentence. Do not count the words in titles or headings. Be sure to count all the words, including initials and numerals. A word is defined as a group of symbols with a space on each side of the group; thus, *Charles, USA, 1980,* and + are each one word.

2. *Count the number of sentences in the 100-word passage.* This procedure is rather simple since you just go through the passage and look for sentences ending with a period, question mark, or exclamation mark. If the final sentence does not stop at the end of the 100 words, determine what proportion of this last sentence you are including in the 100-word count. Estimate the last sentence to the nearest tenth. For example, if the final sentence in a 100-word count has 16 words, and 8 of these are in the 100-word count, the final sentence would be counted as 0.5 sentences. (For additional practice, see Enabling Activity 4.)

3. *Count the number of syllables in the 100-word passage.* You do not need to decide where syllable breaks occur in each of the words. Rather, you simply read the selection aloud and put a slash above each syllable you hear in the words. For example, the word *though* has one syllable, *counted* has two syllables, *determine* has three syllables, and *appropriate* has four syllables. For our purposes, a *syllable* is a phonetic syllable that you actually hear. A word usually has as many syllables as there are vowel sounds. When counting

syllables for numerals and initializations, count one syllable for each symbol. For example, *1980* would be counted as four syllables, *USA* has three syllables, and + has one syllable. (For additional practice, see Enabling Activity 3.)

4. *Refer to Fry's graph.* Notice the grid of intersecting lines. The vertical lines represent the average number of syllables per 100 words. The horizontal lines represent the average number of sentences per 100 words. Where any vertical and horizontal lines intersect,approximate grade levels are indicated. Record the level of your selection at this time. According to Fry, most of the intersecting points will fall near the curved line. If the intersecting point falls in the gray area, conclude that the results are invalid, select another 100-word sample, and refigure.

5. *Remember that these are estimates of readability.* Fry (1977) states that these estimates are probably within plus or minus one year of the true estimates of readability.

Illustrations of Each Step

Suppose you wish to use the following selection, "Teachers Don't Want to Be Labeled," with your students to help them realize that each person has strengths and weaknesses rather than being totally gifted, average, or slow. You want to know at what reading level it is written to determine whether you can require your students to read it.

Step 1: Select a Representative 100-Word Selection.

Usually, the first 100 words in an article are useful if they are fairly representative of the selection. You count every word, including small words such as *a* and *the,* as well as proper nouns, numerals, and initializations. If you use the first 100 words of "Teachers Don't Want to Be Labeled," you will find that the one-hundredth word is *number,* which is in the first sentence of the second paragraph. Remember not to count titles in your word count.

Step 2: Count the Number of Sentences.

The second step in using Fry's graph is to count the number of sentences in the 100-word selection. The one-hundredth word does not always end the selection; therefore, it is necessary to determine the proportion of the last sentence that falls within the word count. Estimate to the nearest one-tenth the fraction of the last sentence that is within the 100-word count.

Our 100-word sample has three complete sentences and part of another sentence. The fourth sentence contains a total of 31 words, of which 24 are in our 100-word count. The fraction of the fourth sentence to be used is $24/31$. The fraction $24/31$ can be changed to a decimal by dividing 31 into 24. The result is the decimal 0.77, which we round to the nearest tenth—0.8. Thus, our sentence count for the 100-word selection is 3.8. You need not do the division when you can estimate the fraction to the nearest tenth.

*Teachers Don't Want to Be Labeled**
(HARRY W. FORGAN)

When teaching a course on tests and measurements at Kent State University recently, I decided to administer an adult group intelligence test to the class. I wanted the students to "feel" what it was like to take such a test and realize what items we use to measure intelligence. I also thought they might be more aware of the short time it takes to obtain a number which is regarded as very important by many educators.

The students were told not to write their names on the test papers, but rather to use a code such as their house number, physical measurements, or any less obvious symbol. I explained that I really didn't have faith in IQ scores; therefore, I didn't want to know their IQs.

The administration of the test required only 50 minutes. The students seemed to enjoy taking it and chuckled at some of the tasks they were expected to perform. I had to laugh myself when I saw some of them looking at their hands and feet when responding to items concerning right and left.

Upon scoring the test I found that the lowest IQ was 87 and the highest 143. The mean IQ for the 48 students was 117. I was not astonished by the 87, even though all of the students had successfully completed the general education courses and student teaching at Kent State and were ready to graduate by the end of the term. After all, IQ tests have many limitations.

Then I got an idea. I decided to prepare a report for each student, writing his code on the outside and "IQ 87" on the inside of each. I folded and stapled each paper—after all, an IQ is confidential information!

At the next class period I arranged all of the folded papers on a table at the front of the room. I wrote the range and the average IQ on the chalkboard. Many students snickered at the thought of somebody getting an 87. The students were eager and afraid as I began by explaining the procedures for picking up their papers. I made a point of telling them not to tell others their IQ score, because this would make the other person feel as if he too had to divulge his "total endowment." The students were then directed to come up to the table, row by row, to find their coded paper. I stood sheepishly—ready to laugh out loud as I watched the students carefully open their papers and see "IQ 87." Many opened their mouths with astonishment and then smiled at their friends to indicate they were extremely happy with their scores.

There was dead silence when I began to discuss the implications of the IQ scores. I explained that in some states a person who scores below 90 on an IQ test is classified as a slow learner. The fact that group intelligence tests should not be used to make such a classification was stressed. I also emphasized the fact that *someone* in this class could have been classified as a slow learner and placed in a special class on the basis of this test.

I told how many guidance counselors would discourage a child with an 87 IQ from attending college. Again I emphasized the fact that one person in this room was ready to graduate from college having passed several courses in history, biology, English, and many other areas.

I then went on to explain that the majority of elementary and secondary school teachers believe in ability grouping. This is usually done on the basis of intelligence tests, so I explained that I would like to try ability grouping with this class—again to see "how it feels." Some students objected right away, saying that "I did not want to know their IQ scores." I calmed them by saying it would be a worthwhile learning experience and assured them that I really didn't believe in IQ scores.

I told the students not to move at this time, but I would like all of those with an IQ below 90 to come to the front so they could sit nearer to me for individual help. I told the students who had an average IQ (between 90–109) to go to the back of the room and then take the seats in the middle of the class. The students with the above average IQ were asked to go to the side of the room and take the seats in the back because they really didn't need much extra help.

"O.K., all those who got an IQ below 90 can come to the front of the room." The students looked around to find those who scored below 90. I said that I knew there was an 87 and maybe a couple of 89's. Again, there was dead silence.

"O.K., all those students whose IQ is between 90–109 go to the back of the room." Immediately, to my amazement, 8 or 10 students picked up their books and headed for the back of the room. Before they could get there I said, "Wait a minute! Sit down! I don't want to embarrass you, but you would lie and cheat—the same way we make our students lie and cheat—because you don't want to be classified as 'slow.' I wrote 'IQ 87' on every paper!"

The class erupted. It was in an uproar for about five minutes. Some of the students cried. Some indicated that they needed to use the restroom. All agreed it was a horrifying and yet valuable experience.

I asked them to do one thing for me: Please don't label kids because we are all "gifted," "average," and "slow," depending on the task at hand. They promised.[1]

---

*Reprinted with permission from the *Phi Delta Kappan*, vol. LV. no. 1. September 1973, p. 98.

Step 3: Count the Number of Syllables.

We illustrate two procedures; choose the one that is easier for you.

Procedure A.   Read the selection subvocally and make a slash to indicate the number of syllables in each word. Remember that it is not necessary to divide the words into syllables. Simply note how many syllables you hear in each word. After making slashes for each syllable, count the number of syllables in each line, and record this number at the right. Add the number of syllables in each line to determine the total number of syllables in the 100-word selection, as you see here:

Syllables

When teaching a course on tests and measurements at Kent __13__
State University recently, I decided to administer an adult group __22__
intelligence test to the class. I wanted the students to "feel" what __17__
it was like to take such a test and realize what items we use to __18__
measure intelligence. I also thought they might be more aware of __17__
the short time it takes to obtain a number which is regarded as very __19__
important by many educators. __10__
 The students were told not to write their names on the test __13__
papers, but rather to use a code such as their house number, |100 words| physical __15__
measurements, or any less obvious symbol.

Total __144__

Procedure B. Assume each word in the 100-word selection has one syllable (that's true!) and simply make slashes for or count the second, third, fourth syllable in each word. Remember to add your subtotal to 100 to determine the total number of syllables in the 100-word selection. An illustration follows:

Syllables

When teaching a course on tests and measurements at Kent __3__
State University recently, I decided to administer an adult group __12__
intelligence test to the class. I wanted the students to "feel" what __5__
it was like to take such a test and realize what items we use to __3__
measure intelligence. I also thought they might be more aware of __6__
the short time it takes to obtain a number which is regarded as very __5__
important by many educators. __6__
 The students were told not to write their names on the test __1__
papers, but rather to use a code such as their house number, |100 words| physical __3__
measurements, or any less obvious symbol.

Subtotal __44__
+ 100 = __144__

Step 4: Refer to Fry's Graph.
Locate the number at the top of Fry's graph that indicates the number of syllables. For our sample, look at 144. Place your right index finger on the vertical line under 144. Locate the number at the left side of Fry's graph that indicates the number of sentences. Our selection has 3.8 sentences, so place your left index finger on 3.8. Move both fingers along the appropriate lines until they meet. Notice the grade-level band within which the two lines intersect. For this selection, the reading level estimate is between ninth and tenth grade. Remember that lines intersecting in the gray areas always reveal invalid scores.

Step 5: Remember, this is an estimate!
Because the estimate for readability using Fry's graph is within one
year of the true estimate, our sample has a true range of ninth or tenth
grade, since it is right in the middle. If the estimate were eighth grade,
the true range would be seventh, eighth, or ninth.

PRACTICUM EXERCISE 1

You learn by doing! Now that you know how to use Fry's Graph for
Estimating Readability, try it on a passage. The following selection
contains exactly 100 words, so the first step has been done for you.
Second, count the number of sentences in the 100 words. Third, count
the number of syllables in the 100 words. Next, refer to Fry's graph to
determine the readability. Finally, consider the estimates you obtain to
be within plus or minus one year of the true estimate of readability. Do
this Practicum Exercise, then compare your results with ours at the end
of this Enabling Element.

Selection for Practicum Exercise 1

Using a Card Catalog

                                                                Syllables

    If you wish to see if the library has a book you want and   _____
where to find it, you will use the card catalog. The card catalog is a   _____
cabinet with small drawers containing alphabetically arranged cards.   _____
Each card tells the title of the book and its classification number.   _____
    To find a book, copy the call number on a slip of paper. The   _____
same call number you copy will be printed on the spine of the   _____
book near the bottom. You will have to find the call number on the   _____
stack of shelves which will lead you to your book. (100 words)   _____
                                                            Total   _____

1. Number of Sentences   _____
2. Number of Syllables   _____
3. Estimate of Readability_____

PRACTICUM EXERCISE 2

The second exercise to help you become skillful in using Fry's graph is
"The Conductor." This article was adapted from a music book and contains more than 100 words. Remember, your first step is always to count
out 100 words. Follow the five steps for using Fry's graph, then check
your answers with the answers for Practicum Exercise 2 at the end of
this Enabling Element.

Selection for Practicum Exercise 2

The Conductor

Syllables

The orchestra is on stage, the house lights have been dimmed, _____
and the audience waits with great anticipation. Soon a person _____
emerges from the wings, walks to the middle of the stage in front _____
of the orchestra and bows to acknowledge the applause of the _____
audience. This person is a conductor who is about to lead the _____
orchestra in an exciting concert of symphonic music. _____
   An orchestra did not need a conductor until it began to in- _____
crease in size. Beginning in the early nineteenth century, during _____
Beethoven's time, the orchestra increased to such a size that a _____
conductor was needed. This was the beginning of the art of con- _____
ducting as it is known and practiced today. _____

Total _____

1. Number of Sentences _____
2. Number of Syllables _____
3. Estimate of Readability _____

PRACTICUM EXERCISE 3

The final Practicum Exercise, entitled "Fry's Graph," includes numerals and symbols as well as words. It contains more than 100 words, so make sure to begin by counting exactly 100 words. Again, remember to count each date as a word and symbols such as + as separate words. After you complete this Practicum Exercise 3, go to the end of this Enabling Element to check your responses with ours.

Selection for Practicum Exercise 3

Fry's Graph

Syllables

The purpose of this selection is to provide you with practice in _____
using Fry's Graph for Estimating Readability. The first edition of _____
Fry's graph came out in 1968, and Fry extended his graph in 1977. _____
The extended graph continues through the seventeenth + grade _____
level. This extended graph was published in an IRA publication enti- _____
tled *Journal of Reading* in December 1977. _____
   Because Fry did not obtain a copyright for his graph, reproduc- _____
tion is permitted. Personally, we feel that Fry has made a worth- _____
while contribution to the field of reading, and we thank him for it. _____
   We believe you will find Fry's graph easy to use and, after _____
practice, will be able to determine readability levels of printed mate- _____

rials within a few minutes. This new competency will enable you to _____
select materials that are appropriate for the ranges of reading levels _____
found among your students. _____

Total _____

1. Number of Sentences _____
2. Number of Syllables _____
3. Estimate of Readability _____

Using Fry's Graph with Textbooks

To determine the readability level of a textbook, you will need to select a minimum of three 100-word passages. One selection should be from the beginning of the book, one from the middle, and one from the last third of the book. Be sure to choose self-contained selections that do not refer to charts or illustrations.

Follow the directions to determine the number of syllables and sentences in each selection. After doing so, find the *average* number of syllables and sentences by adding the three passages together and dividing by three; for example:

100-Word Passages	Syllables	Sentences
First 100 Words	124	6.6
Second 100 Words	141	5.5
Third 100 Words	158	6.8
Totals	423	18.9
Averages	141	6.3

Plot on the graph the average number of sentences and syllables to estimate readability. (The average readability in this example is seventh grade.)

PRACTICUM EXERCISE 4

Determine the average readability of the following three passages, randomly selected from the beginning, middle, and end of a hypothetical basic health book.

1. Count 100 words in each representative passage. Always start counting at the beginning of a sentence and *do* count the proper nouns, numerals, and initializations.
2. Count the number of syllables in each passage.
3. Count the number of sentences in each passage.
4. Determine the reading level of each passage.
5. Determine the average reading level of the health textbook by find-

ing the average number of syllables and sentences in the three selections, then using these averages as you refer to Fry's graph.
6. Check your answers with the answers on page 25 of this Study Guide.

Rabies

Syllables

Since bites by cats, dogs, or any wild animal always present   _____
the danger of infection with rabies, a biting animal should never be   _____
killed unless unavoidable as a matter of safety. It should be caught   _____
and held for observation for at least fifteen days, in order to deter-   _____
mine whether it develops rabies.   _____

If it is necessary to kill the animal at the time of the biting, the   _____
carcass should be sent to the state public health laboratory for an   _____
examination of its brain. If the laboratory finds the animal was rabid,   _____
it is essential that treatment be initiated at once.   _____

Total   _____

Headache

Syllables

The term *headache* is such a part of our everyday vocabulary   _____
that it has become almost synonymous with any unpleasant situa-   _____
tion or problem. But in a medical sense the term quite literally   _____
means a head pain or an aching head and is a symptom rather than   _____
itself an actual disease condition.   _____

Hence, headache can suggest the possibility of a great many   _____
underlying conditions. Perhaps one of the better known types is the   _____
throbbing, devastating headache that sometimes accompanies a   _____
hangover. This differs from the type known as tension headache,   _____
associated with figuring out one's income tax, since they arise from   _____
different causes.   _____

Total   _____

Heatstroke

Syllables

The most important feature of heatstroke, which is some-   _____
times also referred to as sunstroke, is the extremely high body   _____
temperature that accompanies it. It is a far more serious condition   _____
than heat exhaustion.   _____

Heatstroke occurs more often in males than in females and is   _____
more common in elderly people and in those addicted to alcohol.   _____
Physical exertion is a definite contributing factor; and an attack is   _____
much more likely to occur when the humidity is high than when it is   _____
low, even at the same temperature.   _____

The underlying cause of heatstroke is intimately connected   _____
with a cessation of sweating, accounting for the excessive rise in   _____
body temperature.   _____

Total   _____

	Number of Sentences	Number of Syllables	Reading Level	True Estimate Range
"Rabies"				
"Headache"				
"Heatstroke"	_____	_____	_____	_____
Sums	_____	_____	_____	_____
Averages	_____	_____	_____	_____
	_____	_____	_____	_____

The answers are at the end of Enabling Element 2. If your answers are correct, continue reading. If not, repeat steps 1 through 6 and determine why not. Your syllable count may vary by a few syllables because of dialect differences.

PRACTICUM EXERCISE 5

Now try a real-life exercise. Randomly select at least three 100-word passages from a textbook in your teaching area. Determine the average grade level reading ability necessary for reading this material. A chart may be helpful.

	Number of Sentences	Number of Syllables	Reading Level	True Estimate Range
First 100-word Passage	_____	_____	_____	_____
Second 100-Word Passage	_____	_____	_____	_____
Third 100-Word Passage	_____	_____	_____	_____
Sums	_____	_____		
Averages	_____	_____	_____	_____

Here are some follow-up questions you may want to ask yourself. Does the readability estimate match the reading levels of my students? If yes, then you have chosen textual material suitable for your students. If no, you may want to consider changing textual material. Is the readability range among passages less than two years for grades seven through nine and three years for grades ten through twelve? If yes, the range of reading levels should not overtax your students' reading abilities. If not, many passages may frustrate your students, and it may be advisable to consider changing the textual material.

A word of caution: sometimes a book shows great variability either in sentence length or syllable count for all passages. If this is the case, randomly select additional sample passages; average the number of syllables and sentences, and plot as before. If the same variability occurs, conclude that the book has uneven readability and consider changing texts. This type of material is the most frustrating for students.

Applying the Concept of Fry's Graph for Estimating Readability

As a content area teacher, you probably use many printed materials to help students accomplish the objectives of your course. We realize there is not enough time in the day to determine the readability of every single newspaper article, magazine article, pamphlet, or other written material you want to use.

But after you have completed this module on using Fry's Graph for Estimating Readability, you will have a better concept of readability, to apply informally when you select printed materials. In other words, you will be aware that sentence length and word length make the biggest difference in readability levels. When you consider using an article with your students, you can simply glance at sentence length and word length to get a feel for the level of difficulty of the material. If the sentences in the passages are extremely long and have many difficult words, you know the readability level may be beyond many of your students. Now that you have this competency, you can apply it informally when selecting reading materials for your students.

Fry recently published the computerized Fry's Readability Program (Jamestown Publishers, P.O. Box 6743, Providence, RI 02940) to calculate reading levels of materials. To use this computer program, simply type your selections on the computer. The video screen of the computer displays syllable and sentence count as you keyboard each 100-word entry. Of course you will want at least three 100-word selections to determine the readability of a book; however, the computer program can accommodate and average up to 100 passages from a single source. With this computer program, school office personnel can determine the readability of the written materials you are thinking of using.

Competency in using Fry's graph will be most useful when you participate in textbook selection, or when you select articles to prepare and duplicate for your students. Otherwise, you will apply the concept of readability informally as you peruse the reading assignments you are asking students to complete.

Raygor's Graph

Alton L. Raygor developed a graph for estimating readability that is similar to the Fry graph. The major difference in the techniques is that word difficulty is estimated by counting long words (words of six or more letters), rather than by counting syllables. Raygor's graph also takes sentence length into consideration. Thus, Raygor's graph is also based on the two major factors that influence readability: sentence length and word difficulty.

According to our experience in working with content area teachers, if you were unable to develop proficiency in using Fry's graph, chances are you had difficulty counting syllables. If you did have difficulty counting syllables, you will probably prefer using the Raygor graph. Rather than counting syllables to determine word difficulty, you simply circle and count the words in the 100-word passage that have six or more letters. The other procedures for determining readability are the same, except you do not count numerals when using Raygor's graph.

If you look at Raygor's graph in Figure 1–2, you will notice many similarities between the Fry and Raygor graphs. First, the number of sentences is indicated on the left side of the graph, as on the Fry graph.

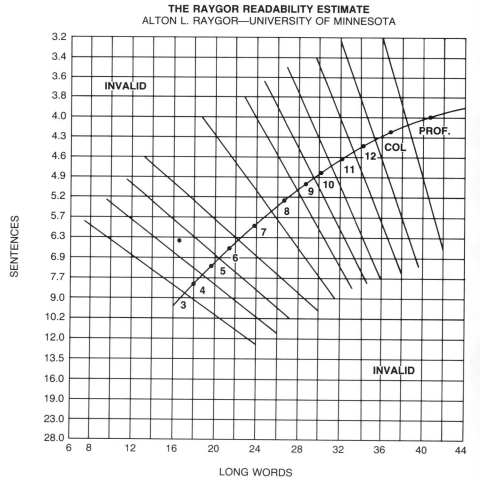

THE RAYGOR READABILITY ESTIMATE
ALTON L. RAYGOR—UNIVERSITY OF MINNESOTA

Figure 1–2
The Raygor Readability Estimate

The major difference is that the longer sentences (3.2 sentences in 100 words) are indicated at the top of the graph and the shorter sentences (28 sentences in 100 words) are indicated at the bottom of the graph. Now look at the bottom of the graph, where the number of long (hard) words is indicated. Notice that the number of long words ranges from 6 to 44. As you look at the grade-level bands in the center of the graph, you will notice that the Raygor graph can be used to estimate the readability of materials from third grade through professional or graduate-school level.

These are the directions for using the Raygor graph:

1. Count out three 100-word passages at the beginning, middle, and end of a book. Be sure to include proper nouns in your word count, but do not count numerals.
2. Count the number of sentences in each passage, estimating to the nearest tenth.
3. Circle and count the words having six or more letters. Words having six or more letters are defined as *long* (hard) *words.*
4. Average the sentence length and the number of long (hard) words over the three samples, and plot the average on the graph.

The directions for using the Raygor graph are exactly the same as for the Fry graph, except that (1) you skip the numerals when you count the 100-word passages, and (2) rather than counting syllables, you determine word difficulty by circling and counting words of six or more letters.

PRACTICUM EXERCISE 6

You can use the Raygor graph on the following selection, "A Positive Use of Fire." Follow these directions:

1. Count the first 100 words in the selection (skip numerals).
2. Count the number of sentences to the nearest tenth.
3. Circle and count those words that have six or more letters.
4. On Raygor's graph, plot a line across from the number of sentences and a line up from the number of hard or difficult words. The grade-level band in which the lines intersect is the estimate of readability.

A Positive Use of Fire

If you look around, signs of fires, long past or quite recent, will be evident. In the southeastern United States, pine forests are a product of fires. If they were not burned periodically by natural or artificial means, hardwoods would replace the pines. Here in the Sanctuary, fire is used carefully under controlled conditions to maintain the pines and keep a proper balance between the pines and the undergrowth. If fire were kept out for a long time, the undergrowth would gain considerable height; then if wildfire swept through, even the fire-resistant pines would be in danger. All of the plants that grow here are "fireproof," coming back rapidly after a burn.

How many sentences are there in the 100-word sample?   _____

How many hard words are there in the 100 words?   _____

What is the readability of this sample?   _____

Answers to the Practicum Exercise

When you counted the number of sentences in this selection, you found approximately 5.1 sentences. Words of six or more letters are defined as *difficult* or *long* words. You circled and counted the number of words with six or more letters, a total of 30 long words. When you plotted these points on the graph, you came across from approximately 5.2 and up from the line indicating 30 long words. You thus found that the readability level for the selection is ninth grade.

A Positive Use of Fire

If you look around, signs of fires, long past or quite recent, will be evident. In the southeastern United States, pine forests are a product of fires. If they were not burned periodically by natural or artificial means, hardwoods would replace the pines. Here in the Sanctuary, fire is used carefully under controlled conditions to maintain the pines and keep a proper balance between the pines and the undergrowth. If fire were kept out for a long time, the undergrowth would gain considerable height; then if wildfire swept through, even the fire-resistant pines would be in danger. All of the plants that grow here are "fireproof," coming back rapidly after a burn.

If you prefer Raygor's graph to Fry's graph because you find it easier to count words with six or more letters than to determine the number of syllables in each word, you may wonder why we introduced Fry's Graph first. We introduced Fry's Graph for Estimating Readability first because there have been more research studies comparing its results to the most respected readability formulas, Dale-Chall and Spache. There have been only a limited number of research studies concerning the validity of Raygor's Graph for Estimating Readability. According to the preliminary studies, the results obtained with the Raygor graph are similar to the results obtained with the Fry graph. For example, Baldwin and Kaufman (1979) found the correlation between the Raygor and Fry readability estimates to be .87. Comparing the results obtained with the Raygor and Fry methods for 100 different reading materials, they found that the estimates for 50 of the materials were exactly the same according to both graphs. For 25 of the books, the Raygor graph indicated estimates one grade level above the results of the Fry graph and one grade level below on 19 of the materials. The mean grade level of all the reading passages was ninth grade according to both Raygor and Fry graphs.

Baldwin and Kaufman also found it faster to determine readability using the Raygor graph; however, there was no significant difference between the Raygor and Fry groups in the errors made using the graphs.

As more research studies are done, we may come to recommend Raygor's graph; however, at this time we continue to feel more comfortable recommending Fry's graph. For the present, we encourage you to use the Fry graph unless you have experienced difficulty counting syllables.

Some educators do not like the idea of using the Fry or Raygor graphs for estimating readability. In Enabling Element 3, an alternative method for estimating readability is presented. If you want to learn a method of estimating readability that does not use a graph, go to Enabling Element 3. If you have sufficient information for estimating readability, you are ready for Posttest items 1–4.

ANSWERS
Enabling Activities 3–6

3. a. very (2)
   b. telephone (3)
   c. ¢ (1)
   d. environment (4)
   e. drenched (1)
   f. basketball (3)
   g. hopeful (2)
   h. ERA (3)
   i. matches (2)
   j. Washington (3)
   k. seventeenth (3)
   l. 1961 (4)
   m. any (2)
   n. $4.98 (4)
   o. let's (1)
4. a. $4/8 = 0.5$
   b. $4/15 = 0.3$
   c. $9/32 = 0.3$
5. The true estimate is ninth-, tenth-, or eleventh-grade reading level.
6. a. Seventh grade
   b. Ninth grade
   c. Invalid estimate (Another sample would have to be used to find the reading level.)

PRACTICUM EXERCISE 1

Using a Card Catalog

	Syllables
If you wish to see if the library has a book you want and	16
where to find it, you will use the card catalog. The card catalog is a	19
cabinet with small drawers containing alphabetically arranged cards.	19

Each card tells the title of the book and its classification number.   _18_

To find a book, copy the call number on a slip of paper. The   _17_
same call number you copied will be printed on the spine of the   _16_
book near the bottom. You will have to find the call number on the   _16_
stack of shelves which will lead you to your book. (100 words)   _10_

                                        Total   **131**

1. Number of Sentences   **6**
2. Number of Syllables   **131**
3. Estimate of Readability   **7ᵀᴴ grade**

PRACTICUM EXERCISE 2

The Conductor

                                            Syllables

     The orchestra is on stage, the house lights have been dimmed,   _13_
and the audience waits with great anticipation. Soon a person   _17_
emerges from the wings, walks to the middle of the stage in front   _16_
of the orchestra and bows to acknowledge the applause of the   _16_
audience. This person is a conductor who is about to lead the   _18_
orchestra in an exciting concert of symphonic music.   _16_
     An orchestra did not need a conductor until it began to in-   _18_
crease in size. Beginning in the early nineteenth century, during   _17_
Beethoven's time, the orchestra increased to such a size that a   _16_
conductor was needed. (100 words) This was the beginning of the   _6_
art of conducting as it is known and practiced today.

                                        Total   **153**

1. Number of Sentences   **5**
2. Number of Syllables   **153**
3. Estimate of Readability   **10ᵀᴴ grade**

PRACTICUM EXERCISE 3

Fry's Graph

                                            Syllables

     The purpose of this selection is to provide you with practice in   _17_
using Fry's Graph for Estimating Readability. The first edition of   _20_
Fry's graph came out in 1968, and Fry extended his graph in 1977.   _21_
The extended graph continues through the seventeenth + grade   _15_
level. The extended graph was published in an IRA publication enti-   _21_
tled *Journal of Reading* in December 1977.   _14_
     Because Fry did not obtain a copyright for his graph, reproduc-   _17_

tion is permitted. Personally, we feel that Fry has made a worth- __17__
while contribution to the field of reading, and we thank him for it. __17__

We believe you will find/Fry's graph easy to use and, after __6__
100 words
practice, will be able to determine readability levels of printed mate- _____
rials within a few minutes. This new competency will enable you to _____
select materials that are appropriate for the ranges of reading levels _____
found among your students. _____

Total __165__

1. Number of Sentences __6.2__
2. Number of Syllables __165__
3. Estimate of Readability __11th grade__

PRACTICUM EXERCISE 4

The average reading level of the three health book selections, "Rabies," "Headache," and "Heatstroke," is 13th level (college freshman). This was found by finding the average number of sentences (4.5) and the average number of syllables (167), and then locating the intersecting point on the graph.

	Number of Sentences	Number of Syllables	Reading Level	True Estimate Range
"Rabies"	4.0	161	12th grade	11–13
"Headache"	4.9	170	14th level	13–15
"Heatstroke"	4.7	169	14th level	13–15
Sums	13.6	500		
Averages	4.5	167	13th level	12–14
(sums divided by 3)				

Rabies

Syllables

Since bites by cats, dogs, or any wild animal always present __16__
the danger of infection with rabies, a biting animal should never be __20__
killed unless unavoidable as a matter of safety. It should be caught __19__
and held for observation for at least fifteen days, in order to deter- __19__
mine whether it develops rabies. __9__

If it is necessary to kill the animal at the time of the biting, the __21__
carcass should be sent to the state public health laboratory for an __18__
examination of its brain. If the laboratory finds the animal was rabid, __23__
it is essential that treatment be initiated at once./*100 words* __16__

Total __161__

Headache

Syllables

The term *headache* is such a part of our everyday vocabulary   *19*
that it has become almost synonymous with any unpleasant situa-   *20*
tion or problem. But in a medical sense the term quite literally   *18*
means a head pain or an aching head and is a symptom rather than   *17*
itself an actual disease condition.   *11*

Hence, headache can suggest the possibility of a great many   *17*
underlying conditions. Perhaps one of the better known types is the   *18*
throbbing, devastating headache that sometimes accompanies a   *16*
hangover. This differs from the type known as tension headache,   *15*
associated with figuring out one's income tax, since they arise from   *19*
different causes.   *100 words*   *0*

Total   *170*

Heatstroke

Syllables

The most important feature of heatstroke, which is some-   *13*
times also referred to as sunstroke, is the extremely high body   *16*
temperature that accompanies it. It is a far more serious condition   *21*
than heat exhaustion.   *5*

Heatstroke occurs more often in males than in females and is   *15*
more common in elderly people and in those addicted to alcohol.   *19*
Physical exertion is a definite contributing factor; and an attack is   *22*
much more likely to occur when the humidity is high than when it is   *19*
low, even at the same temperature.   *10*

The underlying cause of heatstroke is intimately connected   *17*
with a cessation of sweating, accounting for the excessive rise in   *11*
body temperature.   */100 words*

Total   *169*

ENABLING ELEMENT 3
How to Use the SMOG Grading System to Estimate Readability

Specific Objective 3

You will use the SMOG grading system to estimate readability.

Enabling Activities

1. Read Study Guide 3 to learn how to use the SMOG grading procedure for estimating readability.
2. Complete all practicum activities.

3. Practice using SMOG to determine the readability of three text-books in your subject area.
4. Write a paragraph comparing and contrasting the readability procedures advocated by Fry, Raygor, and McLaughlin.
5. Choose a readability procedure and defend its use for determining readability in your subject area.

STUDY GUIDE 3
The SMOG Grading System to Estimate Readability

If you want to determine readability without using a graph, and yet want to base your estimate on sentence length and word difficulty, you may want to use the Simple Measure of Gobbledygook (SMOG), which was developed by McLaughlin in 1969. The SMOG formula is used to determine the readability of materials at the fourth-grade level or above. The formula is based on a sophisticated set of statistical procedures that are incorporated into four simple steps. To estimate readability using the SMOG, follow these four procedures:

Step 1.
Selecting sentences. You must select a total of 30 sentences to use the SMOG grading system. Count ten consecutive sentences from near the beginning of the textual material, ten near the middle, and ten from the last third of the material. Try to select the ten sentence passages that are representative of the printed materials.

Step 2.
Read the 30 sentences aloud and count every word of three or more syllables. A word is defined as any group of letters or numerals beginning and ending with a space or punctuation mark. If a word is repeated, count it again. Remember, it is not necessary to divide the words into syllables, but rather to simply put a check mark over each word that has three or more syllables.

Step 3.
Estimate the square root of the number of words having three or more syllables. To estimate the square root, take the square root of the nearest perfect square. For example, if there were 47 words having three syllables or more, the nearest perfect square is 49 (7 × 7) which yields a square root of 7. If the count lies roughly in between two squares, choose the lower number. For example, if the count is 72, take the square root of 64 (8 × 8) rather than 81 (9 × 9).

Step 4.
Add 3 to the approximate square root. This yields the SMOG grade-level estimate needed to understand the textual material. For example, if 3 were added to 7, you would obtain a readability estimate of 10th grade.

Illustration of the SMOG

To demonstrate how the SMOG grading system is used to determine readability, our first step is to select 30 sentences—ten each from the beginning, middle, and final third of a textbook. For our demonstration, we selected the sentences from a science textbook. Notice there are exactly ten sentences in each passage. The passages did not necessarily conclude at the end of the ten sentences; we stopped, however, because it is necessary to have three samples of ten sentences each.

Viruses (From first third of textual material)
A virus is a complex organic substance that can grow and reproduce itself inside a cell. Since viruses can grow only inside the cell of an organism, every virus is a parasite. The virus may take control and change the normal activities of the cell. When this happens the virus becomes the "master" and the cell becomes a "slave." Sometimes more viruses are produced from the material in the cell. Eventually, the cell bursts and releases the new viruses which then enter other cells.
A virus is made of a nucleic acid, either DNA or RNA, and protein. The nucleic acid is the center or core of a virus. This core is surrounded by a coat of protein. Viruses can have many different shapes such as rodlike, spherical or hexagonal.

Problem Solving (From middle third of textual material)
There are certain procedures which scientists follow to answer questions. The steps they use are called the problem-solving process. The first step scientists take to solve a problem is to make a clear statement of the problem. Scientists usually begin with a question. Secondly, scientists collect information about the problem. Facts and ideas are obtained from journals, books, and other scientists. The third step in the problem-solving process is to form a hypothesis. A hypothesis is the scientists' proposed solution to a problem, or a prediction based on known fact. Finally, the scientists test the hypothesis by making observations. The hypothesis is then accepted or rejected.

Blood Types (From final third of textual material)
Even though all human beings have blood, the type of blood they have is not always the same. Just as people have different colors of hair, skin, or eyes, so do they differ in the kind of blood they have. There are four main kinds or types of blood. The four main blood types are called A, B, AB, and O.
When certain blood types are mixed, a clumping or clustering of the red blood cells occurs. If the wrong type of blood were injected into a person's veins, clumps formed in the blood might slow normal circulation. If the clumps were to prevent circulation, death would result.
A patient who has type A blood can safely receive only type A or type O blood. A patient with type B blood can accept only type B or type O blood. Persons with type AB blood can receive any type of blood.

A person who has type O blood is known as a universal donor, which means type O blood can be injected into people with different blood types.

Our second step was to count the number of words with three or more syllables. We read the passage aloud and put a check over each word having three or more syllables. If the same word reappeared in the passage, we counted it again. Our results were as follows:

Number of words/numerals with three or more syllables
1st ten sentences—Viruses   21
2nd ten sentences—Problem Solving   22
3rd ten sentences—Blood Types   8
                              Total   51

The third step is to estimate the square root of the number of words having three or more syllables. In our sample, there are 51 words with three or more syllables, so the square root is 7. That is, 7 × 7 is closer to 51 than 8 × 8 or 6 × 6. Remember, to estimate the square root you take the square root of the nearest perfect square.

Our final step is to add 3 to the approximate square root which means we add three to seven to get 10. The estimate of readability is tenth grade.

PRACTICUM EXERCISE

Now it is your turn to determine readability using the SMOG grading system to estimate readability. Follow each of the four steps and complete the Practicum Exercise.

Step 1.
Here are three selections from the beginning, middle, and final third of a subject area textual material. Each selection contains exactly 10 sentences.

Step 2.
Read each passage aloud and determine the number of words or numerals containing three syllables in each. Record your answers and the total here:

Human Life   ____
Japanese People   ____
Women's Rights   ____
        Total   ____

Step 3.

Determine the square root for the nearest perfect square.
Record your answer here ___.

Step 4.

Add three to the square root and record your answer here.
___ SMOG Readability Estimate

When you have completed the Practicum Exercise, compare your answers to ours. If any answer differs from ours, recheck your work or consult your instructor.

Human Life

Human life has certain characteristics. People are born in many parts of the world; they usually grow up and learn to get along with each other to a certain degree. People raise families, build societies, and organize their own ways of governing each other. They decide what is acceptable behavior and what is unacceptable. People find ways to express their feelings through art and music. Most people leave written records to share their accomplishments and concerns with future generations. No other creatures on earth can do all the things that human beings can do.

Even though human beings have many similarities, there are many differences. From family organization to government, different people of the world have found different ways to shape society. People are creative so there seems to be no limit as to how and where they live.

Japanese People

The Japanese people have developed a unique way of life over the years. Their customs were quite different during the nineteenth century. The homes of the Japanese were usually made of wood since there was a shortage of stone. The homes were mostly one story because of the earthquakes that frequently occurred to Japan. Sliding panels of heavy paper on wooden frames were used to separate the rooms.

The Japanese homes usually did not have much furniture. A low table was used to serve food. People sat around the low table with their legs crossed.

The floors were covered with straw mats. Since the Japanese people took their shoes off before entering the house, these mats were kept clean.

Women's Rights

Women have not always had the same rights as men. Some people have felt that a woman's role was to take care of the family. In Britain and France women were not allowed to own property. Women could not start divorce proceedings, had no legal claim to their children, and could not vote.

In the mid-1800s some reformers in Europe and the United States wanted equal rights for women. One of the most outspoken women was Susan B. Anthony. Women gradually won the right to vote, but were still not treated as equal. The first country to allow women to vote was New South Wales in Australia (1867). In the United States, Wyoming approved women's suffrage in 1869. It was not until 1918 that women in Great Britain were allowed to vote.

Answers to the Practicum Exercise

Step 1.
Select 30 sentences from the first, middle, and last third of textual material. The sentences were provided for you.

Step 2.
Count the number of words of three or more syllables in the 30 sentences.

Human Life	20
Japanese People	13
Women's Rights	15
Total	48

Step 3.
Determine the nearest perfect square which is 7 ($7 \times 7 = 49$).

Two other close squares were $8 \times 8 = 64$ and $6 \times 6 = 36$.

Since 48 is closer to 49 than it is to 36, or 64, the appropriate answer is 7.

Step 4.
Add 3 to the appropriate square root to obtain the SMOG readability level ($7 + 3 = 10$).

POSTTEST

Directions: Read each of the following statements and complete each Posttest item.

1. State three important factors you should evaluate when selecting textual materials for your classes.
2. Use Fry's graph to determine the reading level of the following selection, "The International Date Line."

The International Date Line

Syllables

    The International Date Line is often referred to as the Sunday- _____
Monday line. It follows approximately the 180th meridian, on oppo- _____
site sides of which the reckoning of the date differs by one complete _____
day. If you travel from west to east, standard time advances one _____
hour for each fifteen degrees, which is one twenty-fourth of a circle _____
of longitude around the earth. In passing around the earth completely, _____
you gain twenty-four hours, or one complete day. If you travel from _____
east to west, it is necessary to turn your clock back one hour for _____
each fifteen degrees of longitude; thus, you lose twenty-four hours _____
in passing completely around the earth. _____

Total _____

1. Number of sentences   _____
2. Number of syllables   _____
3. Readability level   _____

3. Decide if the following directions for using Fry's graph are true or false.
   a. Skip all proper nouns when selecting a 100-word passage.   _____
   b. The estimate of readability is probably within one-half year of the true estimate of readability.   _____
   c. Syllable counts by various people may differ slightly.   _____
   d. If the intersecting points fall in the gray areas of the graph, the results are invalid.   _____
   e. Count only complete sentences when counting the number of sentences in the 100-word count.   _____
4. Use Raygor's graph to estimate the readability level of the selection, "The International Date Line."
5. Specify the procedures you must follow to use the SMOG grading system to estimate the readability of a textual material.

Posttest Answers

1. Three factors that should be evaluated when selecting textual materials are:
   a. content
   b. aids that assist learning
   c. readability
2. The selection, "The International Date Line," has:
   Number of sentences _4.6_
   Number of syllables _148_
   Readability level _9th grade_

Check your syllable count by comparing it line by line with the sample:

The International Date Line

	Syllables
The International Date Line is often referred to as the Sunday-	18
Monday line. It follows approximately the 180th meridian, on oppo-	23
site sides of which the reckoning of the date differs by one complete	17
day. If you travel from west to east, standard time advances one	16
hour for each fifteen degrees, which is one twenty-fourth of a circle	17
of longitude around the earth. In passing around the earth completely,	18
you gain twenty-four hours or one complete day. If you travel from	16
east to west it is necessary to turn your clock back one hour for	17
each fifteen degrees of/longitude; thus, you lose twenty-four hours	6
in passing completely around the earth.	
Total	148

(annotation: 100 words)

3. a. false
   b. false
   c. true
   d. true
   e. false
4. When using Raygor's graph to estimate the readability of "The International Date Line," you should have counted 29 long words. Since there are between 4.6 and 4.7 sentences, the estimate of readability is 9th grade.
5. To estimate the readability level of material using the SMOG grading system, follow these steps:

Step 1. Count ten consecutive sentences from each third of the textual material. This totals 30 sentences.
Step 2. Count every word or numeral with three or more syllables. It is best to count as you read aloud.
Step 3. Determine the nearest perfect square for the total number of three or more syllable words.
Step 4. Add 3 to the square root to obtain the estimate of readability.

FINAL COMMENT

If you have completed this module with 100 percent accuracy, congratulations! You have acquired a set of skills that will enable you to more adequately meet the needs of the students you teach. One word of caution, however. Your new knowledge is of no value unless you use it to select quality printed materials for your students. We hope you enjoy selecting materials!

REFERENCES

Anderson, J. (1983). Lix and rix: Variations on a little-known readability index. *Journal of Reading, 26*(6), 490–496.

Armbruster, B. B., et al. (1985). Readability formulas may be dangerous to your textbooks. *Educational Leadership, 42*(7), 18–20.

Baldwin, R. S., & Kaufman, R. K. (1979). A concurrent validity study of the Raygor readability estimate. *Journal of Reading, 23*(2), 148–153.

Camp, D. J. (1987). Answering middle grade teachers' questions about readability. *Middle School Journal, 19*(1), 8–10.

Dale, E., & Chall, J. S. (1947). A formula for predicting readability. *Educational Research Bulletin, 27*(1), 11–20.

Dale, E., & Chall, J. S. (1948). A formula for predicting readability: Instructions. *Educational Research Bulletin, 27*(2), 37–54.

Danielson, K. E. (1987). Readability formulas: A necessary evil? *Reading Horizons, 27*(3), 178–188.

Evans, C. S. (1987). Use of readability formulas in selecting American history textbooks. *Social Studies, 78*(3), 127–130.

Fry, E. (1968). A readability formula that saves time. *Journal of Reading, 11*(4), 513–516, 575–578.

Fry, E. (1969). The readability graph validated at primary levels. *The Reading Teacher, 22*(3), 534–538.

Fry, E. (1977). Fry's readability graph: Clarifications, validity, and extension to level 17. *Journal of Reading, 21*(3), 242–252.

Fry, E. (1983). *Fry's readability program*. Providence, RI: Jamestown Publishers.

Fry, E. (1987). The varied uses of readability measurement today. *Journal of Reading, 30*, 338–343.

Giordano, G. (1985). Determining the readability of textbooks. *Academic Therapy, 20*(5), 533–538.

Klare, G. R. (1974). Assessing readability. *Reading Research Quarterly, 10*, 62–102.

McLaughlin, C. H. (1969, May). SMOG grading: A new readability formula. *Journal of Reading, 12*, 639–646.

Raygor, A. L. (1977). The Raygor readability estimate: A quick and easy way to determine difficulty. In P. David Pearson (Ed.), *Reading, Theory, Research, and Practice* (pp. 259–263). Twenty-sixth Yearbook of the National Reading Conference.

Schuyler, M. R. (1982). A readability formula program for use on microcomputers. *Journal of Reading, 25*(6), 560–591.

Spiegel, D. L., & Wright, J. D. (1983). Biology teachers' use of readability concepts when selecting texts for students. *Journal of Reading, 27*(1), 28–34.

Taylor, W. L. (1953, Fall). Cloze procedures: A new tool for measuring readability. *Journal Quarterly, 30*, 415–433.

MODULE TWO

Determining Suitability
of Materials

CHAPTER OUTLINE

Overview
  Rationale
  Objectives
Enabling Element 1
  The Informal Suitability Survey
Enabling Element 2
  Constructing an Informal Suitability Survey
Enabling Element 3
  Administering and Scoring an Informal Suitability Survey
Enabling Element 4
  Cloze: An Alternative Procedure for Determining Suitability
Posttest
  Posttest Answers
References

OVERVIEW

Rationale

As a classroom teacher you should use a variety of print materials to expose your students to the subject matter content you teach. You should not allow the textbook to become the only source of printed material from which your students acquire information about your subject.

Textbooks by design are compendiums of facts and are often written like encyclopedias. Sentences and paragraphs are heavily ladened with facts. Paragraphs frequently do not contain a topic sentence. Often the topic or main idea has to be inferred from the information provided in a paragraph. There is no story to make the facts interesting. Rarely do you hear a student say, "That textbook was so interesting, I just couldn't put it down."

If the textbook is the only printed source used to obtain information in your classroom, many of your students will be turned off by your subject. If you want students to enjoy, appreciate, and perhaps love your subject, you had better plan to have them read about it in a variety of printed materials. Magazines, newspapers, biographies, autobiographies, historical novels, science-fiction novels, bulletins of learned societies, and many other materials present information in a more lively and applicable way to enhance the subject's appeal to students.

If you have your students read from a variety of materials, you will need a tool to help you match the students' reading capabilities with the reading requirements of the printed material. In this module, you will learn about a tool that will do just that. It is called the Informal Suitability Survey.

OBJECTIVES

General Objective

You will use an Informal Suitability Survey to determine the suitability of content area materials.

Specific Objectives

1. You will describe an Informal Suitability Survey and state the major purpose for using one with your class.

2. You will construct an Informal Suitability Survey by selecting a representative passage of 200 words, writing a motivation statement, and preparing five appropriate comprehension questions.
3. You will administer and score an Informal Suitability Survey following the procedures described in this module.
4. You will describe how to use the Cloze Procedure as an alternative for determining suitability of content area reading material.

ENABLING ELEMENT 1
The Informal Suitability Survey

Specific Objective 1
You will describe an Informal Suitability Survey and state the major purpose for using one with your class.

Enabling Activities

1. Read Study Guide 1. Determine what an Informal Suitability Survey is and the value of using such surveys.
2. Teaching is both satisfying and frustrating. Think of those things that frustrate you most. Does the fact that some students cannot read the textbook or other required material frustrate you? If so, are you committed to doing something about it?
3. Consider the students who cannot read the textbook or other required reading materials. How do they feel when you make an assignment? How do they feel when others are sharing information gleaned from the reading assignments? How do they respond?
4. Discuss why there is such a wide range of reading achievement among secondary students. Make a list of possible reasons. Module 9, "Identifying and Helping Problem Readers," can help you verify your ideas.
5. Look at the students in your classes to notice the range of their heights. If a standard size of clothing were required, it would be inappropriate for many students. Is there any reason to believe that mental abilities and achievement will not vary as do physical characteristics?
6. Collect the written materials you commonly use in teaching. You will use these reading resources as you complete the other enabling activities in this module.

STUDY GUIDE 1

The first task in bowling is to find a ball that fits. Bowlers move from one rack of balls to another to find a suitable ball. Others go to the expense of having the holes drilled to fit their own fingers, thumb, and span. One bowling ball is simply not suitable for all bowlers.

So it is with textbooks or other reading materials used in content area classes. Materials that are too difficult for some students are suitable for others, because one-third of the students in a classroom commonly read below their current grade level, one-third read at grade level, and one-third read above grade level. The range of reading levels in a typical seventh-grade class is between third and eleventh grade, and the range increases as students advance in grade level.

The wide range in reading achievement is to be expected because of the heterogeneous nature of school populations. Students vary in height, weight, attitudes, and mental ability, to mention just a few factors. Textbooks, on the other hand, vary in readability less than the group of students served in any subject area classroom. The difference between the students' reading levels and the book's reading level produces an instructional problem for subject area teachers. One text is simply not suitable for every student.

Description of an Informal Suitability Survey

For each student in their classes, content teachers must determine the suitability of textbooks or other required material. A useful technique to identify the suitability of a textbook and/or other written material is the Informal Suitability Survey. An Informal Suitability Survey is an informal device to determine if students can handle selected content area printed material.

An Informal Suitability Survey consists of a representative selection from content area material. A motivation statement and comprehension questions accompany the selection. To develop the Informal Suitability Survey, the teacher (1) selects a representative selection from required reading materials, (2) writes the motivation statement to provide a purpose for reading the selection, and (3) prepares comprehension questions covering vocabulary, facts, and inferences to check the students' understanding of the selection. The teacher then administers the Informal Suitability Survey to determine if the textbook is appropriate in terms of the students' reading capabilities. For example, the speech or language arts teacher might use the following Informal Suitability Survey, constructed from a language arts textbook.

Sample Informal Suitability Survey

Name _____ Date _____

Source _____

Circle One: Suitable Unsuitable

Motivation Statement: Many students like to find jobs, and of course, all of you will probably be employed some day. Read the following selection to answer the question, "How do I prepare for a job interview?"

Selection:

Preparing for the Job Interview

An interview is a meeting between two or more parties to exchange information. The purpose of a job interview is to provide opportunities for the employer and prospective employee to exchange information. The employer desires to know if the applicant possesses the necessary capabilities and qualities to handle certain responsibilities. The candidate wants to know if the responsibilities, working conditions, and salary are suitable for his or her needs.

There are two different ways employers interview prospective candidates. In the *open-ended* interview the employer generally begins by saying, "Tell me a little bit about yourself." The prospective employee then has the responsibility of informing the employer of his or her strengths and capabilities as a person. The *closed* interview technique is different in that the employer asks many specific questions. For example, the employer may ask questions about your grades in school, family background, previous responsibilities and interests.

In preparing for a job interview, you should try to learn about the job so you have questions to ask. You may want to discuss the type and responsibilities of the work with your family, friends, or people who have similar jobs. Make a list of the important questions you have.

Another step in preparing for an interview is simply "know yourself." Be prepared to give the interviewer a concise picture of your interests and capabilities. Evaluate yourself to determine those things you do well and the characteristics you have that others seem to like.

Make the appointment for the interview and then plan to arrive a few minutes early. Promptness is generally considered very important by most employers. Evaluate your personal appearance to see if you are creating the image you desire. Usually, simple, conservative clothing is just right for an interview. Be ready to greet the employer with a smile and simply be yourself! **30**

Comprehension Questions:

(*V* = Vocabulary; *F* = Factual; *I* = Inference.)

1. *(V)* What does *prospective* mean?
2. *(F)* What is the main purpose of a job interview?
3. *(F)* What three things should you do in preparing for a job interview?
4. *(F)* What information does an employer usually like to have about an applicant?
5. *(I)* Why do you suppose some employers like to use the open-ended interview technique?

As you can see, an Informal Suitability Survey is a sampling technique to determine if the materials you are considering are appropriate. The preceding selection consists of a 300-word passage; however, you may want to use 200-, 400-, or even 500-word selections. If you have many materials available, you can construct a series of Informal Suitability Surveys, then match the materials to the students. If only one textbook is available, you may need to determine which students are capable of reading the text and then make adaptations for other students. Suggestions for differentiating assignments are presented in Module Three.

You may wonder how many Informal Suitability Surveys you will need. The answer to this question depends upon the availability of textbooks and other commonly used printed materials related to your content area. If you plan to use one textbook with all the students, you need to develop only one Informal Suitability Survey. Of course, you must be aware that the book will be unsuitable for some students. You may want to give each student a copy of the textbook and adapt the reading assignments to the capabilities of the students. For example, if only one textbook is available, you know that some students will be able to read the textual materials to obtain ideas and information. Other students may be able to gain information and ideas from the pictures, diagrams, or other illustrations in the text. Because of the nature of the concepts, some parts of a textbook are easier to read than other parts. If the textbook was written by several different authors, some parts may be easier to read. If you use only one textbook, you must realize from the outset that some students will be unable to complete the reading assignments. Please do not blame the students for not doing their assignments; you are promoting failure by expecting the impossible.

We recommend that you try to find many different reading resources for your content area classes. If you are able to obtain books related to your objectives that are written at different readability levels, you will more effectively help students accomplish the content objectives. Of course, using more reading sources requires making more than one Informal Suitability Survey. The general guideline is to identify the reading resources you *commonly* use and develop one Informal Suitability Survey for each of the materials.

As mentioned in Module 1, you can also match materials to students by comparing the readability levels of the materials to the students' reading levels. To do so, you must have reading scores for all your students, although scores may be either unavailable or invalid. Students exhibit many different reading levels depending upon their interests and the background information they have on a specific topic. For example, a student who is interested in math may be able to read higher level books because he knows the specialized vocabulary and symbols and is highly motivated. This same student may read social studies books at a level two or three years lower because of lack of interest and/or a good background in social studies. Using the Informal Suitability Survey, then, is a more valid technique than using readability formulas for matching specific materials to your students. Enabling Element 2 will help you construct an Informal Suitability Survey.

ENABLING ELEMENT 2
Constructing an Informal Suitability Survey

Specific Objective 2
You will construct an Informal Suitability Survey by selecting a representative passage of 200 words, writing a motivation statement, and preparing five appropriate comprehension questions.

Enabling Activities

1. Read Study Guide 2. This Study Guide provides directions for making your own Informal Suitability Surveys.
2. Do Practicum Exercise 1 to practice constructing an Informal Suitability Survey. Compare your efforts to the answers to Practicum Exercise 1 at the end of this Enabling Element.
3. Select a 200-word passage representative of the textbook most often used in one of your classes, and write a motivation statement and five comprehension questions as directed in Practicum Exercise 2.
4. Evaluate your questions. When writing the factual questions, did you select significant facts? What about your question concerning vocabulary? Is the vocabulary word essential to the meaning of the selection? Does your inference question require knowledge from the selection as well as information from the reader's experiences?
5. What are the advantages of having ten questions as compared to five? Try checking comprehension with ten questions. Are there differences in your findings?
6. Discuss why it is important to provide a statement to motivate the reader. What are the advantages of presenting questions before asking students to read the selection? Are there implications for introducing all reading assignments?

STUDY GUIDE 2

When developing an Informal Suitability Survey, remember that the final product consists of (1) a representative reading selection from any textual material commonly used in the class, (2) a motivation statement giving the student a purpose for reading the selection, and (3) comprehension questions to determine if the student understands the selection. Specific instructions for constructing an Informal Suitability Survey follow.

Step 1: Select a Representative Passage
Select a representative passage from your textbook or other reading materials. The length of the passage will vary with the grade level and nature of the materials. A 200-word passage is generally preferred; however, if it is difficult to find 200 consecutive words (as in some math

books), you can use a 100-word selection. For longer textbooks, you may want to use a 300- or 400-word selection, or two 200-word passages. The selections need not contain exactly 200, 300, or 400 words, but it is necessary to mark the 200th, 300th, or 400th word for scoring purposes. The important fact is that it is essential to choose a selection that is a *representative*, self-contained sample of the material under consideration.

Select two or three passages of 200 words if you are surveying the suitability of a major textbook. The extra passages can be used as alternate forms of the Informal Suitability Survey for students whose scores you doubt.

Skip all proper nouns (capitalized name of a particular person, place, or thing) and numerals when counting words for your passages. Proper nouns are not counted because they are usually introduced to students when regular reading assignments are made. Numerals are not counted because they are not words. Mark the 200th, 300th, or 400th word by making a slash after it.

To illustrate Step 1, suppose as a social studies teacher you chose the following selection. This selection is representative of materials in the major text you would like to use with your students. Your word count (skipping proper nouns and numerals) reveals approximately 200 words.

Sample Selection from a Social Studies Textbook

Becoming a Naturalized Citizen

People who desire to become naturalized citizens of the United States must be at least eighteen years old. The applicant must be able to sign a petition in his or her own handwriting. They must demonstrate skill in reading, writing, and speaking the English language unless physically unable to do so. Those applicants who have been residing in the United States for 20 years are exempted from the English proficiency examination.

A person who desires to become a naturalized citizen must be of good moral character and well-disposed to the good order and prosperity of the United States. There are residence requirements that must be met before filing a petition to become a citizen. The petition must have two credible citizen witnesses who have personal knowledge of the applicant's character, residence, and loyalty. The applicant must demonstrate knowledge and understanding of the fundamentals of United States history and form of government.

Naturalization is denied to any person who within 10 years has been subversive, including Communists or others who favor totalitarian government and who were members of a proscribed organization (unless the petitioner was under 16 or forced under duress).

As with other federal statutes, there are exceptions to the guidelines stated above. Of course, the guidelines are subject to change by the|Congress of the United States.

200ᵀʰ word

Step 2: Write a Motivation Statement

Write a motivation statement for each passage to provide the students with a purpose for reading. The motivation statement usually consists of two sentences. The first sentence is the topic of the passage. This sentence provides the reader with a frame of reference for reading the selection. The second statement is a question or command stating what the reader should try to learn from the passage. For example, a motivation statement for the preceding passage on becoming a naturalized citizen might read as follows:

> People who desire to become United States citizens, but were not born in the United States, can become naturalized citizens. Read this selection to find the requirements for becoming a naturalized citizen.

Step 3: Prepare Five Comprehension Questions

After you have selected the passage and prepared your motivation statement, you will need to write five questions for checking comprehension. Specifically, you should write one vocabulary question, three factual questions, and one inferential question. If you have long selections of 400 words or more, you may want to write ten comprehension questions (two vocabulary, six factual, and two inferential).

Factual Questions. The factual questions require answers that are *directly stated* in the passage. These questions should concern the most important facts in the selection, rather than interesting but picayune details that are not important to remember. The easiest way to prepare factual questions is to read the selection and then list its three most important facts. After identifying the significant facts, you can write questions for each of them.

Vocabulary Questions. Vocabulary questions test the student's understanding of words used in the selection whose meanings are not necessarily obvious in the selection. When writing vocabulary questions, do not choose words that have been set off in italics and precisely defined for the reader; rather, select words that are essential to understanding the selection but are not italicized. Vocabulary questions should relate to the most important concepts in the selection.

Inferential Questions. Inferential questions require some knowledge from the selection as well as some thinking as the reader relates the selection to her experiences. A good inferential question requires the reader to combine information presented in the passage with her experiences to answer the question. The answer to an inference question cannot be stated directly in the selection. Because each student's experiences are different, there may be more than one correct answer to any inference question.

You can determine the format for your questions. Essay and short-answer questions usually require more memory; however, multiple-choice items may be more appropriate when you need to administer and grade the selections for large groups of students. Samples of the three types of questions are given below. The questions are over a 200-word selection concerning becoming a naturalized citizen. Notice the different types of questions and the possible formats (essay or multiple choice).

Sample Questions
Essay or Short Answer
(*F* = Factual; *V* = Vocabulary; *I* = Inference.)

1. *(F)* How old must a person be before he can apply to become a naturalized citizen? (18)
2. *(F)* Name two proficiencies a person must have to become a naturalized citizen. (Skill in using the English language and knowledge of United States history and government)
3. *(F)* Which applicants do *not* have to take a test to demonstrate proficiency in reading, writing, and speaking English? (Those who have been residing in the United States for 20 years and those who are physically unable to do so)
4. *(V)* What does *subversive* mean? (Tendency to destroy or overthrow)
5. *(I)* Why is it necessary for the applicant to have certain proficiencies? (The applicant must know the form of government because he or she will be under its rules and regulations. The applicant must know English so he or she can communicate with others in the country.)

Sample Multiple-Choice Questions
(*F* = Factual; *V* = Vocabulary; *I* = Inference.)

1. *(F)* Circle the letter that indicates how old a person must be to be eligible to become a naturalized citizen.
   a. Seventeen   c. Twenty
   b. Eighteen   d. Twenty-one
2. *(F)* Circle the letter that indicates the two proficiencies a person must have to become a naturalized citizen
   a. Knowledge of English and science
   b. Knowledge of the government of the United States and communistic government
   c. Knowledge of English and the government of the United States
   d. Knowledge of English and mental health
3. *(F)* Applicants who want to become naturalized citizens do not have to demonstrate proficiency in using English if
   a. They are proficient in using some other language.
   b. They are physically unable to do so.
   c. They have resided in the U.S. for 20 years.
   d. Both *b* and *c*
   e. All of the above.

4. *(V)* Circle the letter that indicates the meaning of *subversive.*
   a. communist   c. tendency to disagree
   b. tendency to overthrow   d. tendency not to believe
5. *(I)* An applicant must have certain proficiencies in order to become a naturalized citizen because
   a. The applicant should know the forms of government under which he or she will be living. The applicant needs to know the language to communicate most effectively so that he or she can be a productive citizen.
   b. United States citizens are at a higher intellectual level than citizens in other countries; therefore, all citizens must have certain proficiencies to maintain the high standards found in the United States.
   c. Knowledge of English and history is important so that the person will not feel like a foreigner in his or her own country.
   d. Good moral character and knowledge of English and government are important because the United States already has a high rate of crime and illiteracy.

Now that you know how to develop an Informal Suitability Survey for the major material you hope to use with your students, go on to the Practicum Exercises, which give you an opportunity to apply this knowledge.

PRACTICUM EXERCISE 1

Suppose as a science teacher you want to determine the suitability of a textbook you really like and want to use with your students. You have looked through the textbook and selected a passage representative of the textual materials. You have counted the number of words and indicated the 300th word, skipping all proper nouns and numerals in your word count.

Now it is time to write a motivation statement and five comprehension questions. Read the following selection; then write a motivation statement and five short-answer or essay comprehension questions consisting of three factual questions, one vocabulary question, and one inference question. Then check your response with ours at the end of this Enabling Element.

Sample Science Selection

A cloud is a mass of small water droplets or tiny ice crystals that float in the air. Some clouds have rounded bumps and appear to be piled up. Other clouds appear in layers or sheets.

Seeing clouds does not always mean it is going to rain. Rain clouds only form when so much water vapor gathers that the water droplets become large and heavy. When the water droplets become too heavy, precipitation will occur, usually in the form of rain or snow.

You may wonder where this water vapor comes from. Water vapor comes from water that has evaporated from lakes, oceans, rivers, or from moist soil and plants. When this water evaporates it is called water vapor. Of course, the air can only hold a certain amount of water vapor at any given temperature; when the temperature drops, some of the water vapor begins to condense. *Condense* means to change into a liquid form, or in our case, to change into tiny droplets of water.

Water vapor can rise to form clouds in many different ways. First, some clouds are formed by *evaporation*. When the sun warms the ground, the air next to the ground is heated. Since the warm air is lighter than the same volume of cooler air, the warm air rises. As the air rises, it expands and becomes cooler. If enough water vapor is in the expanding air, the vapor will condense and form clouds.

Second, some clouds are formed by *lifting*. When warm, moist air moves up the side of a hill or over a range of mountains, it is lifted and cooled by expansion. This cooling causes the water vapor to condense and form clouds that seem to hang over the mountains.   **300ᵀʰ word**

Finally, weather fronts where masses of warm and cool air meet each other produce clouds by what is called *frontal activity.* The water vapor in the rising air becomes cooler and condenses, thus creating the water droplets that form clouds.

Motivation Statement:

Essay or Short-Answer Questions to Check Comprehension

1. *(F)*

2. *(F)*

3. *(F)*

4. *(V)*

5. *(I)*

Answers to Practicum Exercise 1

When you check your responses with ours, you may find that they do not exactly match our motivation statement and/or questions. There is more than one purpose for reading this selection and many different questions for determining if the student comprehended the selection. As you compare your responses to ours, keep in mind that the motivation statement should consist of two sentences. The first sentence indicates what the selection is about; the second provides a command or question directing the student to read the selection. When evaluating your questions, see if

1. The factual questions ask for details important to the comprehension of the selection.

2. The vocabulary question asks for a definition for a word that is not defined in the selection but is important for understanding the selection.
3. The inferential question requires the student to combine knowledge from the selection with information from her background of experience.

Sample Answers to Practicum Exercise
    Motivation Statement: Did you ever wonder how clouds are formed? Read this selection to find out what clouds are and how they are formed.
    Sample Essay Questions

1. *(F)* What are clouds made of? (Small water droplets or ice crystals.)
2. *(F)* When do rain clouds form? (When enough water droplets become large and heavy.)
3. *(F)* Name two ways that clouds are formed. (When moist air moves up the side of a hill, it is lifted and cooled. This cooling causes the water vapor to condense and form clouds. Second, sometimes weather fronts are formed because warm and cool air meet each other. Thus, the water vapor in the warm air rises and becomes cooler and condenses.)
4. *(V)* What is precipitation? (Rain or snow, which is made up of water droplets or ice crystals.)
5. *(I)* Why do some areas get more rain than other areas? (It all depends upon the direction of the wind, temperature, and closeness to bodies of water and mountain ranges.)

PRACTICUM EXERCISE 2

Are you ready to prepare an Informal Suitability Survey for your students? You can do so by following these steps:

1. Select a representative 200-word passage. Make sure the passage is self-contained, that is, does not refer to pictures or illustrations. Skip all proper nouns and numerals when you count the 200 words. If the selection does not end with the 200th word, mark the 200th word by putting a slash after it.
2. Write a motivation statement to provide a specific purpose for reading.
3. Prepare five questions to check comprehension: one vocabulary, one inferential, and three factual.

    After you have developed an Informal Suitability Survey, go to Enabling Element 3, which explains how to administer and score this device.

ENABLING ELEMENT 3
Administering and Scoring an Informal Suitability Survey

Specific Objective 3

You will administer and score an Informal Suitability Survey following the procedures described in this module.

Enabling Activities

1. Read Study Guide 3. It provides directions for administering and scoring an Informal Suitability Survey. Do the Practicum Exercise to apply your new knowledge.
2. Administer an Informal Suitability Survey to an individual and to a small group of students. Which procedure seems better suited to your purpose? What are the advantages and limitations of administering the Informal Suitability Survey to an individual? Group?
3. Give examples of the ways comprehension is affected by (a) insertions, (b) substitutions, and (3) omissions.
4. If your instructor has a tape of a student reading a selection, practice recording the word recognition errors.
5. If a student reads a 300-word selection, makes fourteen word recognition errors, and misses one of the five comprehension questions, is the material suitable? Check your response with the Summary Scoring Guide in Table 2–1.
6. If you administer a selection individually and find that the student recognizes the words perfectly but fails to answer three of the five comprehension questions, can you consider the material suitable? Check your response with the Summary Scoring Guide.
7. Make a chart to record the results of the Informal Suitability Survey.

STUDY GUIDE 3

An Informal Suitability Survey can be administered to individuals or groups of students. Content area teachers are advised to administer the survey initially to the entire class, and later, to individual students who exhibit doubtful results.

Before administering an Informal Suitability Survey to a group of students, you must prepare enough copies of the selection so each student will have one. The motivation statement should appear above the selection and the questions after the selection. As an alternative, you can give each student a copy of the text and write on the chalkboard the location of the selection to be read along with the motivation statement and questions. When all the materials are available, you can administer the survey. To administer the Informal Suitability Survey to an individual student, you do not need to duplicate the passage; simply use the actual textual material along with the motivation statement and questions.

Group Administration

1. Be sure to allow at least fifteen to thirty minutes for the test. Suggest work for those who finish early, so they do not disturb others.
2. Explain to the students that you want to determine how well they can read the textual material for the course. Tell them grades will not be given for the survey, but that you will use the results to help determine useful material for teaching the course.
3. Distribute the selection and questions to the students, and ask them to keep the materials face down on their desks. When all the students have a copy of the selection, read the motivation statement to them and tell them they can have as much time as they need to read the selection. When they finish reading the selection, tell them to answer the comprehension questions. If you do not want them to refer to the selection when answering the questions, collect their copies before you distribute the questions. Since students will be able to refer to a text when studying, they should probably be permitted to refer to the selection when answering the questions. The decision is yours.
4. Your main responsibility for step 4 is observing the students to make sure they are taking the test seriously and not simply marking the answers randomly without reading the selection. You can also observe (a) the rate at which different students finish, (b) attitudes toward the task, and (c) reading habits, such as head movements and finger pointing.
5. Check the papers to see how many questions are answered correctly, and refer to the scoring guide to determine for whom the selection is suitable or unsuitable.

Individual Administration

The individually administered Informal Suitability Survey requires more time than group administration, but is also more informative because, in addition to silent reading, the students read orally.

1. Make sure you can spend seven to ten minutes with the student in a quiet place.
2. Tell the student you want to determine how well she can read the course textbook and/or other required reading material.
3. Read the motivation statement to the student, and ask the student to read the selection silently. Tell the student you are going to ask questions after she reads the selection.
4. When the student finishes reading the selection silently, ask the five

comprehension questions you have prepared. Put a check mark after the question if the student's response is incorrect, and leave it blank if the response is correct. If there is more than one part to the answer, you may give partial credit.

5. After checking comprehension, tell the student to read the selection aloud. As the student reads the selection, follow along on your copy. Look for four major types of word recognition errors: substitution, omission, pronunciation, and insertion.

   a. *Substitution*—If the student says, or substitutes, one word for another word, cross out the word the student should have said, and write in the word she did say. Do not mark errors on proper nouns or numerals, because they are not counted in the passage. For example:

   subject
   A *subpoena* is a legal notice to appear as a witness in court.

   b. *Omission*—If a student omits a word or an entire sentence, circle the omitted word or sentence. Again, do not count errors in proper nouns or numerals; if the student omits proper nouns or numerals, simply pronounce them. Count single or multiword omissions (entire sentence) as one error.

   A subpoena is a (legal) notice to appear as a witness in court.

   c. *Pronunciation*—If the student hesitates when attempting to pronounce a word (other than a proper noun or numeral), ask her to try, allowing at least five seconds. If the student does not say the word, pronounce it and write a capital *P* above the word. Also write a capital *P* above a word if the student asks you to pronounce it.

   P
   A subpoena is a legal notice to appear as a witness in court.

   d. *Insertion*—If a student inserts a word, write in a caret where the word was inserted and write the word above the caret.

   expert
   A subpoena is a legal notice to appear as a witness in court.
   ^

6. As you administer the Informal Suitability Survey, observe the student's reading habits and obtain a feeling for her attitude toward reading. Specifically, consider the following questions:

   a. Is the student relaxed and comfortable when reading? Some students display many signs of anxiety or even refuse to read out loud because they are so far behind in reading.

   b. Is it necessary for the student to point or use some marker to keep her place?

   c. Does the student read word by word, or in phrases?

d. How much confidence and enthusiasm are displayed?
7. Refer to the scoring guide to determine the suitability of the selection.

Criteria for Scoring an Informal Suitability Survey

One criterion for classifying materials as suitable is the student's comprehension of at least 75 percent of the information. We do not want students to comprehend *only* 75 percent of what they read, but if they are able to comprehend 75 percent, you can increase their comprehension with these techniques: introduce specialized vocabulary words (Module 4); help with comprehension (Module 5); teach a study strategy (Module 6); and provide specific purposes for reading (Module 8). The other criterion for classifying materials is that students recognize 95 percent of the words. Again, you want the student to recognize all the words, but if he is able to read 95 percent independently, you can help by applying the word pronunciation strategy introduced in Module 7.

Scoring Surveys Administered to Groups

Informal Suitability Surveys usually have five questions; thus, a student who misses one question scores 80 percent for comprehension. Two questions would be 60 percent, and so forth. A selection can be considered unsuitable if the student misses two or more of the five questions. If he misses only one, or one and a half, the material can be considered suitable. Although missing one and a half questions out of five is equal to 70 percent, we have found no significant difference between 70 percent and 75 percent when determining suitability, especially when using only five questions.

If ten questions are used to check comprehension, the selection can be considered unsuitable if a student misses *more than* three of the ten questions. If the student misses three questions or fewer, the material can be considered suitable.

Scoring Surveys Administered Individually

When an Informal Suitability Survey is administered individually, each student receives a score for comprehension and a score for word recognition. Word recognition errors (omissions, insertions, substitutions, and words the teacher must pronounce) are recorded. The general guideline for scoring word recognition errors is that students should be able to recognize 95 percent of the words for the selection to be considered suitable. If students recognize fewer than 95 percent of the words, the teacher can introduce vocabulary (Module 4) and help the students pronounce multisyllable words (Module 7) before asking them to read the selection.

You probably realize by now why we do not mark proper nouns and numerals as word recognition errors. In selecting the passage for the Informal Suitability Survey, you did not count proper nouns because they are usually introduced by the teacher in making reading assignments. Numerals are not counted because they are not words. Since the criterion for word recognition is that the student recognize 95 percent of the words, we can consider only errors on words included in the word count. You should now also understand why you were directed to mark the 200th, 300th, or 400th word in the selection. When marking word recognition errors, you only mark errors up to these lengths. If the selection is longer, do not mark errors past these word limits.

In a 200-word selection, students can make as many as ten word recognition errors and the material is still classified as suitable. In a 100-word selection, the student can make only five word recognition errors for the material to be classified as suitable. A student may make as many as fifteen word recognition errors on a 300-word selection, twenty on a 400-word selection, and so forth. The criterion for comprehension described earlier is used to determine the suitability of an individually administered Informal Suitability Survey.

If the survey is administered individually, both scores will probably indicate either that the selection is suitable or that it is unsuitable. However, a word recognition score may indicate suitability while the comprehension score indicates unsuitability, or vice versa. If the student scores below the suggested criteria (75 percent comprehension and 95 percent word recognition) for *either* word recognition or comprehension, the selection should be considered unsuitable. The Summary Scoring Guide in Table 2–1 can be used to determine suitability of materials.

A student may be on the borderline of the scoring guide in Table 2–1. For example, if a student makes six errors in 100 words, he is on the border. (The limit is five word recognition errors for 100 words.) You need to analyze the types of errors the student made in word recognition, because some errors are more important than others. For example, if the student reads the sentence, "A subpoena is a legal notice to appear as a witness in court," and substitutes the word *subject* for *subpoena*, the meaning of the sentence is lost. But if the student simply substitutes the word *an* for *a*, the word recognition error is not as important. Likewise, if the student inserts the word *the* in front of the word *court*, the meaning is not drastically changed. On the other hand, if the reader inserts the word *supreme* before the word *court*, the meaning does change drastically. If a student is on the borderline of the number of allowable errors, analyze the errors to determine whether or not meaning has drastically changed. You can decide suitability or unsuitability based upon your analysis.

PRACTICUM EXERCISE

Suppose you have administered a group Informal Suitability Survey constructed from the major textbook you desire to use in the course. Of five comprehension questions, Alfredo missed four. You now decide to

Table 2–1
Summary Scoring Guides for Informal Suitability Surveys
Group Administration (Comprehension Only)

Suitable	Unsuitable
5 Questions: 3½–5 correct	5 Questions: 0–3 correct
10 Questions:7–10 correct	10 Questions: 0–6 correct

Individual Administration
(Word Recognition and Comprehension)

Suitable		Unsuitable	
Comprehension		Comprehension	
5 Questions: 3½–5 correct		5 Questions: 0–3 correct	
10 Questions:7–10 correct		10 Questions: 0–6 correct	
Word Recognition		Word Recognition	
Number of words	Errors	Number of words	Errors
100	0– 5	100	6 or more
200	0–10	200	11 or more
300	0–15	300	16 or more
400	0–20	400	21 or more
500	0–25	500	26 or more

Reminder: Errors made when pronouncing proper nouns and numerals are not counted as word recognition errors. If the survey was administered individually, the scores for *both* comprehension and word recognition must meet the criteria for suitability for the material to be classified as suitable.

individually administer an Informal Suitability Survey from a book with a lower readability level.

You call Alfredo aside during your planning period and tell him you want to find materials he will be able to read. You mention that you have a sample selection from another textbook and would like him to read it. You read the motivation statement to him and observe as he reads silently. After the silent reading, you check his comprehension. (Alfredo's responses are presented after the selection.) You then ask him to read the selection aloud and he makes the errors marked. Is the selection suitable?

Venezuela
    Venezuela is located on the north coast of South America. Venezuela's neighbors are Brazil, Colombia, and Guyana. Venezuela was ⟨originally⟩ a part of the Spanish vice royalty of New Granada. It was freed from Spanish rule by Simon Bolivar in 1818. It is now an independent republic.
    The population of Venezuela is approximately twelve million five hundred thousand people. All citizens over eighteen are allowed to vote in the *free* elections that take place every five years.
    Many of the big oil companies—Exxon, Shell, and Gulf—have operations in Venezuela. As a result, the per capita income conceals

P

many disparities in the actual income among the different groups in the population. Some people live in beautiful castles on the hillsides, / *100 TH WORD* whereas others live in shanty huts. About 3 percent of the population own 90 percent of the land.

The comprehension questions you asked, along with Alfredo's answers, are as follows:

1. *(F)* In what continent is Venezuela located? (South America)
2. *(F)* What country originally ruled Venezuela? (Spain)
3. *(F)* Do the people in Venezuela get to elect their own rulers? (Yes. You must be eighteen years old to vote.)
4. *(V)* What does the term *per capita income* mean? (I don't know.)
5. *(I)* Would you like to live in Venezuela? Why or why not? (Yes. If I worked for the oil companies and owned lots of land I would like to live there.)

Answers to the Practicum Exercise
Yes, this material is suitable for Alfredo. He answered four of the five questions correctly and made only three word-recognition errors in 100 words.

Keeping Records of Results from Informal Suitability Surveys
You may want to keep a record of the results from your Informal Suitability Survey. You can use the chart in Figure 2–1, or make a chart that includes the names of your students and a list of the materials you surveyed. You can mark a *U* on the same line as the student's name under each type of material you found unsuitable and an *S* under the material you found suitable. A chart like this is especially helpful if you administer a series of Informal Suitability Surveys to determine the appropriateness of different materials. As we mentioned, it is unlikely you will find one type of material suitable for all students. Your chart will guide you as you select suitable materials for different students.

Another Way to Use the Informal Suitability Survey
You already know that the Informal Suitability Survey can be used to match your students with textual material, as described earlier. There are also situations where a less structured approach can be used, such as when you need to immediately determine suitability of material. For example, you may be working with your students in the library while they locate supplementary material to expand upon the content in their textbooks. You move around the library, helping students find material appropriate to the topic and suitable for them to read. If you find a book you want to suggest to Josephine, you quickly survey the book to find a representative passage. Rather than count 200 words, you simply count

Names of Students	Names of Materials			
1.				
2.				
3.				
4.				
5.				
6.				
7.				
8.				
9.				
10.				
11.				
12.				
13.				
14.				
15.				
16.				
17.				
18.				
19.				
20.				
21.				
22.				
23.				
24.				
Total				

Code: U = Unsuitable
     S = Suitable

Figure 2–1
Material suitability chart

the words in the first two lines, divide by two for the average, and use this figure to determine approximately how many lines you will need to have approximately 200 words. You then give Josephine a purpose for reading and have her read the 200-word selection silently. As she reads the selection, you quickly read it over her shoulder to formulate your five questions. When Josephine finishes, you ask her the five questions. If she answers three and a half or more correctly, you ask her to read the 200-word passage aloud. As she does so, you count her pronunciation errors. You now have all the information you need to determine if the material is suitable for Josephine. If it is, you encourage her to read the material; if not, to find another. This procedure probably takes less than three minutes.

Another technique for identifying suitable reading materials is presented in Enabling Element 4 of this module. If you want an alternative method for matching materials to students, go to Enabling Element 4 and learn about the Cloze procedure.

ENABLING ELEMENT 4
Cloze: An Alternative Procedure for Determining Suitability

Specific Objective 4

You will describe how to use the Cloze Procedure as an alternative for determining suitability of content area reading material.

Enabling Activities

1. Read Study Guide 4. This Study Guide provides directions for using the Cloze procedure as an alternative for determining suitability of content area reading materials.
2. Do Practicum Exercise 1 to learn what it is like to complete a Cloze task. Compare your answers with those provided in Answers to Practicum Exercise 1.
3. Complete Practicum Exercise 2 to practice preparing, administering, scoring, and interpreting results from a Cloze test.
4. Select a passage that is approximately 300 words in length from a textbook in your subject area. The passage should be appropriate for using the Cloze procedure to prepare an Informal Suitability Survey. Prepare a Suitability Survey following the directions provided.
5. Administer the Cloze test you prepared to a group of students to determine if the textbook is suitable.
6. Write a paragraph explaining when it is appropriate to use each procedure you learned for determining suitability of reading material.

STUDY GUIDE 4

An alternative to determining suitability using oral and silent passages and checking for mispronunciation and comprehension errors is a procedure known as Cloze. Cloze is an effective alternative procedure for determining if a match exists between the reading achievement of a student and the reading requirements of textual material such as a textbook.

The Cloze procedure was originally developed by Taylor (1953) for determining the readability of printed material. It can also be used to determine the suitability of printed material for students' reading assignments. Some teachers prefer the Cloze procedure for determining suitability because of its objectivity in scoring. With the Cloze procedure there is no doubt about the correctness of an answer and scoring is much easier. In this module you will learn how to use the Cloze procedure to determine the suitability of textual material.

With the Cloze procedure, students are required to fill in words that have been deleted from a sample of the textual material. By reading and reconstructing the author's intended meaning, students demonstrate how suitable the text is for them.

Examining A Cloze Passage

Here is what a Cloze passage looks like. Notice that the introduction and ending are unaltered. The deletions occur only in the main body of the text. Notice that the text is double spaced rather than single spaced as it would be in a textbook. Also notice that the length of each line is the same for every deletion. Read and complete the Cloze passage by writing the word you believe fits in each blank. Do it now. When you have finished, continue reading Study Guide 4.

PRACTICUM EXERCISE 1

Sample Cloze Passage—52 blanks

As a classroom teacher it is important for you to know why,

when, and how to use an Informal Suitability Survey. This important

teaching tool _____ help you match students _____ textual and library

materials _____ can read. It is _____ undesirable to place advanced,

_____ skilled readers into easy _____ material as it is _____ place

problem readers with _____ expectancy reading skills into _____ that is

too difficult _____ them to read.

When _____ suspect that the material _____ student has chosen to

_____ is too easy or _____ to read, use the _____ survey to determine

suitability. _____ have learned how to _____ a representative passage

and _____ questions over the selection. _____ also have learned how

_____ administer the Informal Suitability _____ to an individual or

_____ groups of students.

In _____ Enabling Element you will _____ an alternative method,

called _____, for determining suitability. The _____ procedure is

particularly good _____ determining the suitability of _____ or library

materials for _____ of students.

You surely _____ find both of these _____ to be useful teaching

_____ for matching students with _____ reading materials. You

will _____ to match students with _____ reading materials in

every _____ of your classes. Even _____ you teach high-achieving,

_____ students you can expect _____ range of reading achievements.

_____ these students there will _____ some with larger vocabularies,

_____ experiences, and greater language _____ and they will be _____ to

read and comprehend _____ difficult material than their _____. By

giving students challenging _____ not overwhelming materials to _____,

you will get your _____ to blossom as fully _____ they are capable

of _____. This is the real _____ of education—getting students to

achieve to their capacity for achieving. You can move toward this goal

by being sure your students are in appropriate reading materials.

Scoring Your Cloze Passage

Look at the Answers to Practicum Exercise 1 to obtain the correct insertions for each blank in the Cloze selection. Compare your insertions with the words in the actual text. Count the number of perfect matches between the words you inserted and the actual words. ONLY perfect matches count as correct answers. In other words, if there is as little as one letter difference between what you wrote and what appears in the actual text you do not have a correct insertion. The only exception is for misspelled words. Misspelled words should not be counted as incorrect insertions as long as they have the correct word endings (hily for highly). Your score is the number of correct insertions.

Answers to Practicum Exercise 1

Sample Cloze Passage
    As a classroom teacher it is important for you to know why, when, and how to use an Informal Suitability Survey. This important teaching tool will help you match students to textual and library materials they can read. It is equally undesirable to place advanced, highly skilled readers into easy reading material as it is to place problem readers with below expectancy reading skills into material that is too difficult for them to read.
    When you suspect that the material a student has chosen to read is too easy or difficult to read, use the informal survey to determine suitability. You have learned how to select a representative passage and prepare questions over the selection. You also have learned how to administer the Informal Suitability Survey to an individual or to groups of students. In this Enabling Element you will learn an alternative method, called Cloze, for determining suitability. The Cloze procedure is particularly good for determining the suitability of textual or library materials for groups of students.
    You surely will find both of these techniques to be useful teaching tools for matching students with appropriate reading materials. You will need to match students with appropriate reading materials in every one of your classes. Even if you teach high-achieving, gifted students you can expect a range of reading achievements. Among these students there will be some with larger vocabularies, broader experiences, and greater language aptitude, and they will be able to read and comprehend more difficult material than their classmates. By giving students challenging but not overwhelming materials to read, you will get your students to blossom as fully as they are capable of doing. This is the real challenge of education—getting students to achieve to their capacity for achieving. You can move toward this goal by being sure your students are in appropriate reading materials.

Constructing a Cloze Passage
Here are the steps you need to follow to prepare your own Cloze passage.

Step 1. Select a Representative Passage.
From a textbook.   Once you have identified the textbook you want to use for your Informal Suitability Survey, your first task is to select the passage you will use for your Cloze test. Select a passage from the front of the textbook. Passages from later sections of the textbook may require vocabulary and knowledge not yet known by the student but to be provided by the teacher. The passage should be approximately 300 words in length.

From a library book.   Anytime you want to generalize to a library book, you must be certain you have selected a passage that represents the book. If you select a passage that is too easy or too hard, you will come to the wrong conclusion about the suitability of the book for your students. Be sure to examine your source book carefully to get a feel for the difficulty level of the book. Then select the passage that best represents the reading difficulty of the library book. The passage should be approximately 300 words in length.

Step 2. Selecting the Words to be Deleted.
Make a photocopy of the passage you have chosen for the Cloze test. Then mark off the first and last 25 words in the passage. No deletions are made in the first or last 25 words in a Cloze passage. After the 25th word, underline every fifth word until you reach the final 25 words in the selection. Then stop. Leave approximately the last 25 words intact.

Step 3. Preparing the Passage.
Type the passage double-spaced with blank spaces for the underlined words. Be sure every blank space is exactly the same length. The blank spaces should be long enough for students to write in the longest deleted word.

Step 4. Duplicate the Passage.
Finally, duplicate the passage so that each student will have a copy. Be sure the duplicated copies are clearly readable.

Training Students for Cloze Tests
If your students have not completed Cloze-type tasks or taken Cloze-type tests, provide them with a number of exercises to familiarize them with Cloze before using your passage to determine the suitability of a textual material. Cloze can present a problem to students who are not familiar with the format or task requirements. Three or four exercises are usually sufficient to acquaint students with Cloze and to develop their confidence with the task.

During the training phase, it is a good idea for the teacher to read the passages aloud and to lead a group discussion on answer choices. Both activities will help students understand how language and meaning are used to decide which word best fits each deletion.

Administering the Cloze Test
To administer the Cloze test do the following:

1. Be sure each student has a pencil and eraser.
2. Give each student a copy of the Cloze selection. Be sure the copies remain face down on the students' desks.
3. Give the directions orally. Tell the students they are to read the following selection and write a word for each deletion in the passage. Tell them to read the selection once silently before filling in any of the blanks.

4. Answer any questions the students have about the task and then ` them to begin.
5. Give the students whatever time is necessary for everyone to complete the passage. Time is not a factor in this test.
6. Since students will finish at different times, be sure every student has something to do when finished with the task. As students complete the task have them turn their papers over and go to their alternate activity. Pick up papers as they are completed. Do not allow students who finish early to move around the room or otherwise cause distractions in the classroom.

Scoring the Cloze Test
Here is how to score a Cloze test:

1. Count the number of perfect matches between words supplied by the student and words in the original text.
2. Misspelled words should not be counted as incorrect so long as they have the correct word endings.
3. The raw score is the total number of correct matches.
4. Count the total number of deletions.
5. Divide the raw score by the number of deletions to obtain the percentage correct score. For example, a student who has 15 perfect matches has a raw score of 15. If there are a total of 30 deletions then 15 is divided by 30 and the percentage correct score is 50 percent.
6. The percentage correct score is what is used to determine suitability.

Determining the Suitability of the Textual Material
Use the following criteria for determining the suitability of textual material:

    0–39%   TOO DIFFICULT, obtain less demanding material.
    40–60%   SUITABLE, adequate for the assignment.
    61–100%   TOO EASY, obtain more demanding material.

PRACTICUM EXERCISE 2

Now it is your turn to prepare a Cloze test. Select a representative passage from a textual source in your subject area. That textual source may be a textbook, magazine, journal, booklet, or any other printed source from which students can obtain information. Prepare the passage so it can be used as a Cloze test. Then administer the Cloze test and determine its suitability.

To verify that you have completed Practicum Exercise 2, provide the following information:

1. Enter the raw score here (total number of perfect matches):

2. Enter the total number of deletions here:

3. Divide the raw score by the number of deletions to obtain the percentage correct score here:

4. Write a statement that explains how the percentage correct score should be interpreted.

Answers to Practicum Exercise 2
Answers to this exercise will vary. Be sure to recheck your counting of correct insertions and total number of deletions. Also check your mathematics and interpretation. In your answer to number 4, you should have indicated what should be done if the material is too difficult, suitable, or too easy.

Final Comment
You have learned two different procedures for determining suitability. Try both and use the one you believe more useful for selecting suitable reading materials for your students. We like to use the oral and silent reading passages and questions when we work with individual students. It's quicker to create and administer this type of Informal Suitability Survey than the Cloze procedure. We like the Cloze procedure when we are working with groups of students and have time to prepare the Cloze test passages.

POSTTEST

Directions: The following questions are designed to test your accomplishment of the objectives in this module. Check your responses with the answers on the following pages. Review as necessary after checking your responses.

1. Describe an Informal Suitability Survey and state the major purpose for using one.
2. Outline and explain the three major procedures in constructing such a survey.
3. What information can you get from an individually administered survey that cannot be obtained when you administer one to a group?

4. Suppose, as a math teacher, you individually administer the following 200-word Informal Suitability Survey to John, who was absent the day you administered the survey to the group. Is the selection suitable? Justify your answer.

Solving Math Problems Stated in Paragraph Form

p The first step in solving mathematical problems written in paragraph form is to read the problems carefully to determine what you are *p* supposed to find. After knowing this, reread the problem to find (the) relevant or irrelevant facts. For example, sometimes problems include facts that are not necessary to find the answer to the problem. The fact that Mrs. Jones waited in line for 12 minutes may be *interest* ~~interesting,~~ but it does not help you determine how much change she should receive, considering her purchase.

The next step is to decide what process you must use to find the answer. Remember that sometimes it is necessary to use two or three processes in order to answer the question. For example, if the problem says that Mrs. Jones bought three cans of milk at 19 cents a can, you must multiply the costs of the milk and then add this to the other groceries. Of course it would be necessary then to subtract the total cost from the amount given to find how much change she should receive. *back*

After you have done the *complete* ~~computation,~~ you should ask yourself if the answer makes sense. If it does not, check your arithmetic and *the* question the process that you used.

Comprehension Questions
(*V* = Vocabulary; *F* = Factual; *I* = Inference.)
1. *(F)* What is the first step in doing math problems that are stated in paragraph form?
2. *(V)* What does *process* mean?
3. *(F)* What are ways of checking your answer?
4. *(F)* After you determine the question that is asked and the relevant facts, what is the next step to solve the math problem?
5. *(I)* Why do math problems stated in paragraph form sometimes include irrelevant facts?

John's Answers to the Comprehension Questions:
1. The first step in doing a math problem that appears in paragraph form is to determine what you are supposed to find.
2. Process means add, subtract, multiply, or divide.
3. You can check your answers by questioning the process you used or by redoing the computation.
4. Decide what process you should use to find the answer.
5. The book tries to get you mixed up. The teacher is trying to fool you.

5. Write a statement that describes the way you will create, administer, and interpret the results from an Informal Suitability Survey using the Cloze procedure.

Posttest Answers

1. An Informal Suitability Survey consists of a representative selection from textual material you plan to use, an accompanying motivation statement, and questions to check comprehension. It is designed to determine if students can handle selected textual material.
2. The major procedures in constructing a survey are as follows:
   a. Select a 200-word passage representative of the reading material in a commonly used textbook or other written material. Skip all proper nouns and numerals when counting the 200 words, and mark the 200th word with a slash. (The selection may be more than 200 words.)
   b. Write a motivation statement to give the students a purpose for reading.
   c. Write three factual questions, one vocabulary question, and one inferential question.
3. Information concerning the student's skill in recognizing words while reading orally is obtained when a survey is administered individually.
4. John's word recognition and comprehension errors for this selection indicate that the selection is suitable. He made seven word recognition errors in this 200-word selection and missed only one of the five questions.
5. Cloze is an alternative procedure for determining suitability of content area reading material. Begin by selecting a passage of approximately 300 words from the beginning of a textbook or a passage that is representative of the reading difficulty in a library book. Mark off the first and last 25 words in the passage. After the first 25 words, underline every fifth word until you reach approximately the last 25 words. Type the passage double-spaced with blank spaces for every underlined word. Be sure the blanks are all the same length.

   Give each student a copy of the passage and a pencil. Have students listen carefully as you explain the directions for completing the Cloze test. Be sure to allow students whatever time is necessary to complete the test. Be sure those students who finish early have something to do so that they do not disturb students still working on the test. Pick up the papers as soon as students complete the test.

   For each student, count the number of perfect matches to get a raw score. Remember that misspelled words should not be counted as wrong so long as they have the correct word ending. Determine the percentage correct. If the percentage correct is between 0 and 39, the material is too difficult, and less demanding material should be found for the student. If it is between 40 and 60 percent, it is suitable for assignment. If it is between 61 and 100 percent, it is too easy and more demanding material should be found.

If you have accurately completed all the Posttest items, you are ready for another module. If not, refer to the appropriate Enabling Element for clarification of your difficulty. If you cannot clarify the difficulty, contact your instructor.

REFERENCES

Barufaldi, J. P., & Daily, R. J. (1986). Enhancing the reading comprehension of secondary school science textbooks: Suggestions for textbook writers. *Science Education in Ohio, 4*(1), 27–37.

Chance, I. (1985). Use Cloze encounters of the readability kind for secondary school students. *Journal of Reading, 28*(8), 690–693.

Dishne, E. K., & Readence, J. E. (1977). Getting Started: Using the textbook diagnostically. *Reading World, 17,* 36–49.

Estes T., & Vaughan, Jr., J. (1978). *Reading and learning in the content classroom.* Boston: Allyn and Bacon.

Graves, M. K., Boettcher, J. A., & Ryder, R. A. (1979). *Easy reading: Book series and periodicals for less able readers.* Newark, DE: International Reading Association.

Johnson, M. S., & Kress, R. A. (1965). Informal reading inventories. *Reading Aids Series.* Newark, DE: International Reading Association.

Kealey. R. J. (1980, Spring). Helping students read the content area textbook. *Reading Improvement, 17*(1), 36–39.

Lovitt, T. C., et al. (1987). Matching students with textbooks: An alternative to readability formulas and standard tests. *B. C. Journal of Special Education, 11*(1), 49–55.

McKenna, M. C., & Robinson, R. D. (1980). *An introduction to the Cloze procedure: An annotated bibliography.* Newark, DE: International Reading Association.

McWilliams, L., & Rakes, T. A. (1979). *Content inventories: English, social studies, science.* Dubuque, IA: Kendall/Hunt Publishing Company.

Rakes, T. A. (1975). A group instructional inventory. *Journal of Reading, 18,* 595–598.

Rakow, S., & Gee, T. C. (1987). Test science, not reading. *Science Teacher, 54*(2), 28–31.

Readence, J., Bean, T., & Baldwin, R. (1981). *Content area reading: An integrated approach.* Dubuque, IA: Kendall/Hunt Publishing Company.

Taylor, W. S. (1953). Cloze procedure: A new test for measuring readability. *Journalism Quarterly, 30,* 415–433.

MODULE THREE

Differentiating
Reading Assignments

CHAPTER OUTLINE

OVERVIEW

RATIONALE

You know one textbook will not serve the information needs or match the reading levels of all your students. Your students will vary in the amount of information they know about any topic in your subject area. They will also vary in their reading achievement. As a subject area teacher, one of your responsibilities must be to provide appropriate reading material to all your students. The textual material must be appropriate in terms of information as well as reading level.

In Modules 1 and 2 you learned how to select appropriate materials for your students to read. In Module 1, you learned how to analyze content, learning aids, and readability to select appropriate textual materials for your students to read. In Module 2, you learned how to use the Informal Suitability Survey to match a student with a specific reading material when you do not know the reading achievement level of the student or the readability level of the material.

Because of the expected range in reading achievement among your students, you will need a variety of reading materials to achieve your content area objectives. In this module you will learn how to organize instruction around unit themes so students with varying reading levels can read from different sources of information and learn yet a common core of information. This module will show you how to specify your unit objectives, organize textual materials, and make differentiated reading assignments. The end result will be that all students will gather information on a common set of objectives, but they will gather the information from sources that are challenging but not overwhelming in reading difficulty.

OBJECTIVES

General Objective

You will use the differentiated reading assignment (DRA) to assign reading materials that are appropriate in reading level.

Specific Objectives

1. You will explain why it is important for a content area teacher to use a differentiated reading assignment (DRA) when making reading assignments and describe the components of the DRA.

2. You will prepare a differentiated reading assignment (DRA) following the guidelines provided.
3. You will specify other ways to help students read textual materials in your subject area.

ENABLING ELEMENT 1
The Differentiated Reading Assignment (DRA)

Specific Objective 1
You will explain why it is important for a content area teacher to use a differentiated reading assignment (DRA) when making reading assignments and describe the components of the DRA.

Enabling Activities

1. Read Study Guide 1 to learn why it is important for teachers to prepare differentiated reading assignments for their students and the major components of the DRA.
2. Look at the reading achievement test scores for the students in one of your classes. What is the range of reading achievement levels for the students in this class? Would one book be appropriate in reading level for all the students in this class?
3. Browse through your school media center and make a list of materials that your students could use in place of the textbook. Be sure to look for both printed and nonprinted sources of information.
4. Ask the school media specialist to help you identify other sources from which your students could obtain information on topics you will cover as part of your course.
5. Visit a bookstore and identify magazines, newspapers, paperback books, and other print materials that can be used by students to obtain information on topics you will cover as part of your course.

STUDY GUIDE 1

One book is not going to match the reading needs of all your students. You know any single book is going to be too difficult in reading level for some of your students, just right for others, and too easy for the remainder. Just as no article of clothing fits all, no book fits all.

One of your responsibilities will be to place students in materials from which they can obtain information relevant to the objectives of your course. Most of the time you will be making assignments in print materials because they are the most readily available. Print is still the least expensive way to mass produce and distribute information. But sources of information should not be limited to print materials. You should use audiotapes, videotapes, films, and the many other sources of nonprint material to get information to your students. You should never deny students access to information merely because they can not read well enough to handle the printed textual material. Denying students access to information because of their reading disabilities is just another form of discrimination.

To provide all students with an opportunity to access information considered important for your course, you will need to prepare differentiated reading assignments. A differentiated reading assignment is a plan for individualizing reading assignments in science, social studies, and other content areas. The teacher has students reading from different sources but for the same purposes. The differentiated reading assignment permits the classroom teacher to have common objectives while varying (differentiating) reading assignments according to each student's reading achievement.

The first part of a differentiated reading assignment is the *unit topic*, a brief statement about the focus of the unit. In the following sample differentiated reading assignment, the unit focuses on the skin; thus, the topic is "Caring for Your Skin."

The second part of a differentiated reading assignment contains the objectives. Objectives tell the teacher what the students must learn from studying this topic.

Reading questions make up the third part of the differentiated reading assignment. The questions are developed from the objectives. There may be one or more questions per objective. Some teachers like to list major questions and have the students add others.

The fourth part of a differentiated reading assignment lists *reading sources* to be used by the students to gather the information they need to answer the questions. Teachers generally use their knowledge of the difficulty of the materials and reading capabilities to assign specific sources to specific students, or they may have students select sources they would like to use and with which they feel comfortable. The readability graphs and the Informal Suitability Survey will be helpful to do this.

The last part of the differentiated reading plan contains the actual *reading assignments*. This section can include the students' names and the appropriate references for each student to read. Although the assignments are differentiated according to the teacher's knowledge of the students' reading achievements, the materials are not designated as "more difficult" or "easy reading." Some teachers make the reading assignments informally by telling each student which resources he or she may want to use, rather than listing reading assignments and distributing copies. We recommend that you jot down possibilities and then suggest these orally to individual students or groups of students.

Here is a sample differentiated reading assignment. Examine each section as to the type of information provided.

Sample Differentiated Reading Assignment

 I. *Unit Topic:* Caring for Your Skin
 II. *Unit Objectives*
    1. To learn the function of skin.
    2. To learn the causes of common skin ailments.
    3. To learn common treatments for skin ailments.
    4. To learn how the appearance of skin can be altered by nature and medicine.
    5. To learn how different skin colors came about.
 III. *Reading Questions*
    1. What are the causes of acne?
    2. What is the best way to treat acne?
    3. What is the easiest and safest way to get a tan?
    4. What causes warts and moles?
    5. How are face-lifts done?
    6. What are some of the best ways to treat impetigo?
    7. Why do some people have birthmarks?
    8. What causes freckles?
    9. How can you best treat athlete's foot and jungle rot?
   10. Why do some people have dry skin and other people have oily skin?
   11. What can you do about caring for oily skin or dry skin?
   12. How is skin grafted?
   13. Why are there different colors of skin?
   14. What is the function of skin?
 IV. *Reading Sources*
    1. *World Book Encyclopedia*—Articles about skin, acne, athlete's foot and warts.
    2. *First Aid*, by the American Red Cross
    3. Film—*Care of the Skin*, by Encyclopaedia Britannica Films
    4. Film—*Healthy Skin*, by Coronet
    5. *The Skin*, by Patrick Hare
    6. *Question and Answer Book About the Human Body*, by Ann McGovern
    7. *Cosmetic Surgery*, by William Brown
    8. *Plastic Surgery: Beauty You Can Buy*, by Harriett LeBarre
    9. Filmstrip—*Caring for Acne*
   10. *Encyclopaedia Britannica*
   11. Pamphlets by The American Medical Association and Dermatology Foundation
   12. Selected articles in *Glamour* and *Today's Health*
   13. *Medical and Health Encyclopedia*, edited by Morris Fishbein, M.D.
   14. *Structure and Function of the Skin*, by W. Montagna
   15. *Fungus Diseases and Their Treatment*, by Ivan Sarkang
   16. Textbook—*You and Your Body*, chapter 7, "Care of Your Hair and Skin"
   17. *You and Your Skin*, by Norman Goldsmith
   18. Filmstrip—*Acne: Cause and Care*

V. *Reading Assignments: Plan 1*

	Students	Reading Sources
Group A:	Nathaniel, Josephine, Harvey, Lara, Rocky, Alfredo	1, 6, 7, 16
Group B:	Ruth, Don, O.J., Susan, Holly, Jorge, Billie	3, 12, 17, 18
Group C:	Mary, Paul, Martha, Rex, Ed, Dalia, Tina	2, 4, 9, 11
Group D:	Jeff, Jackie, Sharon, Nikki, Angie, David, Diane, Bill	10, 13, 14
Group E:	Patricia, Melita, Bob, Dick, Barbara, Ann, Jeff	5, 8, 15

Notice that the last part of the differentiated reading assignment—the actual assignment list—is presented as Plan 1. As you examine Plan 1, you will probably notice that the students in Group B are those who are reading far below grade level. As you peruse the list of reading sources, notice that Group B will be using filmstrips, a low-readability-level book, and articles from magazines to answer the questions. The best readers in the class, those in Group D, will use some of the more difficult reading sources. Regardless of reading level, however, all students will be able to find information to answer some of the questions you planned with them about care of the skin. In this way, each person can make a contribution.

Another way to differentiate reading assignments is to divide students into teams (refer to Plan 2). You will have excellent readers on each team as well as those who read far below grade level. You will then ask each team to find answers using a variety of sources. You can designate particular sources, or discuss all the available sources and ask them to choose some. If you decide to divide the reading sources among the teams, the assignments for your differentiated reading plan might look like this:

V. *Reading Assignments: Plan 2*

	Students	Reading Sources
Group A:	Nathaniel, Ruth, Mary, Jeff, Patricia, Josephine, Don	1, 3, 7, 14
Group B:	Paul, Jackie, Melita, Maria, O.J., Martha, Sharon	2, 5, 10, 15
Group C:	Bob, Harvey, Holly, Rex, Nikki, Dick, Lara	4, 8, 13, 17

Group D:	Jorge, Ed, Angie,	6, 9, 11
	Barbara, Rocky,	
	Billie, Dalia	
Group E:	Diane, Anne,	12, 16, 18
	Alfredo, Tina,	
	Bill, Jeff	

The advantage of Plan 2 is that the groups now include students with many different reading levels. Rather than compete with each other, the students compete as teams. Team A will want to find as many good answers to the questions as the other teams, and frequently, teammates help each other learn. Another advantage of this plan is that students who are poor readers are not categorized as such and given "easy" materials. When students work together as a team, the students in each group will naturally choose the reading resources provided for them. Students who have reading difficulties will prefer to watch filmstrips or read materials at a lower readability level.

We recommend using Plan 2 to allow students of many different achievement levels to work together and compete as teams. We have found that students do learn from each other and can work together well if there are many information sources. We also believe that students' self-concepts are enhanced with a team approach.

You can readily see the advantages of a differentiated reading plan. If you realize that one textbook is not suitable for all, yet want all of your students to accomplish the objectives of your content area, the advantages of a differentiated reading assignment are apparent. The method helps each student use his or her own capabilities to accomplish the objectives you set.

ENABLING ELEMENT 2
Preparing the Differentiated Reading Assignment (DRA)

Specific Objective 2
You will prepare a differentiated reading assignment (DRA) following the guidelines provided.

Enabling Activities

1. Read Study Guide 2 and complete the activities to prepare a simulated differentiated reading assignment.
2. Obtain a copy of a school system curriculum guide. Review the contents to learn what information it contains that will be helpful to you when you prepare a DRA.
3. Check with media specialists and your colleagues to obtain the largest possible set of print and nonprint materials relevant to your topic.

4. Make a list of print and nonprint sources that would be relevant to the topic for which you prepared your DRA and ask students to bring in appropriate materials from home.
5. Share your DRA with colleagues to give and acquire additional ideas for preparing your DRA.

STUDY GUIDE 2

Preparing the DRA

There are a number of steps you must follow when preparing the DRA. For each step you are to complete a simulated differentiated reading activity.

Step 1: Selecting a Topic

Now it is time for you to plan a differentiated reading assignment. Begin by choosing a unit topic you would like to study with your students. You can get ideas for units by looking through the school system curriculum guide. Most school systems have a curriculum guide, which contains a list of topics to be taught in every course at every grade level. Many curriculum guides also contain lists of objectives, learning activities, suggested materials, and recommended evaluation procedures.

You can also obtain ideas for unit topics by browsing through textbooks written for courses similar to those you teach. Most school systems maintain a book depository where copies of all the textbooks used in the school system are kept. The school library or a university library will also have copies of textbooks, reference books, and other print sources from which you can obtain ideas for a unit topic. Of course, teachers, curriculum specialists, assistant principals for curriculum development, and other school personnel can also provide you with ideas for a unit topic.

As soon as you have selected a unit topic, write the unit topic name or description in the appropriate area in the Simulated Differentiated Reading Assignment found at the end of this study guide. After you have recorded your unit topic, continue reading with the next step in the plan.

Step 2: Identifying the Unit Objectives

When identifying unit objectives, the school system curriculum guide, subject area textbooks, and your fellow teachers can be very helpful. Begin by looking in the curriculum guide or subject area textbooks to identify the objectives for your instruction on the unit topic you chose. Some of the objectives will be general statements and some very specific. Review the objectives provided by the school district and select those you believe are appropriate for your students and can be achieved given the amount of time you intend to devote to this topic. Be sure all

---

objectives to be tested on your state competency or knowledge test are included in your list of objectives. Many states require students to pass competency or knowledge tests to graduate from high school.

After you have selected your objectives, share them with your colleagues. Ask your colleagues if, in their opinion, you have gathered too many or too few objectives. Also determine if any important objectives are missing from the cluster you gathered. Once you are satisfied with the objectives, write them in the appropriate section of the simulated DRA found at the end of this study guide. Then, return to this section to learn the next step in preparing the Simulated Differentiated Reading Assignment.

Step 3: Writing the Reading Questions

Study the list of objectives and for each write one or more questions that students need to answer to demonstrate they have acquired the information or skill necessary to achieve the objective. Ask your colleagues to critique your list of questions. Maybe they can think of others to add, some that should be deleted, or ways to state your questions so the intent is clearer. If you are working with students, share the unit topic, objectives, and your questions with them. Ask them to critique and add questions. Allowing students to add questions personalizes the assignment and often contributes to a higher level of motivation for the task. When you are satisfied with your questions, write them in the appropriate section of the simulated DRA found at the end of this study guide. Then return here and continue reading with the next step.

Step 4: Locating the Learning Sources

There are a number of places you can locate good sources of information on almost any topic. Start with the school library, or, as many are called today, the media center. The librarian can show you a number of references you can use to locate material on your topic. The card catalog will provide you with a variety of textual materials you can use. The *Reader's Guide to Periodical Literature* will help you find magazines you can use. Your library probably has a reference to newspaper articles from the *New York Times, Washington Post, Los Angeles Times,* or other popular newspapers. If you browse through the reference section of the library you will find many additional sources of information some of which will be appropriate for studying the topic. If you are near a large regional library or have access to a college or university library you can probably find even more materials for your students to use to obtain information on the topic. Also browse through bookstores for materials. You can also look through related chapters in subject area textbooks for additional sources of information. Your colleagues and friends may also be able to suggest additional materials.

Since your goal is to provide your students with the best possible presentation on the topic, also look for nonprint materials. Pictures, films, videotapes, audiotapes, and other nonprint materials often are excellent for explaining abstract concepts that are very difficult to understand using print materials. Remember, reading is an important way to get information, but it is not the only way. Often nonprint materials must be used to learn difficult concepts or ideas.

When you have compiled your print and nonprint materials, enter the name of each material in the appropriate section of the simulated DRA. Number each material and then return and continue reading with the next step.

Step 5: Making Reading Assignments

Assume you have the following students in one of your classes. Read the information provided for each student. Then, recall or review the two different plans for grouping students for making differentiated reading assignments. This was explained in the last study guide. Complete section 5 of the simulated DRA for each plan.

Plan 1:   Divide the students into four groups according to their knowledge of the subject area and their reading achievement. Then make reading assignments to each group using numbers to designate appropriate materials from your list under Learning Sources.

Plan 2:   Divide the students into four groups according to their knowledge of the subject area and their reading achievement. Next form groups so that each group has one excellent, one high average, one average, and one low average achieving student. Then, make reading assignments to each group using numbers to designate appropriate materials from your list under Learning Resources.

Show how you formed your groups and the assignments you made for each group by completing Section 5 in the Simulated Directed Reading Activity at the end of this study guide.

Students

Mel	Really understands the subject. Excellent reader.
Sally	Very knowledgeable. High average reader.
Gib	Average knowledge and average reader.
José	Average knowledge and average reader.
Marilyn	Excellent knowledge and excellent reader.
Jill	Below average in knowledge and reading achievement.
Sid	High average knowledge and reading achievement.
Pat	Below average knowledge and reading achievement.
Willis	Excellent student and excellent reader.
Sue	Very average student in all ways.
Helene	Low average performance in knowledge and reading achievement.
Barbara	High average student in everything.
Pete	Average knowledge and average reader.
Debbie	High average knowledge and high average reader.

Christin   Excellent achievement in knowledge and reading.
Joe   Has difficulty with everything. Poor reader.

Simulated Differential Reading Assignment (DRA)

Step 1: Unit Topic (Write the topic here)

Step 2: Unit Objectives (List the objectives here)
1.

Step 3: Reading Questions (List and number the questions here)
1.

Step 4: Learning Resources (List and number the resources here)
1.

Step 5: Reading Assignments (Enter student names and assigned resources for each group for both plans)

	Plan 1	
Groups	Students	Learning Resources
A		
B		

C

D

Groups	Plan 2 Students	Learning Resources
A		
B		
C		
D		

You may believe that making a differentiated reading assignment requires too much time. Although extra hours are necessary when using more than one resource with students, you will be more effective if you use a variety of resources. If you continue to develop a repertoire of reading resources for the various topics in your content area, you will soon have a large collection of appropriate reading materials. If you begin by simply suggesting a few sources to your students, you are on the right track!

ENABLING ELEMENT 3
Techniques for Making Print Material More Readable

Specific Objective 3
You will specify other ways to help students read textual materials in your subject area.

Enabling Activities

1. Read Study Guide 3 to learn how to help your students read print materials.

2. Survey Modules 4 on Vocabulary, 5 on Comprehension, 6 on Study Skills and Study Strategies, and 7 on Word Pronunciation to learn what types of knowledge and skills you will be acquiring to help students read textual materials.
3. Survey Module 8 to see what you will need to learn to motivate students to read.
4. Survey Module 9 for additional ideas for identifying and helping problem readers when they lack the reading achievement necessary for most textual materials.
5. Contact the following sources of audiotaped versions of commonly available textual materials to obtain copies of taped textbooks for students classified as learning disabled.
   Recording for the Blind, Inc. (RFB), 215 E. 58th Street, New York, NY 10022; (212) 751–0860.
   National Library Service for the Blind and Physically Handicapped (NLS), the Library of Congress, 1291 Taylor Street NW, Washington, DC 20542; (202) 287–5100.

STUDY GUIDE 3

Other Ways to Help Students Read Textual Materials

In addition to making differentiated reading assignments, what else can you do to help students read the textual materials in your content area? Here are some useful ideas:

- Be sure the material is appropriate by using the Informal Suitability Survey, one of the readability graphs, or the Cloze procedure.
- Introduce the specialized vocabulary that causes difficulty for many students. Module 4 on word meaning gives specific suggestions for helping students develop the meanings of words.
- Teach students how to use the strategy for pronouncing multisyllable words taught in Module 7. This strategy will help them pronounce the many troublesome multisyllable words found in subject area textual materials.
- When introducing assignments, be sure to provide students with purposes for reading. When you give your students a motivation statement as part of the Informal Suitability Survey, you actually provide them with a purpose. It is best to frame the purposes as questions because questions provide the reader with the clearest understanding of the purposes for reading. Module 8, "Motivating Reluctant Readers," gives detailed examples for providing purposes when you introduce reading assignments.
- Ask students to answer post-reading questions and to explain the thinking processes they used to arrive at the answers. Teach students how to think as well as how to acquire information. Having good readers orally explain the processes they use to answer questions is a

good way to help less able readers improve their reading achievement. Module 5 will help you with this.

- Another way you can help students get more from textual materials is to show them how to use appropriate study skills and study strategies. Module 6 reveals some important study skills and study strategies and explains how to teach them.

Additional Techniques for Helping Students Who Cannot Read Available Materials

Suitable content area reading materials are not always available. For those occasions, consider these suggestions:

- If suitable reading materials are not available for all your students, talk to the department chairperson or librarian. See if new books are being ordered that cover the same concepts but are written at a lower readability level. Many publishing companies publish books that include the same information as your textbook, but are written at different reading levels. Write to some of your favorite publishers to see what materials are available. Of course, if the textbook is unsuitable for most of your students, you will want to consider selecting new textbooks. Remember to determine the readability of textual materials you are considering purchasing.
- If you do not have suitable materials for some of the students, perhaps you can have a few of the better readers read the important parts of the text on to a tape to which other students can listen. Often, students understand better through listening than reading.
- There are many ways to gather information other than by reading. Audiovisual materials help students develop concepts by seeing and hearing. Besides offering audiovisual aids, you can provide more involvement activities during class. Students generally enjoy role playing and simulation activities.
- Read some of the most difficult parts of the textual materials to your students. This gives them an opportunity to listen and learn and, at the same time, to observe your model of reading. By varying your rate, volume, and pitch, you can make the textbook come alive. Remember to use the illustrations, charts, and tables in the textbook.
- Have volunteers read the assignments to your students and discuss the concepts with them. Both adults and selected peers can do this. Parents can also help if you provide them with a list of reading assignments and due dates.
- Some of your students with severe reading disabilities may be classified as learning disabled. Students classified as learning disabled can obtain taped textual materials from two major sources of recorded books. Recording for the Blind, Inc. (RFB), 215 E. 58th Street, New York, NY 10022; (212) 751–0860 is a national nonprofit, voluntary organization that provides recorded, educational books free-on-loan. To qualify for this service, a student must be diagnosed as learning

disabled and have difficulty reading printed materials because of visual, physical, or perceptual handicaps. The application must be signed by a physician or learning disabilities specialist.

• A second source of recorded textbooks is the National Library Service for the Blind and Physically Handicapped (NLS), the Library of Congress, 1291 Taylor Street NW, Washington, DC 20542; (202) 287–5100. The application must be signed by a physician and must indicate that the disability is the result of an organic dysfunction. Eligible students may obtain all types of books in addition to textbooks as well as subscriptions to popular magazines. Both RFB and NLS maintain large collections of titles and will record other materials upon request. Usually the request must be submitted several months in advance along with copies of material to be recorded.

Perhaps the most important fact to keep in mind is that students who have difficulty reading can survive in the content areas if you make these adaptations. Poor readers are often labeled as lazy, uninterested, turned off, or slow. If you read the article, "Teachers Don't Want to Be Labeled," found in Module 1, you will realize that everyone is slow, average, gifted, interested, and uninterested, depending on the task at hand. Students and adults generally avoid tasks that are difficult or frustrating. Students who are reluctant to read are not necessarily reluctant to learn. Module 9, "Identifying and Helping Problem Readers," has even more suggestions. Commit yourself to this challenge rather than "writing off" those who cannot read.

POSTTEST

Directions: The following questions are designed to test your accomplishment of the objectives in this module. Check your responses with the answers on the following pages. Review as necessary after checking your responses.

1. Explain why it is important for a content area teacher to use a DRA when making reading assignments.
2. Outline and explain the steps you must follow to prepare a DRA.
3. Specify at least six different ways you can help students read textual materials.

Posttest Answers

1. Students the same chronological age vary in reading achievement just as they vary in physical attributes and cognitive abilities. One way a teacher can provide for the expected range of reading achievement is by using differentiated reading assignments. The content area teacher who tries to use one textbook with all students is using

an unsuitable source for many students. The teacher must use a variety of reading textual materials to provide opportunities for all students to learn about the subject area by reading.

2. Preparing the DRA
   - *Select a topic* from the school system curriculum guide or subject area textbook.
   - *Identify the unit objectives* from the school system curriculum guide. Have colleagues and students evaluate the objectives for completeness and clarity.
   - *Write reading questions* for each of the objectives. For any one objective, there may be more than one question. These questions will be used by your students as purposes for reading in their assigned textual materials.
   - *Locate the learning sources* by looking in your school, community and university libraries, bookstores, and by having students bring materials from home. Gather both print and nonprint materials.
   - *Make reading assignments* so that each student can contribute something unique to the discussion while reading in suitable textual materials. Experiment with different ways of grouping students to capitalize on group motivation and cooperative learning.

3. Different ways to help students
   - Make sure the material is suitable.
   - Introduce specialized vocabulary.
   - Teach students how to pronounce multisyllable words.
   - Provide questions as purposes for reading.
   - Have students share question-answering strategies.
   - Teach study skills and study strategies.
   - Order lower readability materials.
   - Have better readers, volunteers, or parents read aloud to disabled readers.
   - Suggest audiovisual materials students can use to learn the content area concepts.
   - Read the difficult parts of the textual materials to your students in class.
   - Obtain recorded textual materials from RFB or NLS for qualified learning disabled students.

REFERENCES

Alvermann, D. E. (1987). The role of textbooks in teachers' interactive decision making. *Reading Research and Instruction, 26*(2), 115–127.

Carter, B., & Abrahamson, R. (1986). The best of the hi/lo books for young adults: A critical evaluation. *Journal of Reading, 30*(3), 204–211.

Cheek, E. H., & Cheek, M. C. (1983). *Reading instruction through content teaching.* Columbus, OH: Merrill.

Davey, B. (1988). How do classroom teachers use their textbooks? *Journal of Reading, 31*(4), 340–345.

Estes, T., & Vaughan, Jr., J. (1978). *Reading and learning in the content classroom.* Boston: Allyn and Bacon.

Graves, M. F., Boettcher, J. A., & Ryder, R. A. (1979). *Easy reading: Book series and periodicals for less able readers.* Newark, DE: International Reading Association.

Harker, W. J. (1977). Selecting instructional materials for content area reading. *Journal of Reading, 21*(2), 126–130.

Hinchman, K. (1987). The textbook and three content-area teachers. *Reading Research and Instruction, 26,* 247–263.

Kealey, R. J. (1980, Spring). Helping students read the content area textbook. *Reading Improvement, 17*(1), 36–39.

Lamberg, W. J., & Lamb, C. E. (1980). Reading instruction in the content areas. Chicago: Rand McNally.

Mavrogenes, N. A., Winkley, C. K., Hanson, E., & Vacca, R. J. (1974). Concise guide to standardized secondary and college reading tests. *Journal of Reading, 18,* 12–22.

Shepherd, D. L. (1982). *Comprehensive high school reading methods* (3rd ed.). Columbus, OH: Merrill.

Spiegel, D. L. (1987). Using adolescent literature in social studies and science. *Educational Horizons, 65*(4), 162–164.

Stine, D. E. (1971). Tenth grade content—Fourth grade reading level. *Journal of Reading, 14,* 559–561.

Vacca, R. T. (1981). *Content area reading.* Boston: Little, Brown.

MODULE
FOUR

Teaching Word
Meanings

CHAPTER OUTLINE

Overview
  Rationale
  Objectives
Enabling Element 1:
  Levels of Word Meaning
Enabling Element 2:
  Guidelines for Teaching Word Meanings
Enabling Element 3:
  Activities for Teaching Word Meanings
Posttest
  Posttest Answers
References

OVERVIEW

Rationale
No one needs to convince you that teaching word meaning is an important part of your subject area teaching responsibility. You know that without the specific technical vocabulary, students will not be able to read assignments or understand lectures.

Research (Spearitt, 1972) continually demonstrates that to understand reading material, readers must have knowledge of vocabulary. You are aware that subject area word knowledge correlates highly with overall knowledge, success, and grades in the subject. As a subject area teacher, you must systematically expand your students' vocabularies. This module will help you effectively teach word meanings.

OBJECTIVES

General Objective
You will be able to introduce and expand word meanings in your subject area.

Specific Objectives

1. You will list three levels of word meaning and write a definition for a word at each of the three levels of word meaning.
2. You will list the seven major guidelines for teaching word meaning in your content area.
3. You will categorize a list of instructional activities into three levels of word meaning, and you will select activities to develop the fullest meaning of words in your subject area.

ENABLING ELEMENT 1
Levels of Word Meaning

Specific Objective 1

You will list three levels of word meaning and write a definition for a word at each of the three levels of word meaning.

Enabling Activities

1. Read Study Guide 1 to identify four types of vocabulary. Give examples of words in your listening, speaking, and reading vocabularies that are not in your writing vocabulary.
2. Write a statement describing each of the three levels of word meaning. Write a definition of the word *barrier* at all three levels of word meaning.
3. Identify five words from your subject area, and define them at each of the three levels of word meaning.
4. Ask your students to define the word *democracy*. Decide at which of the three levels of word meaning they can define *democracy*.
5. Write a statement describing how a student's understanding of what he hears and reads improves as words move through the three levels of meaning in the student's vocabulary.
6. Teach the five words from Enabling Activity 3 to students at each of the three levels of word meaning. Before teaching, ask the students to define the words; then determine and expand their present levels of understanding.

STUDY GUIDE 1

Everyone has four vocabularies that develop from birth in approximately this order: listening, speaking, reading, and writing. The infant listens to family members and friends as they use words with him. Soon the young child begins to say these words. For example, many parents teach a child the word *ball* by saying the word *ball* as they show the child a ball and place it in the child's hand. The parents repeat this procedure many times. To their amazement, most children begin to say the word *ball* by the time they are eleven or twelve months old. Usually when a child enters school, she begins to learn to read the word *ball* when it is presented in written form, and finally learns to write the word *ball*.

Some words in your listening and speaking vocabularies may not be in your reading and writing vocabularies. For example, you may be able to listen to someone use the word *phlegm*, and can use it to describe mucus in your throat, but perhaps it looked strange to you as you just read it. Likewise, we have found that many people know the word *phlegm* as part of their listening, speaking, and reading vocabularies, but cannot correctly write the word.

A continual task for every teacher is to help students increase these four vocabularies. You will want to make sure students can listen to and understand many words, use them in conversation, recognize them in print, and (if the words are used frequently when writing) learn to spell them. Our concern in this module is helping students develop a *reading* vocabulary, which will in turn help them comprehend.

There is no precise agreement on vocabulary size at various age levels. Research findings for twelfth graders vary on estimates of vocabulary size from 15,000 to 45,000 words. Lack of agreement appears to stem from how "word" is defined. Some educators consider *walk*, *walking*, and *walked* as one word; others consider them three words. Other educators count each definition of a word as a new instance of the word; thus *run*, which has at least 130 definitions, would count as 130 separate words.

High school students, like all of us, constantly add new words to their vocabularies. Although the period of vocabulary growth is most rapid between 2½ and 7 years, growth remains considerable as long as schooling continues. When schooling is discontinued, most adults add only about twenty-five new words a year to their vocabularies. In the middle to later years of life, there is evidence of an overall decline in vocabulary size.

As a word comes into our vocabulary, it generally passes through at least three distinct stages of understanding. At first we have only a specific understanding or association with the word. The learner associates only a single definition, instance, event, or object with the word. For example, the word *sofa* at this level is perceived as a specific object of a precise size, shape, or color, probably located in the living room of the learner's home. The learner is not aware that there are other sofas in other homes, stores, and offices.

At the second stage, the learner has a more than a specific understanding of the word; he begins to develop a functional understanding. Now the learner can answer the question, "What is the function of a *sofa*?" At this level, *sofa* becomes something we sit or recline upon, and *sofa* can be used in a sentence to demonstrate understanding.

At the third and most abstract level of understanding, the learner develops a concept of *sofa*. For our purposes, a concept can be thought of as a cluster of impressions or perceptions for which words are used as labels. At the third level, the learner understands that *sofas* come in a variety of shapes, sizes, and colors, to mention a few things, and are part of a larger category called *furniture*. Sofas are not the only type of furniture; many other things, such as tables and chairs, are also classified as furniture. At this level of understanding, the learner has a more complete understanding of the word *sofa*. Since word meanings are constantly changing, it is probably safe to say that we never acquire complete understanding of a word.

Words, as they come into our vocabularies, do not automatically or naturally rise through the three stages of this hierarchy. Many words become fixed at the specific or functional levels and never reach the general or conceptual level. Students whose vocabularies contain words principally at the specific or functional levels will have serious problems understanding reading assignments, since writers communicate at the general or conceptual level.

It is our responsibility as teachers to encourage and foster vocabulary growth in number of words as well as depth of meaning. Students need to know many words and to understand the fullest meaning possible.

Today's secondary school students take a variety of courses that contain many new words they must learn to master the subject areas. While most subject area teachers are aware of the importance of vocabulary to the understanding of their subject area, many fail to teach for conceptual understanding. Instead, their strategy is to cover as many words as possible, briefly defining each as they go along. Research does not demonstrate that incidental exposure to large numbers of words expands vocabulary or develops conceptual understandings of words. For the most part, teachers who rush through vocabulary lessons, briefly and only orally defining words, waste both their time and that of the students.

A word becomes fixed in the hierarchy of understanding at the specific, functional, or general level depending on how it is experienced or learned. Asking students to look up a list of words in a dictionary generally fixes those words at the specific level. Asking students to define words as used in sentences, to obtain suitable synonyms, and to write a sentence for each word generally fixes words at the functional level of understanding. Providing direct experiences with new words and asking students to incorporate the new words into their written and oral assignments and daily discussions generally fixes the new words at the conceptual level.

As a general rule, the more direct experiences a student has with a word, the more likely the word will become fixed at the conceptual level of understanding. The more vicarious and incidental the experience, the more likely the word will become fixed at the specific or functional level.

As a content area teacher, it is imperative for you to listen to students to learn the levels at which they understand words that belong to your specialized area. When you ask students if they have ever heard a particular word, many will nod their heads. If you take a few minutes to ask for students' definitions of a particular word, you will be able to determine the level at which they understand the word and then plan activities to expand their meanings of the word. For example, if a music teacher asks students if they have heard the word *rhythm*, most will readily say yes. When asked to define it, however, one student may only be able to say, "She has rhythm." After hearing this specific definition, the teacher can expand the students' level of understanding by explaining the functions of rhythm in music. Listen to your students, then clarify and expand their definitions of words.

Defining Words

To be sure you understand the various levels of word meaning, we will take you through the process of defining three words. We all know these common words: *telephone, jump, vote*. Before we define them, let us review each of the three levels of word meaning. At each level we will give you an explanation as well as a sample sentence using the word *book*.

Specific Level of Word Meaning. At the specific level, the student associates a word with a single idea, event, definition, or object. Asked to define the word *book*, a student might respond, "A book is something found in schools."

Functional Level of Word Meaning. At the functional level, the student understands one of a word's major uses or functions. Asked to define the word *book*, a student may respond, "A book is something you read," or may demonstrate understanding by using the word in a sentence, "I like to read books."

Conceptual Level of Word Meaning. At the conceptual level, the student recognizes that a word has more than one meaning or function. The student recognizes that there are many ideas associated with the word and clusters the ideas by some common element. Asked to define the word *book*, he or she responds, "Since books can be used for storing, obtaining, or transmitting information, they are a way of sharing information or a means of communication."

You now should have the levels of meaning in mind and a fair understanding of their distinctions. A detailed look at the words *telephone, jump,* and *vote* will clarify these distinctions.

Telephone. At the specific level of word meaning, a student recognizes that a telephone is a colored object that hangs on a wall, sits on a desk, or the like. At the specific level, the student would define *telephone* as "It hangs on the wall," or "There is one in the office," or a similar statement. At the functional level of word meaning, the student recognizes a major use of a telephone. Asked to define *telephone*, this student responds with something like "I use it to call my friends," or "You talk on it." At the conceptual level of word meaning, the student recognizes that a telephone is one of many different means for communicating with people and that telephones are located in many places throughout the community, nation, or world.

Jump. At the specific level of word meaning, *jump* is what a student does when he or she moves his or her body up and down. It is not uncommon at this level of understanding for a student to actually demonstrate by jumping. At the functional level of word meaning, a student defines *jump* as what she does when jumping rope or making high jumps, pole vaults, and other similar things. At the functional level, the student defines *jump* in terms of some accomplishment, "I like to jump up and down." At the conceptual level, *jump* is defined as a method of exercise or of moving quickly. The student will give examples of prices *jumping*, *jumping* an opponent in checkers, or even *jumping* a dead battery, as in starting a car.

Vote. At the specific level of word meaning, the most common association with the word *vote* is "something done during elections." Remember, at this level a student has only a single association with the word. That association may be an event, a definition, or an instance, to mention just three possibilities. At the functional level of word meaning, probably the most common usage is "a way of getting someone elected." In any event, at this level the student describes the word in terms of its major function or use. At the conceptual level, the student realizes that *vote* is just one part of a complex government process called *democracy* in which decisions or choices are made by the people.

Thus, a student has only a single association with a word at the specific level of word meaning. At the functional level of word meaning, the student can describe a major use of a word or use the word in a sentence that demonstrates understanding. At the conceptual level, the student has many facts and ideas associated with the word and recognizes and uses the word in many different sentences and contexts.

PRACTICUM EXERCISE

Now let us see if you can define a word at the three levels of word meaning, using a word everyone knows—the word *noun*. For each level of word meaning, define the word *noun*. Write your definitions here:

Specific Level of Word Meaning—

Functional Level of Word Meaning—

Conceptual Level of Word Meaning—

Answers to Practicum Exercise
Compare your explanations with ours.

Specific Level of Word Meaning. At this level, the word *noun* can be defined as a word, or some specific noun such as *John* or *dog*. Only a single observation or definition is associated with the word.

Functional Level of Word Meaning. At this level, the word can be defined in terms of a major use or function, or used in a sentence that demonstrates understanding, that is, "a word used in talking or writing about some person, place or thing."

Conceptual Level of Word Meaning. At this level, you have many facts and ideas associated with the word. You may see the noun as one of the major form classes or parts of speech denoting person, place, or thing. You can use and recognize the word *noun* in different sentences, and can identify nouns in written and oral language. At this level, you demonstrate a more complete understanding of the word as you differentiate proper nouns and common nouns and contrast nouns to pronouns.

If you think you can now define words at the three levels of word meaning, you are ready to move to Enabling Element 2. If not, you may want to use a dictionary or thesaurus to further clarify this concept of vocabulary development.

ENABLING ELEMENT 2
Guidelines for Teaching Word Meaning

Specific Objective 2
You will list the seven major guidelines for teaching word meanings in your content area.

Enabling Activities

1. Read Study Guide 2, and prepare a list of generalizations to guide you in teaching word meanings.
2. From your list of generalizations, prepare a second list of key phrases. Examine your list of key phrases and create an acronym to help you recall them as you teach word meanings.

3. With students and teachers, discuss the guidelines for teaching word meaning. Determine if their experiences agree with findings from research and practice.
4. Using the guidelines in this Study Guide, evaluate popular vocabulary development books. For example, one guideline suggests that the study of Latin stems has questionable value for vocabulary development. Look at some of the popular books to see how much they stress the study of Latin stems. Which books would you recommend to your students?
5. List five words from your content area that have both a general meaning and a technical meaning. Write the technical meanings as they are used in your content area. For example, the general meaning of *rich* is "having wealth"; however, the home economics teacher uses the word *rich* to mean "full of choice ingredients."

STUDY GUIDE 2

We once overheard two teachers discuss whether teaching was a science or an art. One maintained that teaching was a science, and therefore required only the application of basic principles and guidelines developed through research. The second teacher maintained that it was really an art, the talents for which were most likely transmitted genetically. After considerable discussion, the two teachers concluded that teaching was both a science and an art. As scientists, teachers read research on teaching and examine their own practices to arrive at generalizations and guidelines for becoming more effective and efficient. As artists, teachers use their creative talents to make the subject of their teaching interesting and relevant to their students' needs.

Manzo and Sherk, in "Some Generalizations and Strategies for Guiding Vocabulary Learning," present an excellent list of guidelines for vocabulary improvement.[1] They developed their list after systematic examination of research on vocabulary acquisition. Teachers who follow the guidelines will improve the efficiency and effectiveness of vocabulary instruction.

Guidelines for Teaching Word Meaning

1. Students learn new words best when they are taught as labels for direct experiences.
2. All classroom teachers must give continued and systematic attention to vocabulary development.

---

[1] Adapted with permission from the *Journal of Reading Behavior* 4, no. 1 (Winter 1971–72): 81–82.

3. Students must encounter a word in many similar and differing contexts before they can learn it.
4. The teacher's attitude toward vocabulary improvement and the superiority of his or her own vocabulary are contagious and vital factors in improving student vocabulary.
5. Study of a limited number of words in depth is more productive than superficial acquaintance with lists of words.
6. It is possible, but may be practically foolish, to teach words that are not part of the student's verbal community. Lack of opportunity for use will result in eventual atrophy.
7. Introducing vocabulary consistently with only one or two activities does not encourage word learning. Teachers who employ a variety of activities help students increase their vocabularies.
8. The wide-reading method of acquiring vocabulary, which stresses little more than wide, free reading with no other attention paid to words, is usually not very effective for influencing rapid and marked improvement.
9. The study of Latin positively influences knowledge of morphemes, but does not seem to influence knowledge of vocabulary.

A review of these guidelines suggests that word meaning instruction must be intensive, systematic, regular, and provided enthusiastically by every subject area teacher. Preferably, words should be introduced with direct and real experiences in a variety of contexts and gamelike situations. The teacher should select words for daily assignments based upon students' needs, and stress continued use of these words in all assignments. Keeping these guidelines in mind as you teach will improve the effectiveness of your vocabulary instruction.

Reread Guidelines 1 through 9, and decide which are the key words in each statement. Make notes to help you remember the guidelines. When you are through, continue with the next paragraph.

In Guideline 1, did you choose *direct experiences?* Students develop the fullest understanding of words when they learn them from real rather than vicarious experiences. A teacher can create situations for teaching words through direct experiences, forcing students to use new words to communicate with each other and with the teacher.

In Guideline 2, the key words are *"continued* and *systematic* attention of all classroom teachers."* Vocabulary development cannot be left up to a few teachers—it is every teacher's responsibility. Content area teachers who have specialized knowledge are the most effective in helping students understand technical words in particular subject areas; the language arts teacher is less effective. Vocabulary instruction is most effective if it occurs daily in all classes and is systematic.

The key words in Guideline 3 are *many encounters . . . in like and differing contexts.* Students need numerous encounters with words in varying types of oral discussions, reading materials, and writing assignments to develop the fullest understanding of the words you want them to learn. Many encounters are also needed to provide the *mass* and *distributed* practice necessary for taking a word and its definition from immediate to long-term memory. Keep in mind that typical beginning readers need at least thirty-eight repetitions to learn one basic sight word. Likewise, middle- and secondary-school students must hear and see a word frequently to make it a part of their listening, speaking, reading, and writing vocabularies.

In Guideline 4, the most important words are *teacher's attitude*. Most research on teaching demonstrates that the teacher is the most important school-related variable in students' success or failure. When teachers approach vocabulary instruction with enthusiasm and positive attitudes, vocabulary growth is considerable; when they approach vocabulary instruction with a casual or negative attitude, vocabulary growth is minimal.

A *limited number of words in depth* is the heart of Guideline 5. Many teachers believe they have too much content to cover and too little time to cover it. These teachers do not develop in-depth word meanings. Often, they assign many words for study at one time, and the burden falls on the students to develop in-depth understanding. The best vocabulary instruction focuses on a few words, their varied meanings, uses, and application in reading, writing, listening, and speaking. A major responsibility as a content area teacher is to decide which words are most important for all students to understand. It is better to select 10 words for in-depth study than to select 100 words the students will define and forget.

Guideline 6 contains two separate but related important ideas. The first idea deals with teaching words that . . . *are not part of the verbal community in which the student lives;* the second is *the lack of opportunity for use must result in eventual atrophy.* This guideline does not suggest that teachers teach *only* those words and meanings common to the students' verbal community, but that they select words for vocabulary instruction that will help students in daily communication of information. Lack of opportunity to use words will cause them to be forgotten.

Some teachers use the same technique for teaching vocabulary words over and over again. A common practice is to list new words for a chapter or unit on the chalkboard or refer to a list of words at the end of a chapter, then ask students to look up the definition of each word and study it for a vocabulary quiz. According to Guideline 7, this is an inefficient way to encourage vocabulary development. It is better to use a variety of activities to introduce words, because some words need more explanation than a simple glossary or dictionary definition.

Some people believe that if students read about a variety of topics from many materials, they will automatically increase their vocabularies. Although it is true that people who read more have larger vocabularies, the point of Guideline 8 is that we must give attention to words so that students learn meanings. We must encourage students to note unfamiliar words and use a variety of techniques to learn their meanings. If the reader does not try to learn the meanings of new words, wide reading does not effectively increase vocabulary.

For years, Latin was a required subject in many junior high and high schools, and students who took Latin enlarged their vocabularies as a result. We now know, however, that unless one is studying a field related to science or mathematics, knowledge of Latin does not necessarily increase vocabulary. Children should probably know some of the common morphemes, but Latin courses are not necessary to expand vocabulary.

The most important guidelines are probably the first seven, because they suggest ways to help students increase their vocabularies. You can remember the seven major guidelines with the help of an acronym. Acronyms are words composed from the beginning parts or beginning letters of other words. Sometimes these are real words and sometimes nonsense words. Select key words for building an acronym for the seven major guidelines to make your vocabulary instruction more effective. Here is our acronym:

Guideline	Acronym	Key Words
6	V	Verbal community; variety of activities
3	O	Opportunities for use
2	C	Classroom teacher
4	A	Attitude
1	B	Build meanings through direct experience
5	S	Study in depth

The Necessity for Applying the "VOCABS" Guidelines

The English language is difficult to master because many of our words have multiple meanings. Many have both a general and a technical meaning. According to the *Guinness Book of World Records*,[2] the word *set* has more meanings than any other word in the English language—at least 194! In a general sense, *set* means "to place," but it also has many technical meanings. Consider the definitions in Table 4–1 from different content areas.

Content area teachers must assume responsibility for vocabulary development. You know the technical definitions of words in your content area better than other teachers in the school; thus, you are the best person to help students learn these technical definitions. If every teacher in your building has a favorable attitude toward vocabulary development, builds meanings through direct experiences, helps the

---

[2]N. McWhirter, *Guinness Book of World Records* (New York: Bantam, 1980), p. 211.

Table 4–1
Definitions of "Set" in Different Content Areas

Content Area	Use or Definition of Set
Art	Describes the process in making a color fast, as in dyeing. In jewelry making, means to cover and encrust with gems.
Business Education	To put down on paper, or in a record book. Also used to describe putting a seal on a document.
Language Arts	May refer to a collection of books.
Health	The teacher refers to "setting" a broken leg or finger.
Homemaking	The students learn proper ways to "set" the table or to let the Jell-o "set."
Industrial Arts	To put a moveable part of a machine in place. For example, you are going to "set" the gears into motion.
Math	A group of things.
Music	The teacher encourages students to "set" down, or write, words to music.
Physical Education	Prepare to begin, "Get set." Also, in square dancing "sets" are formed, and in tennis you can play a "set."
Psychology	A mind "set."
Science	In botany, *set* means to develop after pollination, or to form fruit in the plant's blossom. Science teachers talk about the sun "setting" as it appears to descend below the horizon.
Social Studies	To fix a bond or fine at a certain amount of money; to appoint; or to fix limits or boundries.
Speech and Drama	The scenery, or to make up scenery.

students study a limited number of words in depth, provides opportunities for students to use the words, and uses a variety of activities to help students learn the meanings of words, the students will derive more meaning from their reading assignments.

As you apply the suggestions in this Study Guide, you may want to encourage students to use a strategy for building reading vocabulary, such as this one:

• Be alert for new words when you read.
• Ask me to explain the word to you and/or look it up in a dictionary. Make sure you find the definition that goes with the way the word is used in context.

- Keep a vocabulary notebook. Make a separate entry for each word. Include the pronunciation, the general meaning, and the technical meaning as it applies to our class. For each definition, write a sample sentence using the word.
- Try to use the new word, and listen to hear how others use it.

Enabling Element 3 provides various instructional activities to help students develop technical meanings of words as they apply to the content area. If you encourage students to ask you the meanings of words, you will need a variety of activities to increase their levels of understanding. Enabling Element 3 gives you more than twenty such activities.

ENABLING ELEMENT 3
Activities for Teaching Word Meaning

Specific Objective 3
You will categorize a list of instructional activities into three levels of word meaning, and you will select activities to develop the fullest meaning of words in your subject area.

Enabling Activities

1. Prepare a list of all the activities you can think of for teaching word meanings. Place a plus (+) in front of those you feel develop the most complete understanding of a word. Place a minus (−) in front of those you feel develop the least complete understanding.
2. Read Study Guide 3 to become familiar with a number of activities for teaching word meanings and to determine with which of the three levels of word meaning each activity is associated.
3. Compare the list of activities you prepared in Enabling Activity 1 with those in Study Guide 3. Did you learn new ways to teach word meaning?
4. Do the Practicum Exercise. Choose a word you want all students to know. Now define the word at each of the levels of word meaning— specific, functional and conceptual. Finally, think of activities for teaching the word to your students at levels appropriate for their understanding.
5. Teachers are learners! Many teachers say they always learn more than their students. Make it a habit to continue to increase your vocabulary by looking for new words and/or expanding your level of word meanings. If you can analyze how you learn word meanings, you can pass these techniques on to your students.

STUDY GUIDE 3

This Study Guide provides models for developing instructional activities for word meaning, arranged according to the three levels of word meaning. The three levels of word meaning are:

- *Specific level of understanding.* At this level the student has one object, event, instance, definition, or the like associated with a word. The student can usually only recognize and/or recall the single association. He may associate the word *democracy* with a type of government or the United States, but have no further understanding or associations with the word.
- *Functional level of understanding.* At this level the student states a major use of the word or uses the word in a sentence that demonstrates understanding. At this level the student not only understands that a democracy is a type of government, but understands that in a democracy, people vote to select representatives who pass laws and administer the government. "In a democracy, people select their representatives."
- *Conceptual level of understanding.* At this level the student has many facts and ideas associated with the word. He recognizes and can use the word in a variety of sentences or contexts. The student recognizes that a democracy is government by many people based on the belief that all people have the same rights, freedoms, and responsibilities. He may further understand that the United States has a representative democracy whereby the people elect public officials who act according to the people's wishes.

By classifying activities according to levels of word meaning, we hope to help you evaluate the activities you have been using to develop word meaning. We also hope to give you ideas for selecting future activities. One word of caution before we begin: activities at the specific level are not inherently bad. Coupled with higher level activities, they sometimes form a learning chain from the simple to the complex. They become undesirable when they are overemphasized and are the only activities used to develop word meanings.

Some activities you can use to teach word meanings are described here. We divided the suggestions into three categories according to the level of understanding which will probably be developed.

Activities at the Specific Level
The following activities develop primarily, but not exclusively, the specific level of word meaning. The activities usually lead to a single association between word and object, event, instance, or definition.

1. *Write definitions.* Locate isolated words in a glossary and write a definition.

2. *Write sentences.* Locate isolated words in a dictionary and write a definition and sentence.
3. *Play word games.* Scrabble, Probe, Boggle, Spill and Spell, and such games are generally useful for word identification, although they rarely bring about a discussion of word meaning. When they do, usually only one definition or synonym is mentioned.
4. *Use vocabulary exercise books.* Programmed vocabulary enrichment books introduce a single word at a time, define the word, and use it in a number of sentences. The programmed technique often works for words related to the student's academic or social needs. The problem with most of the programmed texts is that the words do not match the student's academic or social needs; therefore, atrophy results soon after the lesson is completed.
5. *Memorize and associate.* Memorize Latin or Greek stems, prefixes, and suffixes and associate them with single meanings.
   For example:
   the prefix *in* means not.
   The stem *cred* means believe.
   The suffix *ible* means can be.
   Incredible means cannot be believed, or unbelievable.
6. *Give a simple definition* when a student asks the meaning of a word. If a student asks what *picayune* means, and you respond by saying, "petty," the student will have one specific definition.
7. *Show a picture of an object*, or present the object itself, without much discussion. For example, if you show a picture of a conch shell or bring a shell to class and tell the students, "This is a conch shell. It is spiral," they will have a specific level of understanding.

Activities at the Functional Level
The following activities develop primarily, but not exclusively, functional understandings of words. Examples of directions to the students are included with each sample activity. These activities develop and expand a major use or function of a word.

1. *Suggest synonyms.* When defining a word, you can usually suggest many synonyms. You might define *ludicrous* by saying its meaning is similar to those of *comical, ridiculous, laughable*, or *funny*.
2. *Give antonyms.* Frequently, you can tell students words that mean the opposite of the word they are learning. Antonyms of *ludicrous* are *serious, sorrowful*, or *tragic*.
3. *Classify words.* Telling students the group to which a word belongs helps them understand its function. If you tell them *ludicrous* is an adjective that describes situations or ideas, they can suggest situations that are ludicrous or absurd.
4. *Make analogies.* Sometimes you can make comparisons to help students learn words. If a student wants to know what *potable* means, you might say that *potable* is to beverages as *edible* is to foods. You

could carry on the explanation with examples of beverages that are potable as compared with nonpotable beverages.

5. *Explain, give examples, and discuss.* Before reading new material, the teacher selects words that need explanation and usually presents them in phrases or sentences so that *context clues* can be used. Then the teacher explains or checks the students' knowledge of the word meanings, shows illustrative material if available, and gives additional examples. Students should also give additional examples of use. Teachers and students can explain meanings by using different types of sentences or contextual clues.

 a. *Definition clues.* The unknown word is defined in the descriptive content. For example, to teach the word *peruse*, you might say, "I want you to peruse chapter 2 so you will know the material thoroughly."

 b. *Synonym clues.* A synonym clue uses a familiar word with the same meaning to define an unfamiliar word; for example, "I want you to peruse, or study, chapter 2."

 c. *Familiar expression clues.* A common expression is used to relay an idea or offer clarity. "I want you to peruse chapter 2 until you know it forward and backward."

 d. *Comparison or contrast clues.* The unknown word is compared to or contrasted with something known. "I want you to peruse, not survey, chapter 2."

6. *Pictures, graphs, charts, and other visuals.* A collection of visuals associated with an object or event a word represents is useful for developing word meaning if you allow opportunities to discuss similarities, uses, and other explanations. If you show a picture of a conch shell and then explain the uses of the shell, talk about where conch shells are found, and have students note the similarities and differences of conch shells as compared to other shells, you help students understand at the functional level.

7. *Studying functions* of prefixes, suffixes, and stems. Research suggests that this method of vocabulary study is more beneficial for the more able students. Most of this study should occur after the fourth grade.

8. *Demonstration.* At times it may be necessary for you to become an actor or actress to demonstrate a word meaning. Verbs are especially appropriate for demonstrations; you can pretend to be *perambulating* (strolling) or *perusing* (examining something thoroughly).

Activities at the Conceptual Level

The following activities develop primarily, but not exclusively, the conceptual understandings of words. To understand a word at the conceptual level, many different activities are necessary.

1. *Provide real and direct experiences.* To help students understand what

a democracy is, it would be most valuable to have them visit a capitol building to see *democracy* in action. One limitation teachers face is that it is often not possible to provide real and direct experiences. Some students get to visit places with their parents and have many experiences; others never leave their neighborhood during their childhood. If you can take students on field trips, we encourage you to do so.

2. *Use simulation.* Since it is difficult to provide real and direct experiences, teachers attempt to provide simulation experiences. For example, you can set up a mock legislature in your classroom. Although such a simulation requires many hours of work and preparation, it gives students a better understanding of a democracy. The science teacher who wants to teach about the digestive system may dissect a frog or chicken and compare the animal digestive systems to that of human begins. Use as many simulation activities as possible.

3. *Compare meaning.* Comparison of the geographical, historical, social, or psychological significance of words is a good way to develop higher level word meaning. To help the students understand the word *tree* at the conceptual level, you might teach them about the different regions of the world and the fact that different types of trees grow in different temperate regions. You might also talk about the historical significance of trees, about conservation, and how products from trees affect the economy. The more comparisons you and your students make, the higher the level of word meaning.

4. *Use audiovisual aids.* When it is not possible to provide firsthand experiences, movies, slides, filmstrips, or recordings will help students understand a word at the conceptual level. A science teacher may be able to find a filmstrip that defines *chlorophyll* better than any teacher could. A history teacher could use voice recording of historical events to help students better understand the meanings of words such as *war* and *catastrophe.*

5. *Discuss connotations.* Connotations are implied emotional meanings attached to words through stress, gesture, or past experience. Connotations can be positive or negative. Discussions of connotative word meanings should start with denotative (dictionary) meanings. For example, to define the word *yellow,* begin with the dictionary definition of color, and go on to explain the meaning of *yellow* as it is used to imply fear or cowardice. You would need to combine this activity with several others to develop understanding of the word *yellow* at the conceptual level.

6. *Study changes in word meaning.* Studying changes in word meaning over a period of time can create interest in the study of etymology. Most desk dictionaries have a code to indicate obsolete word meaning (obs), Old English meaning (OE), and the like. Study of word changes expands students' associations with a word and moves a word to the conceptual level of understanding.

7. *Use many reference materials.* After students understand a word at the functional level, they may be able to explore different reference materials to understand the word at the conceptual level. For example, students learning about the word *glass* can look in the encyclopedia and specialized books for more information about glass. Pictures and other aids in reference materials help students expand the level of understanding.

8. *Semantic Mapping.* Semantic mapping is an activity that helps students learn the meaning of a word by seeing how other words and ideas are related to the new word. To form a semantic map, you begin by asking the students what they know about a word. For example, if you are a science teacher beginning a unit on the circulatory system, you might ask your students what they know about the word *heart.* Then you would write the word "heart" on the chalkboard or on an acetate for use with an overhead projector and list all the information the students have associated with the word *heart.* At this point, you would be looking for the level(s) of understanding that students have of the word *heart.* Information such as the following might be provided by the students:

heart

size of a fist	some people have heart diseases
pumps blood	smoking makes the heart beat faster
a heart shape means love	needed to stay alive

This information would then be displayed as a semantic map to show the relationships between the various words and ideas. As a semantic map, it would look like Figure 4–1.

After you have determined what the students know about the word *heart,* you can introduce the reading assignment. Do so by providing questions that serve as purposes for reading. Encourage your students to add to the questions.

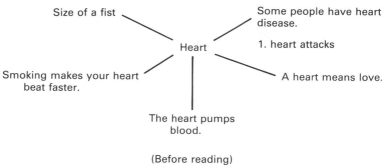

(Before reading)

Figure 4–1
First step of semantic mapping

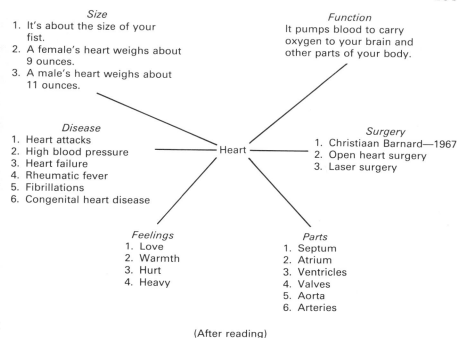

(After reading)

Figure 4–2
Final step of semantic mapping

When the students have completed their reading, ask them what they now know about the word *heart*. Add this new information to the knowledge that was listed earlier. You can organize the information into a semantic map as you write or simply list the new information and organize it into a semantic map later. After the reading and discussion, the semantic map may look like the one shown in Figure 4–2.

9. *Semantic feature analysis.* Semantic feature analysis is an activity that helps students detect differences in words. This activity is particularly valuable when trying to help students make comparisons. When using semantic feature analysis it is necessary to develop a grid or chart similar to the one in Figure 4–3.

The first step in using semantic feature analysis is to select a category that you are dealing with in your content area. For example, if you are a science teacher you may be teaching a unit on animals with backbones. You would list in a column some of the words from the category of animals with backbones (mammals, birds, reptiles, amphibians, and fishes). Next, in a row, you would list some features shared by some of the words in the category (swims, hair, legs, warm-blooded, teeth, beaks, etc.). At this time you would lead a discussion with the class to determine if the words in the column have the features in the row. If the feature is present,

Category	Features ———▶							

Figure 4–3
Grid for semantic feature analysis

put a plus and if it is not present, put a minus. Continue putting pluses or minuses beside each feature to discover the uniqueness of each word. Sometimes you will find a word and a feature that are not always related. If this is true put a plus or minus so as to indicate if the word usually has a given feature. Put a question mark when in doubt. An example is shown in Table 4–2.

Table 4–2
Example of Completed Semantic Feature Analysis

	Warm blooded	Able to swim	Able to fly	Eyes	Teeth	Beaks	Legs	Live on land
Mammals	+	+	—	+	+	—	+	+
Birds	+	? SOME	+ MOST	+	+	+	+	+
Reptiles	—	+	—	+	+	—	+ SOME	+
Amphibians	—	+	—	+	+	—	+	+
Fishes	—	+	— SOME	+	+	?	—	—

Putting It All Together to Expand Word Meanings
As mentioned in Study Guide 2, teachers should use a variety of activities to introduce new words and to help students learn meanings. The following lesson plan uses a variety of activities to teach the meaning of a word.

Demonstration Lesson Plan
Objective: The students will be able to define the word *potable* at a higher level of understanding.

Instructional Procedures:

Write the word *potable* on the chalkboard and pronounce it (po-tə-b-'l). Ask students if any of them have heard the word or seen it written before. Listen to their definitions to determine their present level of understanding. Remember, your task is to help students understand the word at a higher level. For some students, this higher level will be the specific level of understanding; for others, it may be the functional; and for some it may be the conceptual level of understanding.

At the *specific* level, the word *potable* simply means drinkable. At the *functional* level, *potable* is a term used to describe beverages, especially water. A student who understands *potable* at the functional level realizes it describes the quality of water. For example, at a campground you may see the word *potable* when the water is coming from a hose rather than from a water cooler. At the *conceptual* level of understanding, *potable* is one of many words used to describe drinkable beverages in addition to water. The word *potable* is an adjective that may apply to many different types of beverages, such as chocolate, eggnog, ginger beer, punch, lemonade, as well as alcoholic drinks. At the conceptual level of understanding, students also understand why some beverages are potable and others are not potable. These students further understand the results of drinking water or some other beverage that is not potable.

As you begin to teach the word *potable*, you may want to define it with the synonym *drinkable*. After doing so, you can give the students many examples. You might say, "The water in the drinking fountains is potable, or drinkable." This means the water is good for drinking. You may give adverse examples by saying, "The water in some countries is not potable, and if you drink it, chances are you will become sick." Now you are using the word in context.

If students know the meaning of the word *edible*, you may want to compare the word *potable* to the word *edible*. You can make the following analogy: *edible* is to food as *potable* is to water. This analogy may help students who understand the word *edible* to understand the word *potable*.

You might want to ask students to recall direct experiences by having them tell where they have seen the word *potable*. Some students have seen the word in the restrooms of airplanes, others at campgrounds, and others have seen it at mineral springs or near wells. You can provide simulation experiences by having them make signs to put on the drinking fountains in the school. The signs can say, "This water is potable." Students will enjoy watching others' puzzlement at the signs!

Next you may want to have students list beverages that are potable and some that are not. In doing so, students can indicate some of their favorite beverages and contrast them to poisonous liquids such as liquid chlorine.

You may want to have the students look up the word in the dictionary to see if there is a description of the word origin. Some students who are studying foreign languages may be able to provide a foreign word that means the same as *potable* and point out similarities and differences. You may also want to make a semantic map showing how words and ideas are related to the vocabulary word, *potable.*

To help students remember the word and make it part of their listening, speaking, reading, and writing vocabularies, you will have to provide many opportunities for them to use the word. Use the word frequently during the next few days; come into the classroom tomorrow and say, "I had something that was potable." Have the students try to guess what you had that was drinkable to help them review the meaning of *potable.*

Evaluation:

You can evaluate students' knowledge of the meaning of *potable* by having them write a definition or by observing whether or not they use the word in their speaking vocabularies. You might also notice whether or not they use the word in writing and or in conversation with each other.

Did you notice that the lesson plan uses a variety of activities? The teacher defines the word for the students, provides opportunities for students to give definitions, uses the word in sentences, uses a synonym and an analogy, provides a simulation activity, and has students classify ideas associated with the word. Instead of just saying, "Look up the word *potable,*" the teacher uses many different instructional activities to fix the word in students' minds.

PRACTICUM EXERCISE

Now it is your turn to select activities from those in this Study Guide. Choose a word in your content area that you want all students to understand and write a definition at each of the three levels of understanding. Now go through the activities for each level of understanding and select those you could use to teach the meanings of the word. Try to incorporate a variety of activities. Make sure you list activities for each level of understanding, because your students probably have different levels of definitions for the word you have chosen.

Answers to the Practicum Exercise

It is impossible to give an exact answer to this Practicum Exercise, since the words you have chosen are different. We will give a sample answer, to which you can compare your response to see if it meets the criterion of providing a variety of activities to help students understand words.

Suppose you are an English teacher, and have had the students read a short story written by a British author. In this short story, the author uses the word *perambulate,* as in this sentence: "After dinner they decide to *perambulate* around the garden."

In discussing the selection with the students, you ask them what *preambulate* means. As they share their definitions, you listen for understanding of the word at the specific, functional, or conceptual level. A student at the specific level of understanding defines *perambulate* as "to walk or to stroll." At the functional level, a student defines *perambulate* as "a movement that may or may not have a purpose." The student further explains that *perambulate* can be to stroll about without any particular purpose, or to move about as you take a survey of some property. At the conceptual level of understanding, a student says that *perambulate* is a verb that designates moving about, through, over, or around, especially in examining or inspecting something. The student gives examples—you can perambulate in order to fix the boundaries of a forest as well as to scour the ground or to track a course. On the other hand, *perambulate* might mean simply to go for a walk or to push a baby carriage or pram, which is sometimes called a *perambulator.* A student who understands *perambulate* at the conceptual level will be able to compare it to other words that indicate movement or travel, such as *jogging, roaming, driving, hiking,* and *meandering.*

You may want to write *perambulate* on the board and pronounce it, then say that you are going to *perambulate.* Begin to stroll around the classroom and ask the students what you are doing. As they describe what you are doing, write the descriptions on the board. For example, some may say you are walking, some may say you are strolling, others may say you are examining. Through these definitions, you can have them define *perambulate.*

You may want to have the students examine the origin of the word. You can tell them that *perambulate* comes from the root word *ambulare,* which means to walk or to move. The prefix *per* means *through.* So the word *perambulate* means "walk through," especially as in examining or inspecting something.

At this time you may want to ask what the opposite of *perambulate* is. The students may indicate "to stay put or stationary," giving you an antonym; at the same time, you can ask for synonyms for *perambulate.* When the students provide words such as "go over the ground, go for a walk, pace, or cover territory," they will be indicating their understanding of the word *perambulate.*

If you have pictures of people perambulating, you can show them to the students. Throughout the day, you can provide opportunities for students to perambulate, and ask, "Who is that *perambulating* around our class?" This is a good point at which to develop a semantic map for *perambulate.*

Finally, you may want to have the students look up the word in the dictionary to see what definitions are given. Continue to use the word frequently throughout the day in many contexts. You can give sentences with definition clues, such as "They perambulated around the block," or synonym clues, such as "They were perambulating or walking about the school grounds." If you continue to use the word in different contexts during the next few days, the students will soon use it, too.

POSTTEST

Directions: Read the following statements and complete each Posttest item.

1. You must strive to develop the broadest meanings of words specific to your subject area. List and describe the three levels of word meaning, and write a definition of the word *barrier* at all three levels.
2. To teach new words and meanings more effectively and efficiently, you need to follow certain instructional guidelines identified through research and practice. List the seven major guidelines for teaching word meanings to ensure effective vocabulary instruction.
3. You have become familiar with a number of common activities for teaching word meanings. Recall that activities for introducing the meaning of a word can determine the level at which that word is eventually understood. Read the following list of ten instructional activities, and specify the level of word meaning developed by each activity. Use *S* to indicate specific level, *F* to indicate functional level, and *C* to indicate conceptual level of word meanings, then decide which three activities are best for developing the fullest meanings of words.
   a. Suggesting synonyms   ____
   b. Using context clues   ____
   c. Providing real experiences   ____
   d. Looking up words in a glossary and writing sentences   ____
   e. Studying relationships among prefixes, suffixes, and stems ____
   f. Memorizing Latin roots   ____
   g. Playing word identification games   ____
   h. Using vocabulary exercise books   ____
   i. Using films   ____
   j. Semantic feature analysis   ____

Posttest Answers

1. The three levels of word meaning and a description of each follow:
   a. *Specific instance or association level.* At this level the student has only one object, event, observation, or definition associated with a word. Some possible ways to define the word *barrier* at the specific level are (1) "a fence"; (2) "mountains out there"; (3)"the reef in the ocean."
   b. *Functional level.* At this level the student can describe a major use of the word and/or use the word in a sentence that demonstrates

understanding. These are some ways to use *barrier:* (1)"It is like when you put a fence as a barrier in front of a house to keep dogs out." (2)"The mountains were a barrier that made it difficult for the early settlers to get to California from the east coast of the United States." (3)"A barrier reef separates deep from shallow water or warm from cold water."

   c. *Conceptual level.* At this level the student has many facts and ideas associated with the word and recognizes and uses the word in many different sentences or contexts; for example: There are many types of barriers. Barriers to physical movement, barriers to developing personal relationships, and more. Almost anything can be used as a barrier if it is used to block or inhibit something else."

2. The seven major guidelines for effectively teaching word meaning are:
   a. New words are learned best when taught as labels for direct experiences.
   b. Vocabulary development requires the continued and systematic attention of all classroom teachers.
   c. Many encounters with a word in similar and different contexts are necessary before one can acquire the fullest meaning of the word.
   d. The teacher's attitude toward vocabulary improvement and her own superior vocabulary are contagious and vital factors in improving student vocabulary.
   e. Study of a limited number of words in depth is more productive than superficial acquaintance with lists of words.
   f. It is possible, but perhaps impractical, to teach words that are not part of the verbal community in which students live. Lack of opportunity for use results in eventual atrophy.
   g. Use a variety of activities to teach new words rather than only one or two activities.

3. The ten instructional activities for teaching word meaning are categorized into the three levels of word meaning. The circled letters designate the three activities that develop the fullest meaning of words. (S = specific level of word meaning; F = functional level of word meaning; C = conceptual level of word meaning.)

a. Suggesting synonyms	F
b. Using context clues	F
c. Providing real experiences	C
d. Looking up words in a glossary and writing sentences	S
e. Studying relationships among prefixes, suffixes, and stems	F
f. Memorizing Latin roots	S
g. Playing word identification games	S
h. Using vocabulary exercise books	S
i. Using films	C
j. Semantic Feature Analysis	C

Final Comment
You now have more than twenty-five activities to help students learn the meanings of words, and you are aware of the guidelines for increasing vocabulary. If you are enthusiastic, and excited about helping students raise their levels of understanding, they, too, will be more eager to learn. Opportunities to apply your new knowledge will be available every day. We hope you will find these ideas and activities useful.

REFERENCES

Bergman, J. R. (1977, Fall). Reducing frustration by an innovative technique for vocabulary growth. *Reading Improvement, 14*(3), 172–174.

Blanchowicz, C. L. (1985). Vocabulary development and reading: From research to instruction. *Reading Teacher, 38*(9), 876–881.

Dale, E., O'Rorke, J., & Bamman, H. A. (1971). *Techniques of teaching vocabulary.* Palo Alto, CA: Field Educational Publications.

Dupuis, M. M., & Snyder, S. L. (1983). Develop concepts through vocabulary: A strategy for reading specialists to use with content teachers. *Journal of Reading, 26*(4), 287–305.

Fry, E., Polk, J., & Fountoukidis, D. (1985). *The reading teacher's book of lists.* Englewood Cliffs, NJ: Prentice-Hall.

Gipe, J. P. (1978-79). Investigating techniques for teaching word meaning. *Reading Research Quarterly, 14*(4), 624–644.

Johnson, D. D., et al. (1986). Semantic mapping. *Reading Teacher, 39*(8), 778–783.

Johnson, D. D., & Pearson, P. D. (1978). *Teaching reading vocabulary.* New York: Holt, Rinehart, and Winston.

Lange, J. T. (1983). Using S2RAT to improve reading skills in the content areas. *The Reading Teacher, 36*(4), 402–404.

Manzo, A. V., & Sherk, J. K. (1971–72). Some generalizations and strategies for guiding vocabulary learning. *The Journal of Reading Behavior, 4*(1), 78–89.

Spearitt, D. (1972). Identification of subskills of reading comprehension by maximum likelihood factor analysis. *Reading Research Quarterly, 8*, 92–111.

Templeton, S. (1983). Using the spelling/meaning connection to develop word knowledge in older students. *Journal of Reading, 27*(1), 8–14.

Stahl, S. A., & Fairbanks, M. M. (1986). The effects of vocabulary instruction: A model based meta-analysis. *Review of Educational Research, 56*(1), 72–110.

Stahl, S. A. (1985). To teach a word well: A framework for vocabulary instruction. *Reading World, 24*(3), 16–27.

Thorndike, E. L., & Lorge, I. (1944). *The teacher's word book of 30,000 words.* New York: Teachers College Press, Columbia University.

Wood, K. D. (1987). Teaching vocabulary in the subject areas. *Middle School Journal, 19*(1), 11–13.

MODULE FIVE

Helping Students Comprehend

CHAPTER OUTLINE

OVERVIEW

Rationale

As students progress through the educational system, the reading materials they use become increasingly more technical and put greater demands upon their comprehension skills. For many students, the demands eventually overtake their comprehension competencies. Unless these students receive help in deriving meaning from the printed material in subject areas, their performance will dwindle and they may eventually fail.

Subject area teachers are generally the most qualified persons on the school faculty to help these students with their comprehension needs in the subject areas. No other teachers are better acquainted with the nature of the reading material, style of writing, and the strategies for content analysis than subject area specialists. Subject area teachers also know the qualifications of subject area writers and the subtleties with which they communicate. Subject area teachers are the most qualified teachers in our secondary schools to teach subject area-related reading comprehension skills. *Subject area teachers are the best readers of the materials in their respective areas, and the best readers should teach students how to read in their subject areas.*

To help students improve their comprehension of subject area material, subject area teachers need to make only minor instructional changes. This module deals with four basic competencies subject area teachers need to improve the comprehension achievement of their students. First, teachers need to know the basic comprehension behaviors. Second, they need to know how to prepare questions to assess comprehension behaviors. Third, they need to know how to analyze the questions they ask to determine the thinking processes students go through to arrive at answers. In this module, we will refer to this procedure for achieving answers as a "question-answering strategy." Fourth, teachers need to plan ways to teach question-answering strategies that will improve students' comprehension. The purpose of this module is to help subject area teachers attain these four competencies.

OBJECTIVES

General Objective
You will prepare a lesson plan to improve the comprehension achievement of students in your subject area.

Specific Objectives

1. You will name and describe the six major categories of questions in the Classification Scheme for Reading Questions.
2. You will write one question for each of the six categories in the Classification Scheme for Reading Questions.
3. You will write a step-by-step procedure for answering a question.
4. You will list the steps in a plan for teaching question-answering strategies, and you will prepare a lesson plan designed to teach a strategy for answering a specific type of question on a reading assignment.

ENABLING ELEMENT 1
Comprehending Comprehension

Specific Objective 1
You will name and describe the six major categories of questions in the Classification Scheme for Reading Questions.

Enabling Activities

1. After completing Study Guide 1, list the six major categories of questions in the Classification Scheme for Reading Questions.
2. Share the Classification Scheme for Reading Questions with your colleagues. Together determine if there are types of questions for your subject area that are not included in this scheme. If there are, add them to the appropriate list.
3. Randomly select questions from lesson plans in your subject area textbook. Compare them with the questions in the classification scheme. Are there types of questions proposed by the textbook authors that are not listed in the Classification Scheme for Reading Questions? If so, add them to the appropriate list.
4. As you examine the questions asked by the textbook authors, tally the number that fall into each of the six categories of the classification scheme. You may be surprised at how few questions fall into certain categories. It is not uncommon to find that most questions fall into the Recognition and Recall or Translation categories.
5. Use the Classification Scheme for Reading Questions to prepare questions for a future reading assignment. Duplicate the questions and distribute them to your students. Direct your students to use

these questions as purposes for reading. Determine if having purposes that require different levels of comprehension makes the reading assignment more interesting for your students.

STUDY GUIDE 1

Students in your subject area will usually demonstrate their comprehension of printed material with some type of oral or written response, generally to a question you ask. Each day, you will ask your students many questions and receive hundreds of answers.

An inventory of all the questions subject area teachers ask could be used to demonstrate the comprehension behaviors required for success in content areas. Questions could be classified into a few basic types, and the types could probably be arranged in a hierarchy from simple recognition and recall questions to difficult and complex evaluation questions. Subject area teachers could use the classification scheme for developing reading questions and to illustrate for students the types of reading comprehension behaviors they will need in the various subject areas.

The Classification Scheme for Reading Questions included in this Study Guide is a collection of questions classified into six categories, arranged in approximate order from simplest to more difficult and complex. The scheme was developed by Natividad Santos after a thorough examination of taxonomies prepared by Bloom and Sanders.

We include the Santos Classification Scheme for Reading Questions because it is a valuable tool for both assessment and instruction of comprehension behaviors. It has these specific advantages:

It includes most of the questions that teachers ask.
It is divided into six major categories of questions.
Each category requires a different comprehension behavior.
The categories are arranged in approximate order from simple recognition and recall to the more difficult and complex evaluation.

To become familiar with the Classification Scheme for Reading Questions, first skim the classification scheme to identify the six major categories of reading questions. Next, read the introductory statement following each category and ask yourself, "What type of thinking or comprehension behaviors are required to answer questions that fit this category?" Last, look at the specific types of questions that fit each category.

Classification Scheme for Reading Questions
1. *Recognition or Recall Questions.*   A reading question falls in the recognition or recall category if it can be *answered verbatim* with specific information in the reading selection, and if it requires the reader to

locate or repeat the information. When a teacher asks a student to answer a question by locating what the author said, she is asking a *recognition* question. When she asks a student to remember what the author said, she is asking a *recall* question. Recognition questions require a student to locate an answer; recall questions require the student to use only memory. Teachers use recognition or recall questions when asking students to do the following tasks.

1. Respond to direct factual questions when the facts appear in the selection
2. Enumerate or list information in the selection
3. Quote the author or a character in the selection
4. Recall who in a selection made a particular statement
5. Recite a stanza of a poem, an essay, or a rule from memory
6. Read aloud the part of a selection that answers a factual question or some other specified part

B. Translation Questions. A reading question falls in the translation category if it requires the reader to answer a question by *restating* in his own words what the author said. The reader must keep the author's idea and not change facts. When asking a student to give the answer to a question in his own words, a teacher is asking a translation question. Teachers use translation questions when asking students to do the following tasks.

1. Explain in the reader's own words the meaning of technical terms, vocabulary words, and stated meanings
2. Restate a problem, generalization, principle, rule, or procedure the author has described
3. Paraphrase or summarize a selection
4. Retell a selection or describe or retell parts or events of a selection to prove a point
5. Explain printed directions
6. Change poetry to prose or vice versa
7. Change a statement to a question
8. Illustrate or draw information presented verbally
9. Describe a picture, poster, sketch, drawing, painting, or object
10. Present information through a graph, diagram, chart, table, or map

C. Application Questions. A reading question falls in the application category if it requires the reader to use information obtained by reading. Asking students to use information they have just acquired by reading is asking them to apply what they have read. Teachers use application questions when asking students to do the following tasks:

1. Use what they have learned from reading a selection to explain how two or more people, places, or things are alike or different

2. Use what they have learned to explain a situation or outcome or to answer a question
3. Follow directions to complete a task or project
4. Use information they have read to solve a problem
5. Prepare an outline of the information in the reading assignment
6. Group or classify the ideas in a reading assignment
7. Prepare time lines, graphs, charts, and other forms for displaying information

D. Analysis Questions. A reading question falls in the analysis category if it requires the reader to *analyze* what he has read to find information to explain or support a statement. Teachers use analysis questions when asking students to do the following tasks:

1. Find the supporting statements for a main idea, conclusion, or inference
2. Find the steps to follow in solving a problem
3. Locate information for solving a mystery or problem
4. Identify missing information
5. Identify clues that explain a character's actions or traits or a remark the character makes
6. Identify relationships, as in (a) cause-effect, (b) past-present, (c) main idea-details, (d) central theme-main idea
7. Identify statements that reveal an author's bias or viewpoint
8. Identify propaganda devices
9. Identify statements that make a communication false

E. Synthesis Questions. A reading question falls in the synthesis category if it requires the reader to *join or combine information* to form a new communication. Asking a student to generalize over the details in a paragraph to create a main idea statement is an example of synthesis. Teachers use synthesis questions when asking students to do the following tasks:

1. Generalize from details to form a main idea
2. Generalize from facts to form a conclusion
3. Generalize from facts and opinions to form an inference
4. Summarize the main points
5. Substitute words or phrases to make ideas more correct or easier to understand
6. Read a selection aloud showing the author's intended expression
7. Suggest different titles for a story, chapter, side heading, or other item
8. Suggest solutions to a problem
9. Give a different beginning, ending, or title to a story or other piece

F. Evaluation Questions.   A reading question falls in this category if it requires the student to determine whether a communication *meets standards* set up by that student or presented to the student. It requires the student to make decisions and to support his views in his own words. Asking a student to establish evaluation criteria, gather facts to compare with the criteria, judge how well each fact matches a given criterion, and form an evaluation is an example of an evaluation question. Teachers use an evaluation process when asking students to do the following tasks:

1. Evaluate a communication for:

accuracy	completeness
authenticity	practicability
relevance	reasonableness
adequacy	authoritativeness
value	logical consistency
imagination	truth
falsity	merit
agreement	appropriateness
suitability	objectivity, etc.

2. Evaluate pictures for accuracy, appropriateness, suitability, and richness of imagination
3. Evaluate endings to a story, summaries, a performance, a declamation, an oration, or a speech
4. Evaluate statements for ambiguities, overspecificity, omissions, distortions, inconsistencies, inaccuracies, or overstatements
5. Evaluate to determine if a conclusion, inference, main idea, or thesis logically follows the facts; select the best conclusion, inference, etc., from a set of suggested conclusions, inferences, etc.
6. Evaluate to form an opinion or to take a stand on an issue
7. Judge agreement between ideas or sources of information
8. Judge and prove the truth or falsity of statements by pointing out supportive statements or evidence, and justify one's views
9. Judge ideas as similar, different, contradictory, supportive, related, relevant, essential, or in proper sequence
10. Judge the relative merits of information from different sources, or the sources themselves
11. Judge characters in a story

The Classification Scheme in Review
As you read the Classification Scheme for Reading Questions, you noticed that each of the six major categories of questions requires its own comprehension behaviors, or "thinking strategies." You noticed that each level of the strategy tends to build on the preceding level, suggesting a true hierarchy.

Recognition or Recall Questions are the first category in this classification scheme, and questions of this type require the reader to identify or recall exact statements from the passage to give verbatim answers. Since the comprehension behaviors required at this level are rather simple, the question-answering strategy is not elaborate.

Translation questions relate closely to Recognition and Recall questions; the chief difference is that translation questions require the reader to answer the questions in his own words, not verbatim, and are thus a higher level question-answering strategy than Recognition or Recall.

Application questions require that the learner use the information obtained through reading in some new situation. The information can be used in any way as long as a change results. The information can be used to make comparisons, to outline, or to locate information, to mention just a few types of application.

Analysis questions require the learner to analyze a reading selection to locate specific information. Sometimes the information is used to explain, justify, or prove a point; other times, the information is used as a basis for forming generalizations, in which case analysis leads to synthesis. Analysis questions thus require a still higher level question-answering strategy.

Synthesis questions require the reader to combine information to form a new statement or communication. Synthesis is often the other side of analysis; for example, a reader may first analyze a reading selection to find detail and later synthesize the details to form a main idea. The synthesis question-answering strategy builds upon but is more complex than preceding strategies because it requires the reader to combine or synthesize information into a new communication.

Evaluation questions are the final category in the classification scheme. Evaluation questions require the learner to make a decision after reading for information and judging it against evaluation criteria. The decision, information gathered, and evaluation criteria must be justified by the reader. The evaluation question-answering strategy is the most complex and difficult for students to master.

Table 5–1 summarizes factors in the Classification Scheme for Reading Questions, showing the interrelatedness and increased complexity of comprehension behaviors as questions move from Recognition and Recall to Evaluation.

Upon reflection, you will probably realize that the Classification Scheme for Reading Questions is a rather complete model of the reading comprehension requirements of your subject area. The classification scheme probably contains most of the questions you ask your students to answer in your subject area. Because of its comprehensiveness, the classification scheme will be invaluable for preparing questions that will stimulate your students' thinking.

If you can now name and describe the six major categories for classifying reading questions from the Classification Scheme for

Table 5–1
Summary Form: Classification Scheme for Reading Questions

Question Categories	Type of required response					
	Recognize or recall answer verbatim	Change verbatim answer to own words	Use information to alter some situation or product	Separate communication into parts for analysis	Combine information from various sources to form something new	Evaluate and justify the decision
Recognition or Recall	×					
Translation	×	×				
Application	×	×	×			
Analysis	×	×	×	×		
Synthesis	×	×	×	×	×	
Evaluation	×	×	×	×	×	×

Reading Questions, you are ready for Enabling Element 2. If not, complete the task before moving on. If you are having difficulty, reexamine this Enabling Element or see your instructor.

ENABLING ELEMENT 2
Preparing Reading Questions

Specific Objective 2
You will write one question for each of the six categories in the Classification Scheme for Reading Questions.

Enabling Activities

1. Read Study Guide 2. Prepare one question for each of the six categories on the reading selection, "Comprehension Is the Cornerstone of Education."
2. Identify some reading selections from your subject area textbook. Prepare two or three questions for each of the six categories of reading questions. Use these questions to establish purposes for reading the assignment.
3. Make copies of the Classification Scheme for Reading Questions available to your students. Familiarize them with the various kinds of reading questions that can be constructed. Have students construct questions for each of the six categories to use in establishing purposes for reading.

4. Exchange copies of questions with other staff members who have prepared, from common reading assignments, questions in each of the six categories. You may find that some teachers are better than others at writing certain types of questions.

5. Get together with a group of colleagues in your subject area and, using the classification scheme, identify the more important types of questions for your subject area. Arrange the questions in a hierarchy from least to most difficult. This activity will give you a classification scheme for reading questions specific to your subject area. Use this scheme for developing questions when you plan future reading assignments.

STUDY GUIDE 2

Your first step toward improving students' comprehension is to write a variety of questions. Not only is variety necessary, but the questions should range on a hierarchy from Recognition and Recall to Evaluation. The hierarchy in the Classification Scheme for Reading Questions introduced in Enabling Element 1 will be used to prepare questions in this Enabling Element.

It is now time to begin writing questions using the Classification Scheme for Reading Questions. At this point, you should reacquaint yourself with the classification scheme, particularly the variety of questions that fall under each classification. When you have completed this task, read the following selection, "Comprehension Is the Cornerstone of Education."

Comprehension Is the Cornerstone of Education

Comprehension of subject matter materials is one of the major objectives of public and private education. As a major objective of education, it becomes one of the chief responsibilities of every teacher. Many teachers, however, teach as if they believe comprehension to be an innate ability, which students have or have not. Their teaching behavior leads an observer to conclude that developing comprehension abilities is the objective of the student and not of the teacher. Teachers such as these make no attempt to explain the processes involved in obtaining information from textual material. They merely make assignments and leave it to the student to discover the intricate processes that lead to understanding. Given that human beings are our most important natural resource, we can no longer allow miseducation such as this to take place. In the future, subject area teachers will have to assume their rightful responsibility for developing the comprehension skills indigenous to their specific subject areas.

The classification scheme contains six basic categories for questions; each category describes questions that can be classified in the category. Examining each category reveals that it is highly unlikely that all the questions in the category would apply to one reading selection. The nature and the author's purpose will differ for each selection so the types of question will vary.

For the selection, "Comprehension Is the Cornerstone of Education," there are questions for each category, but the number for each is not the same because some questions are appropriate for the passage and some are not. Next to each question is a code number corresponding to a category on the Classification Scheme for Reading Questions; for example, question A1 corresponds to 1 on the scheme, "respond to direct factual questions when the facts appear in the selection." Compare each question with its appropriate classification to see how easy it is to prepare questions using the scheme.

Also notice that we have provided code numbers for preparing additional questions under each category, so you can see which additional categories lend themselves to questions you might prepare.

Outline for Preparing Questions, Form A
"Comprehension Is the Cornerstone of Education"

A. *Recognition or Recall*
  1. According to the author of this selection, what is one of the major objectives of public and private education?
  3.

  6.

B. *Translation*
  1. In your own words, define *comprehension*.
  4.

C. *Application*
  2. Does this selection explain the observation that comprehension scores on standardized tests do not continue to improve as students go through high school? Explain.

  5.

D. *Analysis*
   1. What major facts presented by the author underlie his or her con-
      clusion regarding future responsibilities of subject area teachers?

   4.

   7.

E. *Synthesis*
   2. What is the major conclusion we can reach from the facts pre-
      sented by the author?
   9.

F. *Evaluation*
   1. Did the author objectively present his or her point of view?
   6.

PRACTICUM EXERCISE

Now it is your turn to write some questions. On the Outline for Preparing Questions, Form A, we provide code numbers for questions under
each classification and questions after some of the code numbers. Your
assignment is to formulate questions for the categories that do not have
them. Using the selection, "Comprehension Is the Cornerstone of Education," and the Classification Scheme for Reading Questions, write at
least one question for each of the six categories. You may want to examine the classification scheme to determine if you could prepare still
more questions. When you have finished, begin reading with the following paragraph.

Answers to the Practicum Exercise

Now that you have completed your task, we are sure you will agree that
the classification scheme makes it easy to prepare questions. Now compare your questions with ours. Look at the six categories of questions in
the following Outline for Preparing Questions, Form B. The comparison
should demonstrate the adequacy of your questions as well as reinforce
our point that the classification scheme makes writing questions effort-
less.

Outline for Preparing Questions, Form B
"Comprehension Is the Cornerstone of Education"

A. *Recognition or Recall*
   1. According to the author of this selection, what is one of the major objectives of public and private education?
   3. What did the author say the behavior of many teachers leads an observer to conclude?
   6. Read aloud the sentence in which the author states the future responsibilities of subject area teachers.
B. *Translation*
   1. In your own words, define *comprehension*.
   4. In your own words, state the author's major points.
C. *Application*
   2. Does this selection explain the observation that comprehension scores on standardized tests do not continue to improve as students matriculate through high school? Explain.
   5. How might the author have outlined the facts in the selection?
D. *Analysis*
   1. What major facts presented by the author underlie his or her conclusion regarding future responsibilities of subject area teachers?
   4. Did the author leave any important information out of the selection?
   7. Which statements reveal the author's point of view?
E. *Synthesis*
   2. What is the major conclusion we can reach from the facts presented by the author?
   9. What would be another appropriate title for this selection?
F. *Evaluation*
   1. Did the author objectively present his or her point of view?
   6. How would you defend the author's conclusion?

Now that you are familiar with the Classification Scheme for Reading Questions and can use it to prepare questions in each of the six categories, it is time to look at strategies for answering questions.

ENABLING ELEMENT 3
Strategies for Obtaining Improved
Answers to Questions

Specific Objective 3
You will write a step-by-step procedure for answering a question.

Enabling Activities

1. Read Study Guide 3, and list the steps in your question-answering strategy for an analysis question.
2. For a passage of your choosing, write six questions at the various levels of the Classification Scheme for Reading Questions. When you finish, list the step-by-step procedure you went through to answer each question.
3. Arrange a meeting with a group of colleagues to discuss and refine strategies for answering questions. Share the sample strategies from this Study Guide to initiate the discussion. Group discussion is probably the best way to refine thinking on question-answering strategies.
4. Reproduce the sample question-answering strategies and distribute them to your students. Use the various strategies as a basis for discussing comprehension improvement in your subject area.
5. Discuss with colleagues in your subject area the various strategies students use to answer questions. How well students answer certain types of questions will provide insight into which types of questions you should stress in future reading assignments.

STUDY GUIDE 3

Each question you prepared for the reading selection in Enabling Element 2 has its unique answer; likewise, each question requires a different procedure or thinking process to obtain an answer. This procedure or thinking process is the *question-answering strategy.*

It is your responsibility as a teacher to improve question-answering strategies of students in your subject area. Because your strategies have become highly refined as a result of years of reading and studying in your specialty, you are the most appropriate teacher to improve the students' strategies.

Before you can help your students, however, you need to become more familiar with your own strategies for answering questions. This will take some time, because you probably execute your strategies automatically. The following Practicum Exercise will help you develop an awareness of your question-answering strategies.

PRACTICUM EXERCISE 1

Directions: (1) Read the question that establishes a purpose for reading the selection. (2) Read the essay. (3) Determine your answer to the question. (4) List the step-by-step procedure you followed to arrive at your answer.

Purpose for reading: Is this the correct title for the selection?

The American Red Cross
     The American National Red Cross is part of an organization
found in more than 120 countries throughout the world. The Red Cross
was founded in Switzerland in 1863 for the purpose of relieving human
suffering around the world. The worldwide organization has a paid
professional staff, but consists mostly of volunteers. There are more
than 30 million volunteer members of the Red Cross throughout the
world. The services provided by this multinational organization are
paid for from voluntary contributions.

Write your answer to the question here:

Write the steps in your question-answering strategy here:

Answers to Practicum Exercise 1
Did you write your answer? Did you list the step-by-step procedure you
used to arrive at your answer? If you did, compare your answer and
question-answering strategy with ours.

1. We read the question and surveyed the passage to be sure neither
   contained unfamiliar words, expressions, or ideas. Many questions
   are misunderstood or answered incorrectly because the reader does
   not take time to clarify an unfamiliar word, expression, or idea.
2. Next, we restated the question in our own words to be sure we
   understood the intent. Many students answer questions incorrectly
   because they misunderstand them. In this case, "Is the title for the
   selection the best or most correct title?" can be changed to "Should
   the author have given this selection another title?"
3. Then we examined the passage to find the facts we needed to answer
   the question. Since we were looking for a title that was representative of all the ideas in the selection, we reread the selection sentence-
   by-sentence and found the following:
   a. Sentence 1 explains that the American National Red Cross is part
      of an organization that is found around the world.
   b. Sentence 2 tells where, when, and why the Red Cross was
      founded.
   c. Sentences 3 and 4 tell about the paid staff and volunteers who
      run the global organization.
   d. Sentence 5 explains how the worldwide organization is funded.

4. We believed all the information needed to answer the question was in the passage; therefore, we did not look for additional information from other sources.

5. Next, we studied each sentence to determine if it presented information represented by the title. We found that the sentences gave information about the worldwide organization called the Red Cross. The title was too narrow because it focused on only the American National Red Cross, only one of over 120 organizations that make up the global organization. After examining the facts, we answered the question. "The American Red Cross" was not the correct title for this selection. A more appropriate title would be "The Red Cross Organization," which more adequately represents or explains the information in the selection.

6. Finally, we checked our answer against the facts in the sentence to be sure it was the best answer to the question.

Does your strategy agree with this one? If not, how does it differ? Your answer may agree with ours even if you used a different strategy; strategies can differ even if the answers do not. We do not know enough about the way people think to conclude that only one strategy exists for answering a particular type of question. If the answers agree, it makes little difference that the strategies differ. Different question-answering strategies are important if the answers differ. You will learn more about using your own strategy to help students develop question-answering strategies in the next Enabling Element.

Occasionally, we can find equal support and arguments for two or more answers to the same question. At this impasse, both answers should be accepted as possibilities of equal merit. Remember, however, that your goal is to identify the one *best* answer; emphasizing the need to identify the best answer encourages precise thinking.

You have now had an opportunity to read our question-answering strategy and compare your strategy to ours. If you think your strategy is incomplete, now is the time to refine your strategy so it will be useful in your teaching.

PRACTICUM EXERCISE 2

Now you are familiar with the processes for writing questions and examining your step-by-step procedure for answering questions. From the following selection, formulate one question for each category in the Classification Scheme for Reading Questions, then examine the Sample Question-Answering Strategies. Using the sample Strategies as guides, create a specific question-answering strategy for each of your questions. This activity will further develop insight into your question-answering strategies and enhance your effectiveness in working with your students' comprehension problems.

Fish Propulsion

Fish, like humans, do not all use the same method for propelling, or moving, through the water. Some fish move through the water with snakelike motions. These snakelike motions are caused by muscle contractions throughout the body. Other fish propel through the water using a combination of muscle contraction and the side motion of their caudal, or tail fin. The third type of swimmer uses the caudal fin almost exclusively. This swimmer keeps its body almost rigid while moving through the water. One category of fish has a unique way of propelling through the water. The flying fish emerges from the water, spreads its large pectoral fin, and glides over the water for hundreds of feet. The method used for propulsion seems to be related to the size of the fish and the speed at which the fish swims.

Directions: Using the preceding selection, create one question for each category in the Classification Scheme for Reading Questions.

Recognition or Recall question:

Translation question:

Application question:

Analysis question:

Synthesis question:

Evaluation question:

When you finish preparing questions, read the Sample Question-Answering Strategies. Follow the directions that appear after the sample strategies.

Sample Question-Answering Strategies

These sample question-answering strategies for the six categories of reading questions are *general* strategies. Question-answering strategies for specific questions within each major category will differ slightly from the sample strategies. You will need to alter the strategies slightly to fit the intent of each question.

Recognition or Recall Strategy

1. Check the question and passage to be sure they do not contain unfamiliar words, expressions, or ideas. If you detect an unfamiliarity, clarify it before proceeding.
2. Be sure the intent of the question is clear. Rephrasing the question sometimes serves as a check on understanding.
3. Read the selection and identify the precise statements that answer the question.
4. Reread the selection to verify that you have identified all the information necessary to answer the question.
5. Answer the question in precisely the same words found in the passage.

Translation Strategy

1. Survey the question and passage to see if they contain unfamiliar words, expressions, or ideas. If you detect an unfamiliarity, clarify it before proceeding.
2. Be sure the intent of the question is clear. Rephrasing the question sometimes helps to ensure clarity.
3. Read the selection and identify the precise statements that answer the question.
4. Check the passage to be sure you have identified everything necessary for answering the question.
5. Answer the question in precisely the same words found in the passage.
*6. Restate the answer in your own words.
*7. Compare your restated answer with the quoted answer to be sure it contains all of the facts or ideas.

Application Strategy

1. Determine whether or not the question or passage contains unfamiliar words, expressions, or ideas. If it does, clarify before going further.
2. Obtain a clear understanding of the specific problem or situation contained in the question. Be sure to understand how the information from the reading will be applied to the specific problem or situation. Identify and state the problem or situation. Restate the question so it specifies what information is necessary to solve the problem or change the situation.

---

*Indicates new step(s) not contained in preceding strategy.

3. Read and locate the precise information required by the restated question.
4. Reread the selection to be sure all available information has been extracted.
5. Examine the information to be sure it does not contain new or inaccurate information.
*6. Using the information from the selection, solve the problem or change the situation as directed by the question.
*7. Check the answer to be sure the problem or situation has been appropriately solved or changed.

Analysis Strategy

1. Examine the question and passage to identify unfamiliar words, expressions, or ideas. Clarify before proceeding.
2. Be sure the intent of the question is understood. Restate the question if necessary to clarify the intent.
*3. Read the selection to identify the information needed to answer the question.
*4. If necessary, gather additional information from other sources.
*5. When you have obtained all the necessary information, prepare an answer.
*6. Check your answer to be sure it is the best answer to the question.

Synthesis Strategy

1. Check the question and passage for unfamiliar words, expressions, or ideas. Clarify them before going further.
2. Be sure the intent of the question is clear. Restate the question if necessary.
3. Identify all relevant information available from the passage.
4. Supply information from other sources as needed.
*5. Synthesize the information and compose an answer to the question. The answer should be new, different, and broader than the sum of its parts.
*6. Test the answer to be sure it covers all the information.

Evaluation Strategy

1. Check the question and passage to be sure they do not contain unfamiliar words, expressions, or ideas. Clarify as necessary.
2. Be sure the intent of the question is understood. Rephrase the question, if necessary, to show that you understand its intent.
*3. Establish the evaluation criteria or rules you will use to make the evaluation.

---

*Indicates new step(s) not contained in preceding strategy.

*4. Read and obtain the facts that go along with each criterion or rule.
*5. Compare each criterion to the facts and judge the facts as either conforming or nonconforming to the criterion or rule.
*6. Examine all the judgments and form your evaluation answer to the original question.
*7. Test your evaluation answer to be sure you can defend it.

Use Figure 5–1 to help your students understand the Evaluation Question-Answering Strategy.

1–2 Evaluation question

3. Criteria or Rules	4. Facts or Information	5. Judgments	6. Evaluation Decision
			7. Defend your decision

Figure 5–1
Evaluation Question-Answering Strategy

Directions: Now you are ready to formulate the answer to each of your questions and list the steps in your question-answering strategy.

Recognition or Recall answer:

and strategy:

*Indicates new step(s) not contained in preceding strategy.

Translation answer:

and strategy:

Application answer:

and strategy:

Analysis answer:

and strategy:

Synthesis answer:

and strategy:

Evaluation answer:

and strategy:

Answers to Practicum Exercise 2

Because we could not anticipate what questions you would write, it was impossible to provide strategies for each of your questions. By now, however, you should be able to evaluate your own strategies. Compare your strategies to the samples. Since your strategies are specific to questions within each category and ours are *general strategies* for each category, your strategies probably contain steps in addition to those we have listed. If you are having difficulty listing the steps in your strategy or feel uncomfortable with the strategy you have developed, reread appropriate components of this Study Guide, complete additional Enabling Activities, examine reference sources by Bloom or Sanders, or see your instructor.

You should now be able to prepare questions and develop question-answering strategies. You are now ready to discuss improving students' reading comprehension in your subject area. Enabling Element 4 addresses itself to this topic.

ENABLING ELEMENT 4
Teaching Question-Answering Strategies

Specific Objective 4

You will list the steps in a plan for teaching question-answering strategies, and you will prepare a lesson plan designed to teach a strategy for answering a specific type of question on a reading assignment.

Enabling Activities

1. Read Study Guide 4. When you finish reading it, list the steps in a plan for teaching question-answering strategies.

2. After completing Study Guide 4, prepare a lesson plan to teach a strategy for answering a specific question.
3. Using reading material you will soon assign to your students, prepare questions at each of the six levels in the classification scheme. Assign them to your students. From their answer, identify students who have difficulty answering specific types of questions and group the students according to the type of questions they could not answer. Teach the students a question-answering strategy following the suggested procedure.
4. Organize open discussion groups so students can meet informally and discuss their reading habits and strategies.
5. Teach your aides or more capable students how to teach the question-answering strategies so they can work with students who need additional instruction.
6. Share your lesson plans and materials with your colleagues. By doing so, each of you will gather an excellent collection of lesson plans.

STUDY GUIDE 4

Now that you are familiar with the classification scheme, can prepare questions at different levels in a hierarchy, and have examined your own processes for answering questions, you are ready to teach. Teaching your students to comprehend subject area material with strategies for answering different types of questions is not a long or involved process, nor does it detract from study of the subject area. In fact, teaching students to comprehend reading assignments for different purposes enhances their understanding and appreciation of the subject area.

This Study Guide introduces a simple plan for teaching question-answering strategies that draws heavily on the subject area teacher's background and reading style. The plan is based on the assumption that subject area teachers are the best readers of their subject's materials.

The four steps for teaching question-answering strategies are to:

1. Set the purpose for learning. This step substantiates for your students their need for instruction.
2. Assess the comprehension strategy. This step determines the precise steps in the learner's strategy for answering a specific type of question.
3. Teach the comprehension strategy. This step teaches a strategy for obtaining the best answer to a question.
4. Apply the comprehension strategy. This step determines whether or not the learner understands the strategy you taught.

The procedure for teaching question-answering strategies is the same you would follow when teaching students how to comprehend subject area material. The instructional plan is set in motion when a student *incorrectly* answers a number of questions of the same type: Recognition and Recall, Translation, Application, Analysis, Synthesis, or Evaluation. Study of the instructional plan should begin with a survey of the four steps. Then, read the material under each step.

Plan for Teaching Question-Answering Strategies

A. *Set the purpose for learning.* The purpose of this step is to substantiate the need for instruction. A lesson is taught because a group of students had difficulty answering two or more questions of the same type—probably in similar material. That material would be used for this lesson. Tell the students that their difficulty in answering a type of question is the reason for the lesson; explain that after some instruction, they will be able to answer such questions and, as a result, will improve their comprehension.

B. *Assess the comprehension strategy.* The purpose of this step is to determine what procedure students followed in answering the question incorrectly.
   1. The teacher restates one or two questions and supplies the answers students gave earlier. As an alternative, the teacher may ask students to state their own answers. Write the answers on the chalkboard for reference.
   2. Ask a student to explain step-by-step how she arrived at her answer. You can repeat this procedure with another student.
   3. As the students reveal the steps in their question-answering strategies, list the steps on a chalkboard.
   4. Do not accept "I don't know" answers. Continue to question the students to determine the specific steps they followed.

C. *Teach the comprehension strategy.* The purpose of this step is to teach the necessary components in a strategy for identifying the best answer to a question.
   1. Using the passage in which students demonstrated difficulty, direct them to observe and listen while you read the passage aloud.
   2. As you read the passage aloud, describe and demonstrate how you are determining the preferred answer to the question they answered incorrectly.
   3. As you describe and demonstrate your strategy, write the steps on a chalkboard. (You learned these strategies in Enabling Element 3.)
   4. When you have finished reading, describing, and demonstrating your strategy, review the steps with the students, then cover or remove the steps from their view.
   5. To be sure they understand the question-answering strategy you have just taught, ask selected students to list and explain the steps in the procedure.
   6. Next, have the students compare their original strategies to your strategy to identify similar and different steps.

7. Discuss with the students how they must modify their strategies to obtain the preferred answer to questions of the type they are working with.
8. Have students explain how they would apply the new strategy to similar questions.
9. The students must *understand* and be able to explain the strategy before the teacher goes to the next step.
   Note: A student may arrive at the preferred answer using an equally acceptable but different strategy than the teacher's. If this is the case, the teacher should not attempt to change the student's strategy. Cognitive styles differ, and correct answers can be reached in different ways.
D. *Apply the comprehension strategy.* The purpose of this step is to determine if students understand and can use the strategy presented by the teacher.
   1. Provide students with a reading assignment similar in reading level and content to the initial assignment.
   2. Prepare questions of the same type as those with which the students experienced difficulty.
   3. Direct students to read the passage silently to find the answer to one of the questions.
   4. When they have finished reading, have the students explain how they looked for the answer to the question.
   5. Students should eventually arrive at or near the preferred answer. In some cases, students fail to provide an improved answer. If this is the case, the teacher should return to the teaching step and reteach the strategy with additional demonstrations. Reteaching is most effective when done with new material, if available.
   6. Give students opportunities to answer similar questions in everyday classroom activities and assignments. Help them apply their strategies to answer questions about information in different types of subject area materials, such as newspapers, magazines, and monographs. Remember, students will forget the strategies you teach unless you provide opportunities for continuous application.

The following Teaching Plan explains how comprehension improves through the study of an analysis question. The plan was developed from "The American Red Cross" selection, to which you can refer. Recall that students were asked to answer the question, "Is this the correct title for this selection?" This Teaching Plan demonstrates how to teach students to answer analysis questions of this type.

The American Red Cross
      The American National Red Cross is part of an organization found in more than 120 countries throughout the world. The Red Cross was founded in Switzerland in 1863 for the purpose of relieving human

suffering around the world. The worldwide organization has a paid professional staff but consists mostly of volunteers. There are more than 30 million volunteer members of the Red Cross throughout the world. The services provided by this multinational organization are paid for from voluntary contributions.

Teaching Plan

A. Set the purpose for learning. Assume that a number of students, in answer to the question, "Is this the correct title for this selection?" gave this response: "Yes, because the passage tells about the American Red Cross." Because this answer is not correct, the teacher points out the need for instruction and explains that instructions should improve their comprehension of the passage and help them correctly answer other questions of this type.

B. Assess the comprehension strategy. Write the students' answer on the chalkboard and ask a student to explain how he arrived at the answer. Let other students contribute to the explanation. Write each step on the chalkboard, and probe to elicit as many specific steps as possible. The strategy may resemble this:
  1. "I read the passage."
  2. "The first sentence is usually the topic sentence."
  3. "Since the name, American Red Cross, appears in the first sentence, it must be what the selection is about."

C. Teach the comprehension strategy.
  1. Give the students a copy of "The American Red Cross," and direct them to read silently as you read aloud.
  2. As you read aloud, describe and demonstrate each step in your strategy for answering this question. Use the Analysis question-answering strategy in Enabling Element 3 as your guide. Here is one method:
    a. Have the students read the question and examine the passage for unfamiliar words, expressions, or ideas that will detract from their comprehension.
    b. Have the students restate the question in their own words. Explain that by restating the question they can determine if they understand its intent. If they do not understand the question, they are not likely to answer it correctly.
    c. Read the first sentence aloud. Ask the students to compare the information in the sentence to the title. Ask, "Does the title represent the ideas you find in the sentence?" Repeat this procedure for each sentence.
    d. Remind the students that a title should reflect the ideas of all the sentences in the selection. If one sentence contains ideas not reflected in the title, the title needs to be changed.
    e. Lead the students to see that the sentences tell about a worldwide Red Cross organization, not just the American Red Cross. They will thus come to see that the present title is not correct.

   f. As you explain each step, write it on the chalkboard.
   g. When you have finished, review the steps in the strategy with the students, then erase the steps from the chalkboard.
   h. Ask students to recall and explain each step in the strategy.
D. Apply the comprehension strategy.
   1. Prepare two questions of a similar type dealing with one passage from familiar reading material.
   2. Direct students to read the material silently to answer one question.
   3. Call on one student to answer the question, and ask others to explain the strategy for answering it.
   4. Repeat Steps 2 and 3 to provide additional practice.
   5. Be sure to provide daily practice opportunities to answer similar questions.

PRACTICUM EXERCISE

Now it is your turn. *First,* use the Classification Scheme for Reading Questions to prepare a number of questions on a reading assignment you will soon assign to your students. Prepare questions for each of the six major levels of the classification scheme.

   Second, give students the questions and the reading assignment. After they complete the assignment, ask them to write answers to the questions. You can use a group question-answer discussion technique, but it is easier for students to mislead you with this technique. Analyze the students' answers. Students who have given fuzzy, incomplete, or incorrect answers can be placed in small groups for instruction.

   Third, select one group of students who are having difficulty with a specific type of question, and prepare a lesson following the guidelines.

   Fourth, provide instruction following the steps in the teaching plan.

Teaching Plan

A. Set the purpose for learning.

B. Assess the comprehension strategy.

C. Teach the comprehension strategy.

D. Apply the comprehension strategy.

Answers to the Practicum Exercise

We hope your lesson went well. If not, refer to the discussion to determine why you had difficulty or see your instructor. Since every plan will differ, it is not possible to anticipate answers; therefore, we have not provided answers for this Practicum Exercise.

If you can prepare a plan for teaching question-answering strategies, you are ready for the Posttest. If not, refer to the appropriate Enabling Elements or see your instructor.

POSTTEST

Directions: Read each of the following statements and complete each Posttest item.

1. As part of this module, you were introduced to the Classification Scheme for Reading Questions. Name and describe the six major categories of questions in the scheme.
2. The Classification Scheme for Reading Questions is a useful tool for writing questions. Write one question for each of the six categories based on the following selection.

   Sleep
   > Sleep is an unconscious state from which a person can quickly be aroused. During sleep the function of most vital organs is reduced. This reduction causes a person to become cool and require covers for comfortable sleeping. A sleeping person goes through periods of light and heavy sleep. The person also goes through periods when he or she does and does not dream. Dreaming seems to have an effect upon the quality of sleep. Although the necessary number of hours of sleep varies from person to person, most adults sleep approximately six to eight hours a day. Sleep cannot be stored in a body like energy in a flashlight battery, and therefore most people need to sleep sometime during each twenty-four-hour period.

3. Before you can help students understand their question-answering strategies, you must understand your own. Write the step-by-step procedure for answering the evaluation question you prepared for the preceding selection.
4. A plan for teaching question-answering strategies helps students improve their question-answering abilities. First, list the steps in the Teaching Plan; second, prepare a brief statement describing what occurs at each step of the instructional process.

Posttest Answers

1. The six categories and their descriptions follow:
   a. Recognition and Recall questions. Questions in this category require a verbatim answer.
   b. Translation questions. Questions in this category require the learner to locate the exact answers and translate them into his own words.
   c. Application questions. Questions in this category require the learner to apply what he has read to solve a problem or change a situation.
   d. Analysis questions. Questions in this category require the learner to analyze the information he reads or find support for a statement.
   e. Synthesis questions. Questions in this category require the learner to combine parts to answer a question or create a new idea or product.
   f. Evaluation questions. Questions in this category require the learner to evaluate what has been read and make a decision using specified criteria. The learner must also justify his information, decision, and the evaluation criteria.
2. Compare each question you wrote with the Classification Scheme for Reading Questions. If you have prepared at least one question for each category, you have demonstrated the required competency.
3. Compare your question-answering strategy to the following evaluation strategy taken from the Sample Question-Answering Strategies in Enabling Element 3. If your strategy contains the same steps, you have demonstrated the required competency.
   a. Check the question and passage to be sure they do not contain unfamiliar words, expressions, or ideas. Clarify as necessary.
   b. Be sure the intent of the question is understood. Rephrase the question if necessary.
   c. Establish the evaluation criteria or rules.
   d. Obtain the facts that go along with each criterion or rule.
   e. Judge how well the facts match with the criterion or rule.
   f. Study your judgments and form your evaluation answer.
   g. Check your evaluation answer to be sure you can defend it.

The following graphic will be helpful.

Evaluation Question

Criteria or Rules	Facts or Information	Judgments	Evaluation Decision
			Defend Your Decision

4. Teaching Plan
   a. Set the purpose for learning. At this step, the teacher establishes the need for instruction.
   b. Assess the comprehension strategy. Here the teacher asks students to explain how they answered a question, to assess the adequacy of the learners' strategy for answering a specific type of question.
   c. Teach the comprehension strategy. This step contains the procedures for teaching the question-answering strategy.
   d. Apply the comprehension strategy. This step determines if the strategy taught is understood by the learners.

Final Comment
You have now acquired a competency that will help you substantially improve students' comprehension in your subject area. Using this competency requires only minor instructional effort by most subject area teachers. We hope you will make this minor adjustment.

If you have satisfactorily completed all Posttest items, you are ready to move to another module. If not, refer to appropriate Enabling Elements, see your instructor, or see the Reference list.

REFERENCES

Axelrod, J. (1974). Some flaws in commercial reading comprehension materials. *Journal of Reading, 17*(6), 474–479.

Bloom, B. S., et al. (1956). *Taxonomy of educational objectives: Handbook I, cognitive domain*. New York: David McKay.

Conley, M. W. (1986). The influence of training on three teachers' comprehension questions during content area lessons. *Elementary School Journal, 87*(1), 17–28.

Dale, E. (1976, Spring). Develop critical reading. *Reading Improvement, 13*(1), 30–33.

Dixon, N. P. (1980, Spring). A test to help improve instruction in reading comprehension. *Reading Improvement, 17*(1), 22–25.

Duffy, G. G., Roeheler, L. R., & Mason, J. (Eds.). (1983). *Comprehensive instruction: Perspective and suggestions*. New York: Longman.

Durkin, D. (1978-79). What classroom observations reveal about reading comprehension instruction. *Reading Research Quarterly, 14*(4), 481–533.

Elrod, G. F. (1987). Turning passive readers into active readers in content area subjects. *Reading Horizons, 27*(3), 197–201.

Flood, J. (Ed.). (1984). *Understanding reading comprehension*. Newark, DE: International Reading Association.

Johnson, K. L. (1987). Improving reading comprehension through pre-reading and post-reading exercises. *Reading Improvement, 24*, 81–83.

Johnson, P. H. (1983). *Reading comprehension assessment: A cognitive basis*. Newark, DE: International Reading Association.

Manzo, A. V. (1975). Guided reading procedure. *Journal of Reading, 18*(4), 287–291.

Mize, J. M. (1978). A directed reading strategy for teaching critical reading and decision making. *Journal of Reading, 22*(2), 144–148.

Montague, M., & Tanner, M. L. (1987). Reading strategy groups for content area instruction. *Journal of Reading, 30*(8), 716–723.

Nist, S. L., & Kirby, K. (1986). Teaching comprehension and study strategies through modeling and thinking aloud. *Reading Research and Instruction, 25*(4), 254–264.

Ortiz, R. K. (1977). Using questioning as a tool in reading. *Journal of Reading, 21*(2), 109–114.

Pearson, P. D., & Johnson, D. D. (1978). *Teaching reading comprehension.* New York: Holt, Rinehart and Winston.

Sinatra, R. C. (1977, Summer). The Cloze technique for reading comprehension and vocabulary development. *Reading Improvement, 14*(2), 86–92.

Smith, R. J. (1987). A study guide for extending students' reading of social studies materials. *Social Studies, 78*(2), 85–87.

Wood, K. D. (1987). Helping students comprehend their textbooks. *Middle School Journal, 18*, 20–22.

MODULE
SIX

Helping Students Use
Study Skills And Strategies

CHAPTER OUTLINE

OVERVIEW

Rationale

To read a textbook, your students need study skills and a study strategy. In fact, in a number of content area textual materials, they need *many* study skills and strategies. Study skills are necessary for locating, organizing, and interpreting information; study strategies are plans for reading textual materials that help the reader comprehend and retain more of the information while adjusting rate and style of reading according to its purposes. If you want your students to read textual materials effectively and efficiently you must teach the appropriate study skills and study strategies. In this module, you will learn the major study skills and an appropriate study strategy for your content area, and how to teach them to your students.

OBJECTIVES

General Objective

You will specify the major study skills from your content area, prepare a plan for teaching a study skill, and apply three study strategies.

Specific Objectives

1. You will specify the major study skills in your content area and prepare a lesson to teach a study skill.
2. You will write the associated words for each step in the SQ3R Study Strategy, write a paragraph describing each step in SQ3R, and describe a plan for teaching the strategy.
3. You will write the associated words for each step in the PQRST Study Strategy, write a paragraph describing each step in PQRST, and describe a plan for teaching the strategy.
4. You will write the associated words for each step in the SQRQCQ Study Strategy, write a paragraph describing each step in SQRQCQ, and describe a plan for teaching the strategy.

ENABLING ELEMENT 1
Teaching Study Skills

Specific Objective 1

You will specify the major study skills in your content area and prepare a lesson to teach a study skill.

Enabling Activities

1. Read Study Guide 1 to identify the major study skills in your content area and learn a plan for teaching study skills.
2. After reading Study Guide 1, prepare a plan for teaching a study skill from your content area by completing Practicum Exercise 2.
3. Examine your textbook to identify the study skills students need to acquire in order to efficiently use print material in your content area. List the skills.
4. Together with colleagues, identify the study skills required for understanding and using the various textual materials in your subject area. Divide the responsibility of developing plans for teaching the study skills. Share plans with each other. After using the plans in class, meet with your colleagues to revise the plans as necessary.
5. Ask students how important it is for you to teach them the study skills necessary for locating and understanding textual materials in your subject area. Let their comments guide you in preparing future plans for teaching study skills.

STUDY GUIDE 1

In addition to being able to understand word meanings (Module 4), comprehend ideas (Module 5), and pronounce multisyllable words (Module 7), students need to understand the basic skills for locating, organizing, and interpreting information. We refer to this cluster of skills as *study skills*.

If you fan through the pages of any textbook in your area, you will notice it is full of information, pictures, graphs, charts, diagrams, worksheets, and other useful aids. The textbook also has a table of contents, and probably an index, glossary, and other front and back matter sections that are important for students to use effectively and efficiently when they study. Now consider that the textbook is only one source of information students use when they study. They also use dictionaries, encyclopedias, thesauruses, references, and guides. You can see that students need to master many study skills to study effectively and efficiently. Your students must be taught the specific study skills for reading textual materials in your content area. It is your job to teach these skills because you are most qualified. You know how to use the study skills for your content area, and through your demonstration, students will learn to study the way you do.

Study Skills

We have listed major study skills common to most textual materials; however, some study skills are unique to specific textual materials or subject areas. To make a complete list of study skills, you will need to (1) examine the following list of General Study Skills, and (2) examine textual materials in your subject area. From this examination, you should be able to compose a list of the skills students need to study textual materials in your content area.

General Study Skills

Locate information through:

1. Card catalog
2. *Reader's Guide to Periodical Literature*
3. Dictionary, to pronounce and define words
4. Encyclopedias
5. Thesaurus
6. Aids in the front and back of textbooks
   a. Title page
   b. Copyright page
   c. Table of contents
   d. Preface
   e. Index
   f. Glossary
   g. Bibliographies or References
   h. Appendixes
7. Government publications
8. Common references for your content area

Organize information by:

9. Preparing outlines
10. Writing summaries
11. Classifying topics
12. Associating whole to parts
13. Cause-effect relationships
14. Compare-contrast relationships
15. Problem-solution relationships
16. Time line

Interpreting information from:

17. Diagrams
18. Illustrations

19. Graphs
20. Charts
21. Time lines
22. Drawings
23. Cutaway patterns
24. Pictographs
25. Flowcharts
26. Pictures
27. Maps
28. Specific types of worksheets and/or balance sheets
29. Cartoons
30. Advertisements

PRACTICUM EXERCISE 1

Directions: List the five most important study skills for your content area. Be sure to first examine all the skills listed.

1.

2.

3.

4.

5.

Answers to Practicum Exercise 1
If you (1) referred to the list of study skills in the Study Guide, (2) examined your textual materials for other important study skills, and then (3) listed the five major study skills, you have a good list.

Teaching Study Skills
When you introduce the textbook to your students, share with them the various study aids that are important for using the textbook. Most textbooks contain aids such as a title page, copyright page, table of contents, glossary, and index. Many also contain pictures, graphs, charts, and similar graphic aids. When you introduce the textbook, the first set

of study skills you should teach students are those for understanding the purposes and uses of the title page, copyright page, table of contents, glossary, and index. As you move through the textbook, you will want to teach students how to use specific graphic aids to understand information presented in the various chapters.

The basic lesson plan for teaching study skills contains four steps. (1) objective, (2) instruction, (3) evaluation, and (4) extension activities. A sample lesson plan shows you how to teach a study skill. Read the plan to see how instruction occurs. This plan can be used with a whole class or with only those students who cannot demonstrate the skill.

Demonstration Lesson Plan

Objective—The first step in any lesson plan is to state the purpose or objective. To do so, you need to determine what you want students to do after a lesson that they could not do before the lesson. Suppose students were not able to answer questions about the various sections of the textbook, perhaps because they have not seen a textbook of this type, or because they have never been taught to use the study aids in similar textbooks. The object of the lesson becomes, "Given a textbook, students will identify the major study aids and state the purpose of each."

Instruction—Here are steps to help students accomplish the stated objective:

1. Ask students to survey the textbook to identify its various sections or parts. As they identify them, list them on the chalkboard. They should identify front cover, title page, copyright page, preface, table of contents, chapters, glossary, index, and possibly other parts specific to your textbook.
2. Ask students to share what they know about each of the sections of the textbook. As they mention key points for each section, write them after the section title on the chalkboard. For example:
   a. Front cover—tells the name of the book and the author
   b. Title page—tells the name of the book, name of the authors, location of the authors, and publishing company and its location
   c. Copyright page—tells when the book was copyrighted, which is assumed to be the date the book was first available, and whether the book was previously copyrighted, which shows that this is a newer version of an older book
   d. Preface—the author explains the purpose for writing the book; may identify the audience for which the book was written and acknowledge those who helped with it
   e. Table of contents—outline of the various chapters or topics, showing how the book is organized
   f. Glossary—author defines generic and/or technical words she considers important for understanding the book
   g. Index—alphabetical listing of the various topics in the book, a finer breakdown of the topics than found in the table of contents;

names of people, places, or things mentioned in the book are also included in the index

3. Now lead students through an examination of each section of the book. As you examine each section, discuss the information found there and how students can use it effectively and efficiently; as time permits, continue this way until you move through the whole textbook.

4. As you work through the textbook sections, it will be obvious that some students do not know how to use some of the more technical sections, such as a glossary and index; you will need to group them for additional study skills lessons.

Evaluation—You can determine how effective instruction was by calling on students by name and asking them to explain the various sections of the textbook.

Extension Activities

1. To reinforce what students have learned about the various sections of the textbook, you will want to give assignments requiring them to use the textual aids. For example, you may want to give a list of questions that refers them to the table of contents or index to find sections where they can read to answer the questions. Some questions may ask them to define words in the glossaries. Also ask them questions that require them to read the copyright or title page.

2. Have students look through other content area textbooks to determine if they contain the same textual aids. Ask students how the textual aids will be useful, and allow them to support their statements by examining the textual aids.

PRACTICUM EXERCISE 2

One lesson usually leads to another, and it is likely that you will have a number of students who now understand the various sections of a textbook but do not understand how to use the more technical aids such as a glossary or an index. Suppose the students do not know how to use the index. On the sample lesson plan, write an objective for a lesson to teach how to use the index. Write the objective now.

Lesson Plan
Objective:

Instruction:

Evaluation:

Extension Activities:

Next, decide how you are going to demonstrate and what you are going to have students do to acquire an understanding of an index. Outline what you will do, say, and require of students to accomplish your objective under the *Instruction* section.

When you have finished teaching, you need to evaluate the effectiveness of instruction. Write what you will do to evaluate how well your students have learned the purpose and use of an index. This will be not only an evaluation of how well the students learn, but also of the effectiveness of your instruction. Write your ideas under *Evaluation*.

Finally, you will need to provide students with activities for reinforcing and extending what they have learned about an index. Under *Extension Activities*, specify your ideas for helping students solidify their understanding and become more skillful at using an index.

Answers to Practicum Exercise 2

The following lesson plan is one example for teaching students what an index is and how to use it. Compare it to your responses to see if you have provided a clear objective, appropriate instructional activities, useful evaluation techniques, and extension activities that truly reinforce and develop skill in index use.

Lesson Plan

Objective—Given a textbook index, students will state its purpose and demonstrate how to use the index to locate specific material in the textbook.

Instruction

1. Have students refer to the table of contents to locate the page on which the index begins, then have them turn to the index. Point out that each page of the index has two or more columns of information.
2. Have students use their index fingers to skim down each column on each page of the index, and point out that the index is organized in alphabetical order.
3. Next have students read the columns of information on the first page of the index, while you explain that major topics and subtopics are included in an index. Major topics are capitalized, and aligned on the far left of every column; subtopics are usually not capitalized, and are indented under major topics. Also point out the page references for topics and subtopics.
4. Direct students to a topic that has a number of subtopics. They should first read the topic and subtopics, then refer to the pages on which the subtopics appear. Lead the students to understand that a major topic may be dealt with in a number of places in a textbook, and the various page numbers after the major topic show which pages have information about it. The various subtopics are ideas that relate to the major topic; they too may be discussed on various pages, and the numbers after the subtopics in the index indicate the text pages on which they are mentioned.
5. Have students skim the major topics to see what kinds of information are included in the index. Point out that the index may mention names, places and topics.
6. Point out any other features the index has.
7. Ask students to tell where they would locate information on various topics in their textbooks. Such an exercise gives students practice in rapidly locating topics and subtopics in the textbook.

Evaluation—Question the students to determine if they understand the purpose of an index, then give each student a topic and watch as the students use the index to evaluate them for effectiveness and efficiency.

Extension Activities

1. At another time, ask students to locate information using the indexes in their textual materials.
2. Incorporate into your assignments activities that require your students to use the index to locate information in their textbooks.
3. Hold time drills in which students compete with each other to locate information in their textbooks.

Now you should understand the basic skills that students need for independent study in your content area. You should also know how to prepare a lesson plan to teach these study skills. Some of the study skills should be taught when a textual source is introduced; others, when the need arises. The best time to teach study skills is *when students need them.*

Now that you are familiar with the basic study skills in your content area and know how to teach them, you are ready to learn about study strategies. You will learn about a different study strategy in each of the following three Enabling Elements.

ENABLING ELEMENT 2
The SQ3R Study Strategy for Social Sciences

Specific Objective 2
You will write the associated words for each step in the SQ3R Study Strategy, write a paragraph describing each step in the process of using SQ3R, and describe a plan for teaching the strategy.

Enabling Activities

1. Read Study Guide 2 to identify the five key words associated with this strategy and to learn how to use each step in SQ3R with a reading assignment in social science and humanities materials.
2. Select a reading passage with side headings from a student textbook in social science or humanities. The reading passage should be approximately six to ten pages, *or* require approximately twenty to thirty minutes of sustained silent reading by the students. Follow the recommended procedures for "Using the SQ3R Study Strategy," and study read the selection.
3. Use the recommended procedure in "Teaching SQ3R," to prepare a plan. Following your plan, teach SQ3R to a group of students.
4. Practice using the SQ3R Study Strategy with reading assignments containing few or no side headings. Prepare a plan for teaching students to use this strategy with reading assignments that have few or no side headings.
5. Reproduce the section entitled "Components of SQ3R," and distribute it to your colleagues. Discuss the possibilities for teaching this study strategy in all social science and humanities courses.
6. Compare reading rate and comprehension scores after students read two similar assignments, one using SQ3R and the other using their present reading strategy. What do your findings suggest?

STUDY GUIDE 2

Francis Robinson, concerned about the reading comprehension level of his students, found that the typical reader remembers only about half of

MODULE SIX

what she is asked for on a quiz immediately following a reading assignment. This was the case for both average and superior high-school students. To deal with the problem, Robinson devised the SQ3R Study Strategy as a technique to increase immediate understanding and prolong retention. The strategy is well supported by results of studies investigating the learning process.

SQ3R is a five-step strategy: *Survey, Question, Read, Recite,* and *Review.* The first three steps evolved from research that demonstrated (1) the value of skimming over and summarizing headings before reading and (2) the value of knowing the comprehension questions before reading an assignment. Skimming to obtain an overview of the textual material orients one to the material and provides clues to what information will be presented. Questions provide specific purposes for reading and directions on how to read. Furthermore, the questions are generally connected by a thread of logic that makes them easier to remember. Because questions tell us the specific information we are looking for, they help us remember the information.

When Robinson's students applied the first three steps, Survey, Question, and Read, to assignments, the result was a higher level of immediate understanding. This result did not satisfy Robinson, because he knew that approximately 80 percent of what was read would be forgotten within two weeks. He also knew that retention could be improved by test-type reviews after the reading assignment. When test-type review sessions were held after reading, forgetting was reduced from 80 to 20 percent after a two-week period. Because of this substantial change in retention, Robinson added the last two components to his study strategy: Recite and Review.

The SQ3R Study Strategy that Robinson introduced many years ago has withstood the test of time. It has been widely accepted because the strategy serves as an advance organizer, provides specific purposes for reading, provides self-comprehension checks, and fixes information in memory. The SQ3R Study Strategy does not require additional reading time; in fact, after the technique is mastered, it generally requires less time.

Components of SQ3R

The student follows the five steps in the order they occur in the formula statement SQ3R: Survey, Question, Read, Recite, and Review. Here is an overview of the five components:

- *Survey.* When reading material includes side headings, the Survey consists of reading the title, introduction, all side headings, and the final or summary paragraph. If the material does not have side headings, the Survey consists of skimming paragraphs for topic sentences until a transition point is located. When the reader locates a transition point, she is to stop and reflect on the ideas in the last set of paragraphs and formulate a question about those ideas. This process continues until the end of the assignment.

- *Question.* Now the headings or major points are changed into questions. A question is used because, of all sentence forms, it probably provides the reader with the most specific direction. Questions serve as advance organizers for the total assignment, and each specific question provides immediate and specific direction for reading.
- *Read.* Taking each question in turn, one reads to locate the answer. The reader may skim, skip, or reread material as she chooses. The style of reading should vary with the purpose for reading.
- *Recite.* Recitation checks on clarity of ideas and fixes ideas in memory. After an answer to a question has been located or reasoned out, the reader should pause and recite the answer. Most students should recite their answers aloud. Students, like most of us, are more critical of their ideas when they are spoken aloud.
- *Review.* A review fixes in memory the overall organization as well as the specific ideas. Generally, one review should occur immediately after completing the reading assignment, second review within the next twenty-four hours, and a third, twenty-four hours later. Students with memory difficulties should periodically review throughout the reading assignment as well as continue the daily reviews.

Using the SQ3R Study Strategy

Before you can teach SQ3R to others, you must understand how to use it. So that you will have no difficulty teaching this strategy, follow our suggestions for using it on a reading assignment in one of the student textbooks in your subject area.

PRACTICUM EXERCISE

Identify a six- to ten-page selection in the textbook. The reading assignment should take approximately twenty to thirty minutes for your average reader to complete. Choose a selection you would like your students to read, because we will later ask you to use this passage with your students.

- *Survey.* Begin by surveying headings, charts, graphs, and pictures, then read the introductory and final paragraphs or summary. Surveying consists of a rapid reading of side headings or topic sentences if side headings are not provided to give the reader an overview of the content and the thread of organization. Stop reading and complete this step, then go to step 2.
- *Question.* After completing the survey, use the information you have obtained from headings and/or topic sentences to formulate questions.

For most of us, questions provide a clearer focus than other types of sentence constructions. A well-formulated question cuts down considerably on the amount of time it takes to locate information. Stop reading and complete this step, then go to step 3.

- *Read.* Now read to locate the answers to your questions. Reading here is not defined as looking at every word on every line of every page. It is legitimate to skim material, skip material, and reread material. The objective is to obtain the information necessary to answer your questions. Your style of reading should vary dramatically as the nature of the questions changes. Just as there is more than one type of question, there is also more than one style of reading. Stop reading and complete this step, then go to step 4.

- *Recite.* After you locate the answer to each question, look away from the textbook and recite the answer in your own words. It is important to recite the answer in your own words to be sure you understand what you have read and to avoid parroting. Depending on how important the information is, you may want to write a brief phrase to help you later recall the information. Stop reading and complete this step, then go to step 5.

- *Review.* When you finish the assignment, review the ideas you derived from the reading. Remember, immediate recitation followed by periodic reviews reduces memory loss from 80 to 20 percent at the end of a two-week period. Stop reading and complete this step.

Answers to the Practicum Exercise

How was it? If you are like most teachers, you found it very easy to apply this study strategy. You also found that you remembered more of what you read. If you timed yourself, you probably found it took you less time than you expected to complete this assignment. You surely noticed that your reading style varied with the nature of the question you asked— and it should! Remember, effective and efficient readers vary their reading style with their purpose for reading.

You are now familiar with the SQ3R Study Strategy and have applied it to a textbook in your teaching area. Now we will prepare to teach the SQ3R Study Strategy.

Teaching SQ3R

The instructional procedures for the SQ3R Study Strategy are divided into five steps.

Select Materials

1. Select a reading assignment six to ten pages in length or one requiring twenty to thirty minutes of sustained silent reading by your students. Select reading assignments from suitable textbooks. For your first lesson, you can use the material you identified for the practice lesson from the Practicum Exercise in Study Guide 2 if it is suitable.

2. Prepare and duplicate copies of "Components of SQ3R" for each student.
3. Collect copies of nontextbook materials without side headings. You will need one copy for each student in your group. All students should have a copy of the same material.

Apply SQ3R
1. Read the six- to ten-page textbook selection using the SQ3R Study Strategy.
    a. *Survey* the selection.
    b. *Question* the material.
    c. *Read* and answer the questions.
    d. *Recite* answers.
    e. *Review* questions and answers.
2. Be sure to apply SQ3R with the same care and completeness you expect from your students.

Schedule Instruction. Schedule three fifty-minute periods for teaching the study strategy to your students. If possible, teach the three lessons within the same week.

Provide Instruction.
1. During the first fifty-minute period
    a. Explain to your students that you are going to introduce them to the SQ3R study strategy that they are to use when reading assignments in your class. Tell them the SQ3R strategy will raise their level of understanding, extend retention, and save study time. You may want to share other facts about how Francis Robinson developed the strategy.
    b. Distribute copies of "Components of SQ3R" to each student. Discuss each component so your students understand its function.
    c. Demonstrate the application of SQ3R with the selection you prepared. Answer any questions.
    d. Assign the same selection to the students, and direct them to apply SQ3R as they read it.
    e. When students finish reading the assignment, record their reading time and check their comprehension. Use this information in the following discussion.
    f. Begin a group discussion comparing SQ3R to prior reading strategies. Point out the advantages of study strategies such as SQ3R.
2. During the second fifty-minute period
    a. Review the SQ3R components.
    b. Demonstrate application of SQ3R with another textbook selection.
    c. Assign a different selection than you used for demonstration purposes and direct students to apply SQ3R as they read.

    d. When the assignment is completed, record reading times and check comprehension. Review the advantages of SQ3R.

    e. Assign another, shorter selection for additional practice using SQ3R.

  3. During the third fifty-minute period

    a. Discuss application of SQ3R to materials without side headings.

    b. Demonstrate application of SQ3R to materials without side headings.

    c. Help students use SQ3R with material that does not contain side headings.

    d. When the assignment is completed, record reading times and check comprehension. Discuss advantages of SQ3R with this type of material.

Practice.

    Schedule ten- to fifteen-minute class periods for additional demonstrations and student practice sessions. You will need at least twenty teacher-directed practice sessions to raise this study strategy to the automatic performance level. It is just as easy on this level to apply SQ3R as it is to use any other strategy.

    In stress situations, students have a tendency to resort to their most secure and automatic behavior patterns, so students may apply SQ3R in practice activities but not in actual assignments unless you provide sufficient practice to raise the skill to the automatic level of behavior. Encourage the use of the SQ3R Study Strategy in every assignment by providing time for surveying and suggesting questions that can be used to guide reading. Whenever you use a new type of instructional reading material, demonstrate how to apply the strategy to the new material. Always stress and reward improved comprehension and extended memory as a result of using SQ3R.

    Review and list here the five steps for teaching the SQ3R Study Strategy.

  1.

  2.

  3.

  4.

5.

We hope you now know how to use and teach the SQ3R Study Strategy. Take the next step and teach the strategy to someone.

ENABLING ELEMENT 3
The PQRST Study Strategy for the Physical Sciences

Specific Objective 3
You will write the associated words for each step in the PQRST Study Strategy, write a paragraph describing each step in PQRST, and describe a plan for teaching the strategy.

Enabling Activities

1. Read Study Guide 3 to identify the five key words associated with the strategy and write a paragraph describing each step in using PQRST with a reading assignment.
2. In textual materials from various physical science subject areas, locate selections appropriate for your students. Identify selections that are approximately six to ten pages in length or require approximately twenty to thirty minutes of sustained silent reading by your students. Follow the recommended procedures in "Using the PQRST Study Strategy" to study the selection.
3. Identify some reading selections in physical science materials that do not contain side headings. Practice the PQRST Study Strategy with these selections.
4. The plan for teaching SQ3R can be adopted for teaching PQRST. Write a paragraph that explains each of the basic steps for teaching PQRST and follow the plan to teach PQRST to a group of students.
5. Share with your colleagues the section "Components of PQRST." Show them how you used the strategy to improve comprehension and retention of information.
6. Contrast SQ3R and PQRST as study strategies to clarify how the strategies are applied differently to social science and physical science textual materials.

STUDY GUIDE 3

Physical science materials are written in a style that may require a unique study strategy. Although SQ3R may be useful for studying physical science materials, George Spache (1952) and Leo Fay (1965) recommend the PQRST Study Strategy. The difference between the SQ3R and

PQRST Study Strategies is more than semantic; and we concur with Spache and Fay that PQRST be taught for studying physical science materials.

Scientific textual materials are written in a different style than most of the textual materials students are accustomed to reading. Science textbooks, for the most part, are not designed with the express purpose of imparting information. Their emphasis is on developing a way of thinking referred to as the *inquiry* or *scientific method*. The reader is generally required to follow a presentation of details that the author formulates into a generalization, theory, or concept. Once the generalization, theory, or concept has been formed, the student is shown how to test it through a series of experiments. Keep this in mind as you read to understand the components of the PQRST Study Strategy, and as you see how the PQRST Study Strategy is applied to science textual reading materials. The science selections in this module are typical of, but shorter than, most selections in science textbooks.

Components of PQRST
Five steps form the PQRST Study Strategy. The reader applies the steps in the same order as they occur in the formula statement PQRST: Preview, Question, Read, Summarize, and Test.

- *Preview.* The student begins by reading the title, introduction, side headings, and captions for pictures and other visuals to identify the generalization or theory the writer is presenting and supporting. The student cannot move to the next step and form questions until she identifies the writer's generalization or theory.
- *Question.* Next, the student seeks out the questions the writer is going to answer to supply information to support the generalization or theory. The student uses these questions as purposes for reading.
- *Read.* Then the student reads the selection to obtain answers to the purpose-setting questions. When there are more questions and facts than the student can trust to memory, she should write them down. Sometimes it is necessary to complete experiments before the student can obtain and understand answers to questions.
- *Summarize.* Now the student summarizes the information, preferably in written form. The facts related to each question are grouped together, and a summary statement is prepared for each question.
- *Test.* Finally, the student tests the generalization against the supporting information. He must determine if the author answered the appropriate questions with sufficient information to support the generalization or theory. As students grow in age and scientific understanding, the criteria they use for testing generalizations will and should change.

You should now be familiar with the basis and components of the PQRST Study Strategy. Read on to see how the strategy is applied when reading scientific textual materials. First read the selection, "Your Nervous System," and then the explanation of how you should apply the strategy.

Your Nervous System

In your body the nervous system regulates all other systems. The nervous system can be divided into three separate but related systems. First is the *central nervous system*, which includes the brain and the spinal cord. Second is the *peripheral nervous system*, which includes the outward extension of nerves from the spinal cord to the base of the brain. Third is the *autonomic nervous system*, which controls both the central and peripheral systems through conscious activity and sensations. When we think of these three systems, it is best not to think of them as separate systems, but as interrelated systems, the interrelationship of which is necessary to sustain good health and life.

Here is how you should use PQRST to study-read this passage:

Preview. Skim the title and selection to gain an overall impression. You notice that the selection deals with the *nervous system*. The generalization the author is making is that the nervous system regulates all other systems in the body. The author has highlighted some important points for your attention. Anything that appears in capital letters or italics should be given special attention during previewing.

Question. There are at least one major and three minor questions to ask that are relevant to the author's basic generalization. What is a nervous system? How does the central nervous system relate to the nervous system? How does the peripheral nervous system relate to the nervous system? How does the autonomic nervous system relate to the nervous system?

Read. Using the questions as guides, slowly read the selection. Carefully attend to the facts that relate to your questions. Remember that facts are very important in scientific writing. Although many facts are needed to substantiate a theory, only a single fact is needed to refute it.

Summarize. Take the facts you have gathered and organize them into clusters around the four questions. First, summarize the facts around the three questions concerning the central nervous system, peripheral nervous system, and autonomic nervous system. Second, summarize all the facts related to the major questions on the nervous system.

Test. Examine the questions and answers to determine if the appropriate questions were asked and sufficient information was supplied to support the author's basic generalization. If the generalization passes the test, it can cautiously be accepted. If it fails, then additional information may be needed, or perhaps the generalization should be

166 MODULE SIX

rejected. Remember, as students grow in age and scientific sophistication, their criteria for testing generalizations or theories will and should change.

PRACTICUM EXERCISE

Now it is your turn to apply the PQRST study strategy. Read the following selection using PQRST. The key words in the PQRST study strategy follow the selection; for each, describe the procedure you used to read "Weather Symbols."

Weather Symbols
The weather map used by meteorologists contains a variety of information. The quantity of information and ease of reading require that the information be codified. Three major classes of weather symbols are codified under (1) precipitation, (2) cloud cover, and (3) barometric change.

The precipitation code includes an asterisk for snow, a dot for rain, and an inverted triangle for showers. The symbols may be combined. For example, a dot over an inverted triangle means rain showers. An asterisk over an inverted triangle means snow showers.

The cloud cover code is a simple one. It uses only a circle. A clear circle indicates clearness or no clouds. A half-shaded circle indicates partly cloudy weather. A fully shaded circle means cloudy.

The barometric code is also simple. A horizontal line means steady. A line rising to the right indicates rising barometric pressure. A line falling to the right indicates falling barometric pressure.

Your knowledge of these signs will enhance your understanding of weather reporting. It will also improve your map-reading ability.

Preview:

Question:

Read:

Summarize:

Test:

Answers to the Practicum Exercise

The PQRST formula is a helpful mnemonic device for remembering the key words that will help you understand scientific writing. You should have found these key words helpful as you read "Weather Symbols." This is how you should have applied the PQRST study strategy to this passage:

1. *Preview.* You skimmed the title and the selection to gain an overall impression. As you were skimming, you noticed a sequence of three numbers used in the selection. The numbers should have alerted you to something important. If you stopped to read the sentence containing those numbers, you learned a great deal about the selection. You learned that the selection discussed three different types of codes. A quick glance at each of the succeeding paragraphs should have verified that observation. The generalization you searched for is in the last paragraph, where the author proposed that your understanding of weather reporting will be enhanced by an understanding of weather symbols or signs.
2. *Question.* At least two major and three minor questions should have come to mind. Although your questions may not have been exactly like ours, they were probably similar. What are weather symbols? What are weather symbols used for? What are the weather symbols for precipitation? For cloud cover? For barometric change?
3. *Read.* Using the questions as guides, you read the selection slowly, and carefully clustered the facts around the questions.
4. *Summarize.* You took the facts you gathered and organized them into clusters around the questions you raised. You summarized the minor questions, then the major questions.

5. *Test.* You examined the questions and facts supporting each question to determine if they supported the writer's generalization. If the questions and their answers passed your test of reasonable support for the generalization, you cautiously accepted that generalization. If they did not pass the test, you reread the selection for additional questions and answers, or sought additional information from other sources, or rejected the writer's generalization.

If your answers and explanations agreed basically with those presented here, you are ready to try PQRST on scientific material of your own choosing. We hope that after you try the strategy, you will share it with your students.

Teaching PQRST

The instructional procedures outlined at the end of Enabling Element 2 for teaching SQ3R are also appropriate for teaching the PQRST Study Strategy. To teach the strategy, you first need to *select an appropriate reading assignment.* The assignment probably should be no more than six to ten pages in length or require no more than twenty to thirty minutes of reading time. Prepare and duplicate copies of "The Components of PQRST" from this study guide so that each student has a copy.

Second, apply the PQRST Study Strategy to the reading assignment you plan to use for teaching students how to use the strategy. Apply all the steps as you did in the preceding practicum activities.

Third, schedule instruction. Instruction probably should occur over three fifty-minute periods, preferably within the same week.

Fourth, provide the instruction by following the guidelines suggested for teaching SQ3R. Be sure your explanations and demonstrations are clear to your students.

Finally, provide opportunities for students to practice the PQRST Strategy both in school and home reading assignments. Remember, at least twenty teacher-directed practice sessions will be necessary before students become comfortable with the strategy. When they achieve a comfortable and automatic level, students will probably use the strategy without you reminding or prodding them. To encourage them to continue using PQRST, always stress and reward improved comprehension and memory that results from applying PQRST.

You now know how to use and teach the PQRST study strategy in physical science textual reading materials. Now teach it to someone to help him become a more effective and efficient reader.

ENABLING ELEMENT 4
The SQRQCQ Study Strategy for Mathematics

Specific Objective 4
You will write the associated words for each step in the SQRQCQ Study

Strategy, write a paragraph describing each step in SQRQCQ, and describe a plan for teaching the strategy.

1. Read Study Guide 4 to identify the six key words associated with this strategy and to write a brief description of each step in the strategy.
2. Locate a number of math reasoning problems that require reading and following the procedures in "Using the SQRQCQ Study Strategy." Read and solve the problems. Did you find the study strategy helpful for solving the problems?
3. Demonstrate the use of the SQRQCQ Study Strategy to a small group of students. This will give you an opportunity to practice teaching the SQRQCQ Study Strategy in a controlled environment.
4. Have students who successfully use the SQRQCQ Study Strategy explain and demonstrate it to students who are still mastering the study technique.
5. Select two mathematical reasoning problems that require reading and are of equivalent difficulty. Assign students to read the first problem using their traditional reading approach and to read the second problem using the SQRQCQ Study Strategy. After students have completed both, discuss the merits of a study strategy and when it might or might not be appropriate to use one.
6. Place your explanation of the SQRQCQ Study Strategy and an example of how it is applied to solve a math reasoning problem on an audiotape. Let students who are having difficulty answering reasoning problems and not consistently using the study strategy listen to the audiotape. Also, use the audiotape to introduce the strategy to new students who arrived after your initial explanation.

STUDY GUIDE 4

Students who have no difficulty with straight mathematical computations often have considerable difficulty solving problems that require reasoning and reading. This difficulty begins to appear in the intermediate and middle-school grades and continues throughout the school years. For the most part, students have difficulty with math reasoning problems because they do not know how to systematically approach and solve these problems. Leo Fay (1965) proposed a strategy for helping students solve mathematics problems requiring reasoning and reading, the SQRQCQ.

Components of SQRQCQ
The six steps in the SQRQCQ Study Strategy are *Survey, Question, Read, Question, Compute,* and *Question.*

- *Survey.* Begin by rapidly reading through the entire mathematics reasoning problem to visualize the situation or problem. Ask yourself a question or two about the problem to determine its intent.
- *Question.* Once you identify the intent of the problem, put the intent into question form. In addition, restate the problem, and attempt to further your understanding by visualizing, drawing, or speaking aloud.
- *Read.* Next, read to find the facts and relationships necessary for solving the problem.
- *Question.* With the facts and relationships clearly in mind, decide upon the processes for reasoning through or solving the problem by asking yourself, "What mathematical processes must I follow to obtain the correct answer to this problem?"
- *Compute.* At this point, you are ready to do the actual computation, but you must first set up the problem or problems on paper.
- *Question.* Finally, look at the answer to the problem and ask, "Does the answer appear correct? Did I answer the original question?" To answer the first question, check the computation. To answer the second question, examine the answer to verify its relationship to the intent of the problem.

Apply the SQRQCQ Study Strategy to this word problem:

> John has been earning $55 a week working for Mr. Tomilson. With the money he earns, John wants to purchase a new motorcycle, which costs $330. How many weeks will John have to work to earn enough money to purchase the motorcycle on a cash sale?

1. *Survey.* Read the problem rapidly but carefully to determine the intent or outcome. From a survey of this problem, we learn that (a) John wishes to purchase a motorcycle with his weekly earnings and (b) he would like to know how long it will take to buy the motorcycle if he applies the full $55 each week to the sale price.
2. *Question.* Now that the intent or outcome is clear, put it into question form. Remember, a question provides the most specific direction to the reader and serves as an advance organizer for sifting and locating key information. The question raised by this problem is, "With John's present weekly earnings, how long will it take him to buy the motorcycle?"
3. *Read.* Now it is time to look through the problem to identify the pertinent facts, which are that (a) John earns $55 a week, and (b) the motorcycle John wants to buy costs $330. Although no other substantiated facts are needed, there are some implied facts: first, that there will be no weekly deductions from John's $55 salary; second, that his weekly earnings will continue at $55 a week as long as it takes him to accumulate enough money to purchase the motorcycle.

Third, it is assumed that the motorcycle cannot be purchased for a discount, nor will it increase in cost during the time John is acquiring his money.

4. *Question.* Now it is time to ask, "What mathematical process must I follow to obtain the correct answer to the question?" If the total cost of the motorcycle ($330) is divided by the weekly earnings ($55), we will obtain the number of weeks John has to work to accomplish his goal.

5. *Compute.* The computation is now carried out, resulting in an answer of six weeks.

$$55 \overline{)\frac{6 \text{ weeks}}{330}}$$
$$\underline{330}$$

6. *Question.* At this point, one should ask, "Does the answer appear to be correct?" A simple check can determine correctness. Realizing that division is verified through multiplication, the participant multiplies six weeks times a weekly earning of $55 and obtains total earnings for the six weeks of $330.

PRACTICUM EXERCISE

Now apply the SQRQCQ Study Strategy to a mathematics problem.

Peter borrowed $95 from his father at an 8-percent annual interest rate. He agreed to repay the loan along with the interest at the end of three months. How much must he repay?

Describe the procedures you followed to solve this problem.

Survey.

Question.

Read.

Question.

Compute.

Question.

Answers to the Practicum Exercise

- *Survey.* Your quick but careful survey of the problem revealed that Peter borrowed money, which he would have to pay back at a specific time, along with a certain amount of interest for its use.
- *Question.* The question raised in this problem is "What is the total principal and interest to be paid at the end of three months on a $95 loan at an 8-percent annual interest?"
- *Read.* The facts are: (1) the total amount borrowed was $95; (2) the loan is to be repaid in three months; (3) the 8 percent interest is a yearly rate, and Peter only has to pay interest on his loan for the three-month period of time he used his father's money. An assumed fact is that all the conditions of the loan will remain constant.
- *Question.* Next, ask "What mathematical processes must I carry out to solve this problem?" First, what is the yearly interest at 8 percent? This is a multiplication task. Second, what fraction of one year is three months? This is a process of reducing fractions. Third, how much is the interest for three months? This is a division process. Fourth, how much is the total principal and interest for three months? This is an addition process.
- *Compute.* The yearly interest at 8 percent is $7.60. Three months equals one quarter of a year. ($\frac{1}{4}$ of $7.60 = $1.90) ($95 + $1.90 = $96.90)

- *Question.* At this step, ask yourself "Is the answer reasonable?" Next, check each step of your answer to see if it is correct. Your verification revealed that the total principal plus interest payment of $96.90 is correct.

Teaching SQRQCQ

Now is the time to learn how to teach SQRQCQ to students who are having difficulty solving mathematics reasoning problems that require reading. An adaptation of the outline for teaching SQ3R and PQRST can be used to teach SQRQCQ Study Strategy. The instructional procedures are divided into five steps.

Select Problems.

1. Select a mathematics reasoning problem that requires reading and is typical of those with which your students are having difficulty. The best way to demonstrate the value of the SQRQCQ Study Strategy is to show students how it makes it easier to solve problems.
2. Prepare and duplicate copies of "Components of SQRQCQ" for each student.

Apply SQRQCQ.   Apply the study strategy to the reading problems with the same care you expect from your students. Be sure to:

1. *Survey* the problem to determine what is to be accomplished.
2. Ask yourself a *question* that captures the intent of the problem.
3. *Read* to find the facts and relationships necessary for solving the problem.
4. Ask yourself a *question* regarding the mathematical processes necessary for solving the problem.
5. *Compute* as necessary.
6. *Question* the accuracy of your answer and its appropriateness for your original question.

Schedule Instruction.   Schedule three fifty-minute periods for teaching the study strategy to your students. They will not master the strategy after a single lesson, so you will need to prepare additional lessons with other problems to help them develop mastery.

Provide Instruction.

1. During the first fifty-minute period
   a. Begin by explaining that you are going to teach the students how to use the SQRQCQ Study Strategy, which is designed for studying mathematics reasoning problems. Tell them the SQRQCQ Study Strategy will give them a structure for answering mathematics reasoning problems effectively and efficiently.

   b. Distribute a copy of "Components of SQRQCQ" to each student. Discuss each component so that students understand its function.
   c. Demonstrate how SQRQCQ is used to solve a mathematics reasoning problem. Answer any questions.
   d. Now have students work independently through the same problem, applying the SQRQCQ Study Strategy as they read to solve the reasoning problem.
   e. Have students write a statement describing how they use each step in the SQRQCQ Strategy to solve the problem.
   f. Hold a group discussion comparing SQRQCQ to prior reading strategies. Bring out the advantages of this study strategy.
2. During the second fifty-minute period
   a. Review the SQRQCQ components.
   b. Demonstrate application of SQRQCQ with another mathematics reasoning problem.
   c. Assign a different mathematics reasoning problem for students to read using the SQRQCQ Study Strategy.
   d. When the assignment is completed, call on students to explain how they applied the various steps in the strategy. Discuss their feelings about how they have grown in effectiveness and efficiency by using SQRQCQ.
3. During the third fifty-minute period
   a. Again, discuss the components of SQRQCQ.
   b. Assign a number of reasoning problems to different individuals in the group. Tell the students to solve the problems with the SQRQCQ Study Strategy.
   c. As students work, circulate among them to answer questions and ensure that they are applying the steps in the strategy as you have taught them.
   d. When the assignment is completed, allow students to share with each other how they applied the study strategy to solve the problems.

Practice.   Continue to provide students with opportunities to practice SQRQCQ under your supervision. As with the previous study strategies, it will take at least twenty teacher-directed practice sessions before students reach the automatic performance level. You will know they have reached the automatic performance level when they begin to apply the strategy without your reminder. Always stress and reward the improved mathematics reasoning that results from using SQRQCQ.

Now it is your turn to identify a mathematics reasoning problem that requires reading and prepare a lesson for teaching SQRQCQ to a group of students. After you do this, you will have a good feeling about the new study strategy you have learned to teach. If you now understand and can apply SQ3R, PQRST, and SQRQCQ, you are ready for the Posttest. If you cannot, you should reexamine the appropriate Enabling Elements or talk with your instructor.

Final Comment

A few words of caution are necessary before we leave the discussion of study strategies. SQ3R, PQRST, and SQRQCQ Study Strategies are all effective study tools; however, to be successful, students must (1) be familiar with the vocabulary, (2) be able to comprehend ideas, and (3) be able to pronounce the words. For the strategies to succeed, the material must be generally suitable for the students. The strategies should not be used to force students through material that is basically unsuitable for them. If textual materials are unsuitable, all the teacher can do is select new materials or rewrite the old; the first is the better solution.

Of course, to apply PQRST, a student must also be familiar with the scientific method as applied to the various areas of the physical sciences. Similarly, to use SQRQCQ successfully, the student must have mastered the basic mathematical operations.

POSTTEST

Directions: Read each of the following statements and complete each Posttest item as directed.

1. Study skills are techniques students use when they read textual assignments. List the five major study skills in your content area, then identify the components of a lesson plan to teach study skills.
2. The SQ3R Study Strategy was introduced by Francis Robinson to help students study social science reading assignments. We propose teaching this strategy to students for studying reading in social science and humanities materials. Write the key words associated with each letter in the SQ3R formula statement and write a brief description of each step.
3. PQRST was introduced by George Spache to help students read physical science textual materials. Write the key words associated with each letter in the PQRST formula statement, then briefly describe each step.
4. SQRQCQ was proposed by Leo Fay to help students solve mathematical reading/reasoning problems. Write the key words associated with each letter in the SQRQCQ formula statement, then describe each step.
5. Identify and briefly describe the steps in the instructional procedure for teaching any one of the three study strategies.

Posttest Answers

1. Check your list of study skills against what you wrote for the Practicum Exercise in Study Guide 2. The four lesson plan components are *objective, instruction, evaluation,* and *extension activities.*
2. The key words associated with the SQ3R formula statement are:
   Survey
   Question
   Read
   Recite
   Review
   These are the procedures for applying SQ3R to reading assignments:

   Survey   Begin by making a quick survey of the reading assignment to get a general idea of the selection. Refer to side headings and/or topic sentences as appropriate.

   Question Turn each heading into a question. If there are no headings, key topics should be turned into questions.

   Read   Read to answer each question. Answer questions in the order they occur.

   Recite   Recite the answer to the question with eyes averted from the passage. It is often beneficial to write key phrases in outline form.

   Review   Review your questions and answers immediately after reading the assignment. Periodic reviews enhance retention.

3. The key words associated with the PQRST formula statement are:
   Preview
   Question
   Read
   Summarize
   Test
   These are the procedures for applying PQRST to reading assignments:

   Preview   Skim the selection for an overall impression and to identify the writer's generalization or theory.

   Question   Form questions to use as purposes for reading.

   Read   Using the questions as guides, read the selection.

   Summarize Organize information and summarize, preferably in writing.

   Test   Test the generalization or theory against the supporting information.

4. The key words associated with the SQRQCQ formula statement are:
   Survey
   Question

Read
Question
Compute
Question

These are the procedures for applying SQRQCQ to math problems that require reading:

Survey   Read rapidly to determine the problem's intent.
Question   Determine what question the problem is asking or what problem needs to be solved.
Read   Read for facts necessary to answer the question to solve the problem.
Question   Decide what process to use.
Compute   Do computation.
Question   Ask yourself, "Does the answer appear correct?" Check the answer against the problem and facts.

5. The five steps for teaching any of the three strategies are:
   a. *Select* materials or math problems.
   b. *Apply* the strategy to the materials or problem.
   c. *Schedule* instruction for appropriate number of periods or length of time.
   d. *Provide instruction* following the suggestions provided.
   e. *Hold practice sessions* after instruction to help students apply the study strategy automatically.

REFERENCES

Askov, E. N., & Kamm, K. (1982). *Study skills in the content area*. Boston: Allyn and Bacon.

Cheek, E. H., & Cheek, M. C. (1983). *Reading instruction through content teaching*. Columbus, OH: Merrill.

Davis, E. D. (1986). Selected high school English teachers' suggestions for teaching reading and study skills needed in high school classes. *American Secondary Education, 15*(3), 25–27.

Fay, L. (1965). Reading study skills: Math and science. In J. A. Figurel (Ed.), *Reading and inquiry*. Newark, DE: International Reading Association.

Lamberg, W. J., & Lamb, C. E. (1980). *Reading instruction in the content areas*. Chicago: Rand McNally.

McClain, L. J. (1981). Study guides: Potential assets in content classrooms. *Journal of Reading, 24*(4), 321–325.

Pyrczak, F. (1978). Knowledge of abbreviations used in classified advertisements on employment opportunities. *Journal of Reading, 21*(6), 493–497.

Riley, J. D., & Pachtman, A. B. (1978). Reading mathematical word problems: telling them what to do is not telling them how to do it. *Journal of Reading, 21*(6), 531–533.

Rinehart, S. D., et al. (1986). Some effects of summarization training on reading and studying. *Reading Research Quarterly, 21*, 422–438.

Robinson, H. A. (1978). *Teaching reading and study strategies: The content areas,* (2nd ed.). Boston: Allyn and Bacon.

Roe, B. D., Stoodt, B. D., & Burns, P. C. (1978). *Reading instruction in the secondary school* (rev. ed.). Chicago: Rand McNally.

Singer, H., & Donlan, D. (1980). *Reading and learning from text.* Boston: Little, Brown.

Smith, C. B., Smith, S. L., & Mikulecky, L. (1978). *Teaching reading and subject matter in the secondary school.* New York: Holt, Rinehart and Winston.

Smith, C. F. (1979). Read a book in an hour: Variations to develop composition and comprehension skills. *Journal of Reading, 23*(1), 25–29.

Spache, G. D. (1963). *Toward better reading.* Champaign, IL: Garrard.

Stahl, N. A., & Henk, W. A. (1985). Teaching students to use textbook-study systems. *Reading Horizons, 25*(3), 153–161.

Tadlock, D. F. (1978). SQ3R—Why it works, based on an information processing theory of reading. *Journal of Reading, 22*(2), 110–112.

MODULE SEVEN

Helping Students Pronounce Multisyllable Words

CHAPTER OUTLINE

OVERVIEW

Rationale

One characteristic of subject area textual material is its unique vocabulary. Generally, this vocabulary will consist of hundreds, if not thousands, of multisyllable words, such as *dispensation, tambourine,* and *horticulture.* Your students must learn to pronounce these words as well as acquire their meanings. Module 4 explained how to develop word meanings for technical words in your subject area; this module addresses pronunciation of technical words.

Most middle-school and secondary-school students will have acquired the necessary skills for pronouncing multisyllable words, but there will be some who have not. These students will rely on you to provide them with the necessary word-pronunciation strategy to read the textual material in your subject area.

This module will not acquaint you with the word-pronunciation skills taught in the primary grades; if you have students who need primary-grade reading skills, Module 9 offers suggestions for helping problem readers. For the most part, this group of students needs the help of trained reading specialists.

The purpose of this module is to provide subject area teachers with a brief but useful strategy for helping students pronounce multisyllable words. You will teach this strategy to students who did not acquire this strategy in the upper-elementary grades. Soon they will be able to handle reading materials that would previously have been difficult.

OBJECTIVES

General Objective

You will determine the word-pronunciation strategies students use and help them use a strategy for pronouncing multisyllable words.

Specific Objectives

1. You will prepare a written list of steps that make up the word-pronunciation strategy in this module.
2. You will prepare and use the Quick Test of Word Pronunciation, Word-Pronunciation Strategy Test, and Class Record Form.

181

3. You will list the major organizational steps and their purposes in lesson plans for teaching word-pronunciation skills and strategy.

ENABLING ELEMENT 1
A Word-Pronunciation Strategy

Specific Objective 1
You will prepare a written list of steps that make up the word-pronunciation strategy in this module.

Enabling Activities
1. Read Study Guide 1 and list the seven steps in the strategy.
2. On a sheet of two-by-three-foot newsprint or similar material, record the word-pronunciation strategy. Display the strategy permanently in the classroom. When students have difficulty pronouncing words, refer them to the strategy. Students will find the chart a valuable aid. Look at the "Strategy Chart" at the end of this Study Guide for suggestions.
3. Students who struggle to pronounce longer words may benefit from a discussion and examination of the more common prefixes and suffixes. You can use the lists of common prefixes and suffixes in this module.
4. You may wish to do a content analysis of your subject area material to identify its many prefixes and suffixes. A form, the "Subject Area Inventory," at the end of this Study Guide will help you with the analysis. Also, *The New Reading Teacher's Book of Lists* (1985) includes an extensive list of prefixes and suffixes. Exposure to the isolated prefixes and suffixes will help students identify them in unrecognized words.
5. Provide small-group practice sessions for pronouncing multisyllable words from textual material. Spend one or two minutes daily in such groups to increase students' pronunciation effectiveness and efficiency.
6. Duplicate the word-pronunciation strategy on bookmarks and distribute them to every student. Give the extras to the librarian or other teachers.
7. Use the word-pronunciation strategy to practice pronouncing these words: *temperature, legislature, dramatic, stationary, exercise, inclination, bilingual, urbanize.*
8. Do Practicum Exercise 1 to identify long words in your subject area.

STUDY GUIDE 1

By the end of sixth grade, some students will not have acquired all the necessary skills to identify some of the longer, technical words in the various content areas. If you wish to assign content area reading material to these students, you will need to provide word-pronunciation instruction. After you provide this instruction, you will find that students complete more reading assignments.

Characteristics of Problem Words

Some students struggle with reading assignments because they cannot pronounce all the words. Analyzing words the students have difficulty pronouncing will reveal that:

1. Many words begin with a prefix and/or end with a suffix.
2. Many words contain stems composed of two or more syllables. A stem is a base word or unit to which a prefix and/or suffix is affixed, such as *pay* in re*pay*ment.
3. Students who have difficulty pronouncing words approach unrecognized words in a haphazard way rather than with a definite strategy.
4. Many of the struggling students have the elementary phonics skills to pronounce the common one- and two-syllable words.

Word-Pronunciation Strategy

Using what we know about the kinds of difficulties students have pronouncing words, we can develop a strategy that will help many of them pronounce longer and more complex words. Teach students to:

1. Look for a prefix.
2. Look for a suffix.
3. Locate the stem.
4. Divide the stem into syllables.
5. Try the word in context.
6. Look in a glossary or dictionary.
7. Ask someone how to pronounce the word.

Prefixes are language units that occur *before* a stem to change its meaning. Examples are *un-* in *uncertain* and *pre-* in *preview.* Many of the longer words that perplex struggling readers contain prefixes. Since prefixes are easy to spot, occur frequently in words that present pronunciation problems, and have highly reliable pronunciations, teaching prefixes is a likely place to begin a strategy.

Suffixes are language units that occur *after* the stem to change the function of a word. Examples are: *able* in *portable,* *-ly* in *miserly,* and *-tion* in *education.* Many of the longer and more perplexing words also contain suffixes. Since suffixes are also easy to spot, occur frequently, and have highly reliable pronunciations, locating them is the second step in the word pronunciation strategy.

When the prefix and suffix are removed from a word, the *stem* remains. The stem is the next component of the word that must be identified. It is a base word to which a prefix and/or suffix may be added; it is the underlying language unit. Examples are *dance* in *dancer,* *fair* in *unfairly,* and *skill* in *unskillful.* A stem may not always be recognized as a word, however, as with *trac* in *subtraction* or *cep* in *perception.*

After isolating the stem, the reader must determine whether it has more than one syllable. If the stem is only a single syllable, chances are the student can pronounce the syllable, and can skip this step. Stems containing more than one syllable have more than one vowel, usually separated by one or more consonants; for example, mis-*cal-cu-late,* re-*fur-bish,* and uni-*lat-er-al.* When the stem is two or more syllables, it is necessary to divide it into separate syllables before pronouncing it. These are helpful guidelines for dividing stems:

- Stems following the consonant-vowel-consonant/consonant-vowel-consonant (CVC/CVC) pattern usually divide between the double consonants; examples are *but/ton, can/cel,* and *nor/mal.* This rule works well as long as the middle two consonants are not consonant clusters (*ch, ph, th, bl, st, cr*); natural clusters are usually not divided.
- Stems following the consonant-vowel/consonant-vowel (CV/CV) pattern usually divide after the first vowel; examples are *la/bor, fla/grant,* and *fi/nite.* After dividing the stem into syllables, the student can pronounce each syllable using reading skills acquired in earlier grades.
- Sometimes stems that follow the consonant-vowel/consonant-vowel (CV/CV) pattern do not divide after the first vowel, but rather after the consonant that follows the vowel; examples are *cab/in, pun/ish, trag/ic, plan/et,* and *man/age.* When CV/CV does not work, the students should be encouraged to try CVC/V.

When prefix, suffix, and stem have been identified and pronounced, the student should again read the word in the sentence. *Sentence sense,* or *context clues,* can be the most useful and reliable word-pronunciation clues if the word is in the student's listening vocabulary.

If these steps in the word-pronunciation strategy do not help, the student should be directed to use a textbook glossary or a dictionary to look up the pronunciation. If this fails, he should be directed to ask someone for the correct pronunciation.

Now you have the components of a word-pronunciation strategy. These instructional aids will help you teach the strategy.

1. *The Strategy Chart.* This is an abbreviated list of key components of pronunciation strategy. You can duplicate the strategy and distribute it to students, or construct a larger chart for display in the classroom.

Key Terms to Remember
1. Prefix
2. Suffix
3. Stem
4. Syllables
   a. CVC/CVC
   b. CV/CV or CVC/V
5. Context
6. Glossary or Dictionary
7. Ask

2. *List of Most Common Prefixes.* Bring this list to the attention of your students to ensure that none of these prefixes is causing word-pronunciation difficulties (Stauffer, 1942).

ab	dis
ad	en
be	ex
com	in
de	pre
pro	sub
re	un

3. *List of Most Common Suffixes.* This list can also be introduced to ensure that none are causing word-pronunciation difficulties. Pronunciation difficulties occur more often with suffixes than with prefixes (Thorndike, 1941).

ness	ant	ing	ed (d)
er	ment	ful	ly
tion	est	able	ed (ed)
ily	al	ed (t)	ent
y	ive	ance	ous

4. *Subject Area Inventory.* This form can be used to compile a list of additional important prefixes and suffixes from your subject area materials.

Subject Area Inventory

Source:		*Source:*	
Prefixes	Suffixes	Prefixes	Suffixes

The technical words you want students to pronounce in textual materials must be in their listening vocabularies before they can successfully use the word attack strategy, so you must first introduce the words orally in sentences. Second, write the words on the chalkboard for the students to see and study. Third, have the students say the words aloud to hear how they sound when they say them. Finally, for further reinforcement have students write the words that are likely to be most troublesome.

PRACTICUM EXERCISE 1

Look through textual materials in your content area to identify 20 words that are potentially difficult to pronounce. Write the words, then use the seven-step word-pronunciation strategy to see how it would help students pronounce the words. To use the context-clues step in the strategy, read the sentences in which the words appear.

Answers to the Practicum Exercise 1
Answers will vary according to the words you chose, so check them over with a colleague and, as necessary, with your instructor.

If you know the steps in the word-pronunciation strategy, you are ready for Enabling Element 2, to help you identify students who need to develop their strategy. If not, review the elements as necessary or talk with your instructor.

ENABLING ELEMENT 2
Assessing Word Pronunciation

Specific Objective 2
You will prepare and use the Quick Test of Word Pronunciation, Word-Pronunciation Strategy Test, and Class Record Form.

Enabling Activities
1. Read Study Guide 2, then prepare the Quick Test of Word Pronunciation, Form A; Word-Pronunciation Strategy Test; and Class Record Form.
2. Prepare the Quick Test of Word Pronunciation, Form B. Follow the same guidelines as for Form A.
3. Do Practicum Exercise 2. This exercise will help you interpret test results.
4. Administer the Quick Test of Word Pronunciation and the Word-Pronunciation Strategy Test to two students. Fill out the Class Record Form for these students.
5. After providing instruction following the suggestions in Enabling Element 3, administer Form B of the Quick Test of Word Pronunciation to see how students have grown in word pronunciation achievement. Readminister the Word-Pronunciation Strategy Test to see how they have grown in awareness of the strategy.
6. Do Practicum Exercise 3 to construct and use tests of word pronunciation with words from your content area.
7. You may discover that some students lack the basic pronunciation skills taught in the primary grades. You can refer to *Phonics in Proper Perspective* by Arthur Heilman for suggestions in teaching these skills.

STUDY GUIDE 2

A characteristic of subject area material is the introduction of specialized vocabulary—words used to label concepts in the subject. Specialized vocabulary is one element that differentiates one subject area from another.

Generally, specialized vocabularies consist of multisyllable words formed with prefixes, suffixes, and compound stems. Prefixes alter the meaning of words, suffixes change the function of words, and compound stems form new words.

Students often learn to pronounce new subject area words by looking at a word while listening to the teacher pronounce it. If there are only a few new words to learn, the student can memorize them. When there are many new words, memorization is inappropriate for most students; they must have another method or strategy to help them pronounce words.

During elementary school, many students acquire adequate methods or strategies for pronouncing unfamiliar words. These students will probably not need additional instruction. Others will need assistance to acquire a workable word-pronunciation strategy. If you take the time to identify these students and teach them the strategy in this module, they will be better able to accomplish the course objectives.

This Study Guide will familiarize you with simple tests to identify students who need word-pronunciation skills and strategy. Enabling Element 3 contains detailed lesson plans for teaching skills and strategy to help students pronounce words.

Preparing Tests and Record-Keeping Materials
1. *Quick Test of Word Pronunciation, Form A*
   Print or type each of these nonsense words on the unlined side of a three-by-five-inch index card. Print or type the "dictionary" spelling on the back of each card.

Front of Card	*Back of Card*
pronabment	pro/năb/ment
abstraimance	ab/strāīm/ance
comteationaly	com/tēa/tion/ly
subsumptarant	sub/sŭmp/tär/ant
demomenence	de/mō/mĕn/ence or de/mŏm/ĕn/ence

   You can use Form B of the *Quick Test of Word Pronunciation* at the end of this Study Guide for students who were absent or to evaluate achievement after instruction.

2. *Word-Pronunciation Strategy Test*
   Take one three-by-five index card and print or type the following question on one side.

   When you come to a word in a sentence that you do not immediately recognize, how do you go about pronouncing that word?

(What do you do first, second, third, etc., may be asked if further elaboration is necessary.)

3. *Class Record Form*

   Prepare a Class Record Form as in Table 7–1 for recording students' word-pronunciation difficulties. You will need one record form for each class.

Table 7–1
Quick Test of Word Pronunciation Class Record Form

Names of Students	Skills Unknown						Strategy Not Known
	Prefix	Suffix	Single Syllable Stems	Multiple CVC/CVC Stems	Multiple CV/CV CVC/V Stems	Context Clues	

Test Administration, Interpretation, and Record Keeping

1. On a Class Record form, record the name of every student in the class you have decided to test.
2. Arrange your class schedule to allow about three minutes for testing each student.
3. Each student must be tested separately, where other students cannot hear what is said. It is not necessary to be out of sight.
4. When the student arrives at the testing center, explain that you want to determine whether he has the necessary word-pronunciation skills and a strategy for pronouncing longer words in the textual material.
5. Begin by exposing, one at a time, the cards containing the multisyllable nonsense words. Explain that these are nonsense words and you want the student to pronounce them as if they were real words.
6. As the student pronounces each nonsense word, look for the following difficulties. As a difficulty is identified, place a check mark after the student's name under the appropriate category on the Class Record Form.

Nonsense Word	Sources of Difficulty
pronabment	pro—prefix
	nab—stem
	ment—suffix
abstraimance	ab—prefix
	straim—stem
	ance—suffix
comteationly	com—prefix
	tea—stem
	tion—suffix
	ly—suffix
subsumptarant	sub—prefix
	sump/tar—stem (CVC/CVC)
	ant—suffix
demomenence	de—prefix
	mo/men—stem (CV/CV or CVC/V)
	ence—suffix

These are how the nonsense words were pronounced by a student. Look at the errors, then see how they are classified on the Class Record Form.

Nonsense Word	Pronounced by Student	Errors
pronabment	pro/nab/ent	1 suffix
abstraimance	ab/strum/ent	1 stem; 1 suffix
comteationly	com/tea/tal/ty	2 suffixes
subsumptarant	sub/sumpt/ent	1 CVC/CVC; 1 suffix
demomenence	de/mome/nence	1 CV/CV; 1 suffix

The errors are recorded on the Class Record Form in Table 7–2.

Table 7–2
Quick Test of Word Pronunciation Class Record Form

Names of Students			Skills Unknown				
	Prefix	Suffix	Single Syllable Stems	Multiple CVC/CVC Stems	Multiple CV/CV CVC/V Stems	Context Clues	Strategy Not Known
Jack		✔✔✔ ✔✔✔	✔	✔	✔		✔

7. To determine whether students are using context clues to pronounce words, you can observe them as they read, as well as ask them if they use the clues. Students who use context clues should be able to demonstrate how they use them.

8. Next, place the single three-by-five card containing the Word-Pronunciation Strategy Test in front of the students. Ask the student to read aloud and answer the question on this card. It is acceptable to read the question to the student. (It may be necessary to probe for a student's most complete answer.) Compare the student's answer with the strategy in this module:

    a. Look for a prefix.
    b. Look for a suffix.
    c. Locate the stem.
    d. Divide the stem into syllables.
    e. Try the word in context.
    f. Look in a glossary or dictionary.
    g. Ask someone who knows.

It is not necessary for the student's answers to contain precisely the same words, or the same number of steps, or give the steps in the same order. There are other acceptable ways to state the strategy, and you will have to use your professional judgment as to whether the strategy is expressed adequately. You will become better at this with practice. If a student omits a step, place a check mark after his name in the column "Strategy Not Known." For example, we asked Jack, "When you come to a word in a sentence that you do not immediately recognize, how do you go about pronouncing that word?" He responded, "Look for a beginning and ending that I know and divide the word into syllables." When Jack was asked to tell more about how he pronounced words, he said, "That's all I know." Jack appeared to be aware of prefixes, suffixes, and syllabication, but did not demonstrate awareness of context clues, glossary or dictionary, nor his responsibility to ask for the pronunciation of an unknown word.

    Now it is time to identify word-pronunciation skill and strategy errors and classify them appropriately in the Class Record Form, Table 7–3.

PRACTICUM EXERCISE 2

Latisha pronounced the following words as indicated. Classify her errors in the Class Record Form in Table 7–3.

Nonsense Word	Pronounced by Student	Summary of Errors
pronabment	pro/na/bent	_____
abstraimance	ab/strum/any	_____

Table 7–3
Quick Test of Word Pronunciation Class Record Form

Names of Students	Skills Unknown						Strategy Not Known
	Prefix	Suffix	Single Syllable Stems	Multiple CVC/CVC Stems	Multiple CV/CV CVC/V Stems	Context Clues	
Jack		✔✔✔ ✔✔✔	✔	✔	✔		✔
Latisha							

comteationly   com/tea/ton/ty   _____
subsumptarant   sub/sumt/ance   _____
demomenence   de/mon/en/ed   _____

Latisha said her strategy is "I look for a beginning that I know and guess." Record your assessment.

Latisha did not appear to use context clues to pronounce unrecognized words. When asked, she agreed with the observation.

Answers to the Practicum Exercise 2

Examination of Latisha's errors revealed the following conclusions. Check marks should appear in the appropriate columns on the Class Record.

Nonsense Word	*Pronounced by Student*	*Summary of Errors*
pronabment	pro/na/bant	1 stem; 1 suffix
abstraimance	ab/strum/any	1 stem; 1 suffix
comteationly	com/tea/ton/ty	2 suffixes
subsumptarant	sub/sumt/ance	1 CVC/CVC; 1 suffix
demomenence	de/mon/en/ed	1 CV/CV; 1 suffix

Latisha's strategy is inadequate. It is limited to looking for prefixes and guessing. A check mark should be placed in the Class Record Form in Table 7–4 under Strategy Not Known.

Retesting

You will want to retest students from time to time to determine if they have improved in word-pronunciation skills and strategy. Since

Table 7–4
Quick Test of Word Pronunciation Class Record Form

Names of Students	Skills Unknown							Strategy Not Known
	Prefix	Suffix	Single Syllable Stems	Multiple CVC/CVC Stems	Multiple CV/CV CVC/V Stems	Context Clues	
Jack		✔✔✔ ✔✔✔		✔	✔		✔
Latisha		✔✔✔ ✔✔	✔✔	✔	✔	✔	✔

students may become familiar with the nonsense words used for the Quick Test of Word Pronunciation, Form A, we have given an equivalent list for retesting. Prepare the Quick Test of Word Pronunciation, Form B, in the same manner and format as Form A. It is not necessary to prepare another Word-Pronunciation Test or Class Record Form.

1. *Quick Test of Word Pronunciation, Form B*
   Print or type each of the nonsense words on the unlined side of a three-by-five index card. Print or type the "dictionary" spelling on the back of each card.

Front of Card	*Back of Card*
premeply	pre/mĕp/ly
exsceemest	ex/scrēέm/est
subpeedtionous	sub/pēέd/tion/ous
unpetsuming	un/pĕt/sum/ing
besimenable	be/sī/mĕn/able or be/sĭm/ĕn/able

Nonsense Word	*Source of Difficulty*
premeply	pre—prefix
	mep—stem
	ly—suffix
exscreemest	ex—prefix
	screem—stem
	est—suffix
subpeedtionous	sub—prefix
	peed—stem
	tion—suffix
	ous—suffix

unpetsuming   un—prefix
                           petsum—stem (CVC/CVC)
                           ing—suffix
besimenable   be—prefix
                           simen—stem (CV/CV or CVC/V)
                           able—suffix

2. *Word-Pronunciation Strategy Test*

Use the three-by-five index card you prepared for Form A for this test also. Since the test is basically a question the student answers, it can be used with both Form A and Form B.

3. *Class Record Form*

Use the same Class Record Form you used with Form A to record the results on Form B. You can thus rapidly identify the growth areas for each student you test.

Form C of the Quick Test of Word Pronunciation

If you want to construct your own form of a word pronunciation test, you can use some of the long words that you identified for your content area (see Practicum Exercise 1). To prepare a Form C of the Quick Test of Word Pronunciation, select five long words. Obtain five three-by-five cards and write one word on one side and the dictionary respelling on the other of each.

Because these words are real words, you can present them in a paragraph to see if your students can use context clues to identify the words. Each paragraph can be printed below the word on the front of the card.

Form C of the test is administered following the same procedure as used for Forms A and B; however, you will need to tell the examinees that the words are real words and typical of the long and more difficult words found in textual materials in your content area. Have each student read the word or the sentence that includes the word. Note any difficulties as the student pronounces the words and use the Class Record Form to record results.

PRACTICUM EXERCISE 3

Construct a Form C of the Quick Test of Word Pronunciation by selecting five long words from your content area. After you have selected the words, write each word on the front of the card and the dictionary respelling on the back. Remember to include a paragraph on the front of the card if you want to evaluate the use of context clues.

Answers to Practicum Exercise 3

It is not possible to provide answers to this exercise since the words you select will be specific to your content area and the textual material you use. However, here are some sample responses for mathematics, social studies, and science.

Mathematics

Front of Card   Back of Card

Front of Card	Back of Card
denominator	di-näm-ə-nāt-ər
approximately	ə-präk-sə-mət-li
equiangular	ē-kwi-aŋ-gyə-lər
quadrilateral	kwä-rə-lat-ə-rəl
commutative	kə-myōu-tə-tiv

Social Studies

Front of Card   Back of Card

Front of Card	Back of Card
proclamation	präk-lə-mā-shən
reconstruction	rē-kan-strək-shən
unconstitutional	ən-kän-stə-tū-shən-əl
monotheism	män-ə-thē-iz-əm
discrimination	dis-krim-ə-nā-shan

Science

Front of Card	Back of Card
extraterrestrial	ek-strə-tə-res-trē-əl
electromagnetic	i-lek-trō-mag-net-ik
deoxyribonucleic	dē-äk-si-ri-bo-naō-klē-ik
precipitation	pri-sip-ə-tā-shən
metamorphosis	met-ə-mor-fə-səs

If you have prepared the Quick Test of Word Pronunciation, Forms A and B, Word-Pronunciation Strategy Test, and Class Record Form, and have classified errors correctly in the Practicum Exercises, you are ready for Enabling Element 3. Enabling Element 3 provides directions and lesson plans for teaching word-pronunciation skills and strategy. If you have difficulty with any of the Enabling Elements, re-examine them, or see your instructor.

ENABLING ELEMENT 3
Teaching Word-Pronunciation Skills

Specific Objective 3
You will list the major organizational steps and their purposes in lesson plans for teaching word-pronunciation skills and strategy.

Enabling Activities
1. Read Study Guide 3 to learn the major organizational steps in seven lesson plans for developing a strategy for pronouncing multisyllable words.
2. Teach the seven plans to one or two students who need this instruction.
3. Look through textual material to locate prefixes and suffixes not included in the lesson plans in this Study Guide. Modify the plans to include these prefixes and suffixes.

4. If you have an aide or school volunteer, familiarize him or her with the instructional procedure in this Enabling Element. Have the aide teach students who need a word-pronunciation strategy.
5. Peer teaching has been found effective in many situations, so you may want to use some of your better students as tutors.
6. Do Practicum Exercises 4–6 to apply your newly acquired competence.

STUDY GUIDE 3

Word-Pronunciation Strategy

The lessons in this Study Guide are designed to develop a precise word-pronunciation strategy. The strategy applies to longer, multisyllable words that often perplex subject area students when the words are in students' listening vocabularies but *not* in their reading vocabularies. If the word is not in their listening vocabularies, the problem is word meaning, not pronunciation, and you should refer to Module 4, "Teaching Word Meanings." If the problem is pronunciation, the lesson plans in this Study Guide will help students improve pronunciation. The lesson plans are designed to develop an understanding of specific word-pronunciation skills, which make up a word-pronunciation strategy.

1. Look for prefix.
2. Look for suffix.
3. Locate the stem.
4. Divide the stem into syllables.
5. Try it in context.
6. Refer to glossary or dictionary.
7. Ask someone.

There are seven lessons in the instructional set, and each lesson requires twenty to thirty minutes to teach, depending on the amount of teacher direction and discussion. The lessons should be taught in the sequence in which they appear in this instructional set.

There are three major organizational steps in each lesson plan: purpose, instruction, and generalization. The information in the purpose section substantiates the need for this skill. This instruction step contains directions and information for developing word-pronunciation skills and strategy. At the generalization step, the student is led to conclude that the pronunciation skill he has just acquired is one of several skills that form the strategy. The student soon learns that with each succeeding lesson, the generalization gets longer, until it consists of all seven steps in the strategy.

Choosing Your Lessons

Not every student needs every lesson in the set. For example, the Class Record in Study Guide 2 reveals that Latisha needs instruction in identifying suffixes, identifying single syllables, and with all syllabication generalizations. She also needs to become familiar with the steps in the word-pronunciation strategy. She appears to recognize prefixes so she does not need instruction in this step of the strategy. Since Latisha does not know the word-pronunciation strategy, her first lesson should give an overview of the strategy. She should be shown how to use the seven steps in the strategy to recognize a written word that is in her listening vocabulary. Then Latisha should receive instruction in suffix recognition (lesson 2), single syllable stems (lesson 3), and syllabication generalizations (lessons 4 and 5) and context clues (lesson 6). Begin with the suffix lesson plan and proceed in order.

When students are familiar with the pronunciation strategy and have only specific skill difficulties, you need to teach only the specific skill lessons that correspond to their difficulty. They should be taught in the order they occur in the lesson plans that follow. When students know all the pronunciation skills but are unfamiliar with the strategy, you need to show them only the strategy. Now complete Practicum Exercise 4 to demonstrate that you understand these last guidelines for planning instruction.

PRACTICUM EXERCISE 4

If Marty demonstrates the needs shown in Table 7–5, where and how should you begin instruction?

Answers to Practicum Exercise 4

Since Marty does not know the word-recognition strategy, you must review it with him. Then begin teaching, using lesson 2 for suffixes, lesson 3 for single syllable stems, and lessons 4 and 5 to teach the basic syllabication generalizations.

PRACTICUM EXERCISE 5

Now look at the information in the Class Record Form for Alfredo. How would you provide instruction?

Answer to Practicum Exercise 5

Alfredo is aware of all the steps in the word-pronunciation strategy, but has difficulty with one word-pronunciation skill. He needs instruction in the generalizations of CV/CV and CVC/V for syllabication.

Table 7–5
Quick Test of Word Pronunciation Class Record Form

Names of Students	Skills Unknown						Strategy Not Known
	Prefix	Suffix	Single Syllable Stems	Multiple CVC/CVC Stems	Multiple CV/CV CVC/V Stems	Context Clues	
Jack		✔✔✔ ✔✔✔	✔	✔	✔		✔
Latisha		✔✔✔✔ ✔✔	✔✔	✔	✔	✔	✔
Marty		✔✔✔	✔✔	✔	✔		✔
Alfredo				✔			

Now you know how to use the Class Record Form to differentiate instruction. You are also aware that some students will need to be taught only the word-recognition strategy, and others will need both the strategy and specific word-pronunciation skills. Still others will need to be taught only specific skills. You are ready to read the seven lesson plans in the instructional set. Read each lesson, giving your full attention to the three organizational steps and to the directions and information under each step.

Word-Pronunciation Lesson 1—Prefix

1. *Purpose:*
   Being able to detect a common prefix can enable a student to unlock an unknown word. This lesson (1) acquaints students with common prefixes and (2) builds recognition of prefixes as pronunciation units.
2. *Instruction:*
   a. Write the following stems on the chalkboard. Have students read them, then discuss the meaning of *stem* as a base word to which a prefix is added. You may wish to have students find additional examples in the dictionary.

sent	come	verb	press	grace
fine	done	side	forest	fix
noun	ability	act	camp	

   b. Here are some common prefixes. Write each one on the chalkboard. Direct students' attention to each prefix as you pronounce it. You may wish to discuss the meaning of the prefix, but this is not necessary, since the primary purpose of the lesson is prefix identification and pronunciation.

ab	ad	be	com	de	pro	re
dis	en	ex	in	pre	sub	un

   c. Attach the common prefixes to the known root words presented in step 1 and have students pronounce the new words.

absent	become	adverb	compress	disgrace
define	undone	subside	reforest	prefix
pronoun	inability	exact	encamp	

   d. Now that the students are familiar with the common prefixes and have had an opportunity to see them in words, a practice activity will be useful. Place the following words on the chalkboard; as you do so, direct students to (a) identify and pronounce the prefix, (b) identify and pronounce the stem, and (c) blend the two to pronounce the affixed word.

abnormal	defame	prorate	adjoin	degrade
adjust	prewar	export	beside	bespeak
commit	unwed	disarm	input	submit

   e. Tell students that many words begin with patterns that look exactly like these prefixes. In some cases, the beginning patterns are not prefixes, but some of the words can nevertheless be pronounced in the same way as the prefixed words. (Example: *pre*ach, *per*k, *de*al, *de*an.)

   f. Locate words in subject area materials that contain other prefixes and teach the prefixes as you did in this lesson.

3. *Generalization:*

Through discussion, lead students to conclude that looking for prefixes is the first step in a word-pronunciation strategy. You may wish to record this step on a chart or chalkboard for reference before introducing the second lesson, or have students record it on a sheet of notebook paper reserved for the word-pronunciation strategy, as follows:

First: Look for a prefix.

Word-Pronunciation Lesson 2—Suffix

1. *Purpose:*

Being able to detect a common suffix can enable a student to decipher an unknown word. This lesson (1) acquaints students with common suffixes and (2) builds recognition of suffixes as pronunciation units.

2. *Instruction:*

   a. Write the following stems on the chalkboard. Have students read them. If some students are still unclear about the meaning of *stem*, clarify its meaning. It may be necessary to have students locate examples in a dictionary.

hope	happy	move	educate	walk
mail	high	skill	arm	act
love	talk	nerve	want	

b. Here are some common suffixes. Write each suffix on the chalk-board. Direct students' attention to each suffix as you pronounce it. You may wish to discuss the meaning of the suffix, but this is not necessary, since the primary purpose of the lesson is suffix identification and pronunciation.

ness	ily	est	y	tion
ly	ous	er	ant	ent
able	ance	ed (ed)	ed (d)	ive
al	ing	ed (t)	ful	ment

c. Attach the common suffixes to the known stems presented in step 1 and ask students to pronounce the new words.

hopeful	higher	active	happily
mailable	talked (t)	nervous	happiness
lovely	movement	education	wanted (ed)
walking	army	happiest	skilled (d)

d. Now that the students are familiar with the common prefixes and suffixes and have used them to build words, they need a practice activity to help build their recognition of prefixes and suffixes to the automatic recognition level. Write the following words on the chalkboard and ask students to (a) identify and pronounce the prefix, (b) identify and pronounce the suffix, (c) identify and pronounce the stem, and (d) blend and pronounce the affixed word.

reloading	prepayment	inactive	department
refreshment	enjoyment	preheated	unfairly
preschooler	abnormally	unskillful	prolonged

e. Locate words in subject area materials that contain other suffixes. Teach the suffixes as you did in this lesson.

3. *Generalization:*

Through discussion, lead students to conclude that looking for suffixes is the second step in a word-pronunciation strategy. You may wish to record this step on a chart or chalkboard before introducing the third lesson, so students can refer to it during the lesson, or have them record it on a sheet of notebook paper reserved for the strategy. Show students that they have now developed a two-step strategy, and have them record it:

First: Look for a prefix.
Second: Look for a suffix.

Word-Pronunciation Lesson 3—Stems

1. *Purpose:*

Identification of stems precedes their pronunciation. This lesson (1) acquaints students with one- and two-syllable stems and (2) builds recognition of stems as pronunciation units.

2. *Instruction:*
   a. Write the following words on the chalkboard, pointing out that they contain prefixes and/or suffixes. Identify the stems through analysis of each word, first for the prefix and then for the suffix. Point out that once these elements have been identified, the remaining word or syllable is the stem.

camping	mainly	installment	entrenchment
discovering	enrichment	predisposition	undesirable
reboarding	unsinkable	removed	unknowingly

   b. Show students the procedure for pronouncing the words. First pronounce the prefix, then pronounce the suffix, then pronounce the stem; next, blend and pronounce the word. Now direct the students to pronounce the words using this strategy.
   c. Either teacher or students can locate words in subject area materials that contain other prefixes and/or suffixes. The words can be analyzed with the strategy in this lesson.

3. *Generalization:*
   Through discussion, lead students to conclude that they should use the following strategy when they encounter an unknown word in their reading. You may wish to record this third step on the strategy chart or chalkboard before introducing the fourth lesson, so students can refer to it during the lesson, or have students record it on a sheet of notebook paper reserved for the strategy. Their strategy should now contain these three steps:
   First: Look for a prefix.
   Second: Look for a suffix.
   Third: Look for a stem.

Word-Pronunciation Lesson 4—Syllabication CVC/CVC

1. *Purpose:*
   After identifying a prefix and/or suffix, students often must pronounce a multisyllable stem. A few general guidelines for dividing stems into syllables will help. This lesson (1) acquaints students with one of two common techniques for dividing stems into syllables and (2) provides practice in using this technique to pronounce words.

2. *Instruction:*
   a. Ask students to listen closely as you pronounce some words. Tell them you will be pronouncing two-syllable words and want them to identify the separate syllables after you pronounce each word. Elongate each syllable as you pronounce these words:

cargo	cattle	pencil
person	summer	circus

   b. After you pronounce the words and students identify the separate syllables in each, write the words on the chalkboard. Then review pronunciation and re-identify the separate syllables. Draw a slash mark (/) between the two syllables in each word.

car/go   cat/tle   pen/cil
per/son   sum/mer   cir/cus

c. Show students that each word divides between two consonants, and that each word follows the consonant-vowel-consonant/consonant-vowel-consonant pattern (CVC/CVC). Have students draw from this observation a generalization they can apply to similar words.

d. They should draw a generalization such as this: In multisyllable stems of the CVC/CVC pattern, the separate syllables usually divide between the two consonants. (The exact words need not be used.)

e. Now that students are familiar with the first syllabication technique, a practice activity is necessary to improve their skill in applying it. These words are useful for practicing this technique.

carrot   center   donkey   picnic   valley
corner   settle   barrel   follow   grammar
napkin   silver   garden   suggest   bottle

f. Have students skim the pages in their most recent reading assignment to locate multisyllable words that follow the CVC/CVC pattern. You can locate words in subject area materials that contain this pattern for additional practice for the students.

3. *Generalization:*

Through discussion, lead students to conclude that the CVC/CVC pattern is useful for dividing multisyllable stems into their separate syllables. Record this step on a chart or a chalkboard, or have students record it in their notebooks. Show students that the strategy is now one step longer.

First: Locate the prefix.
Second: Locate the suffix.
Third: Identify the stem.
Fourth: Divide into syllables using CVC/CVC pattern.

Word-Pronunciation Lesson 5—Syllabication
CV/CV or CVC/V

1. *Purpose:* Even when a prefix and/or suffix has been identified, the stem can still be difficult for a student to pronounce, particularly if it has two or more syllables. Three-syllable stems are unusual, but two-syllable stems are quite common. One syllabication technique has already been introduced; the purpose of this lesson is to (1) familiarize students with a second syllabication technique and (2) provide them with practice in applying the technique.

2. *Instruction:*

a. Tell students to listen while you pronounce the following words, elongating and stressing each syllable as you do so. After you pronounce each word, have a student pronounce each syllable separately and indicate where the syllable division takes place.

CV/CV		CVC/V	
famous	station	river	habit
hotel	direct	damage	rigid

b. Now write the list of words on the chalkboard, and pronounce each word as you would in normal speech. Next, have a student pronounce the word and divide it into separate syllables on the basis of auditory experience. Draw a slash mark between the separate syllables:

CV/CV		CVC/V	
fa/mous	sta/tion	riv/er	hab/it
ho/tel	di/rect	dam/age	rig/id

c. Show students how multisyllable words that follow the CVCV pattern can be divided according to either the CV/CV or CVC/V generalizations. Explain that one must often apply both generalizations to achieve the correct pronunciation. Have students draw a generalization from this observation that they can apply to similar words.

d. A generalization containing the following information is appropriate: Multisyllable words following the CVCV pattern usually divide CV/CV or CVC/V. Try CV/CV first and then CVC/V.

e. Now that your students are familiar with the CV/CV and CVC/V patterns for syllable division, they need practice to improve their skill. The following words lend themselves to these division techniques.

pupil	locate	image	devil	blatant
spider	cement	pirate	dozen	timid
petal	seven	comic	final	novel

f. You may wish to locate other words that follow these patterns in your subject area material.

3. *Generalization:*
Through discussion, lead students to conclude that the CV/CV and CVC/V patterns are useful for dividing multisyllable stems into their separate syllables. Record this step on a chart or a chalkboard, or direct students to record it in their notebooks.
First: Locate the prefix.
Second: Locate the suffix.
Third: Identify the stem.
Fourth: Divide into syllables using the CVC/CVC, CV/CV, or CVC/V pattern.

Word-Pronunciation Lesson 6—Context Clues

1. *Purpose:*
Sometimes a reader can extract a clue to pronunciation from the context surrounding a word. Context clues are phrases, sentences, or paragraphs that provide clues to an unknown word. This lesson acquaints students with these clues.

2. *Instruction:*
   a. Write the following two sentences on the chalkboard. Point out that a word is missing, for a reason you will reveal shortly.
      (1) To pronounce an unknown word, all learners at all levels must learn how to_____
      approach the unknown word. (*systematically*)
      (2) The_____
      strategy being taught with these lessons is a systematic approach for identifying unknown words. (*pronunciation*)
   b. Have students silently read the sentences, then write what they think is the missing word.
   c. Discuss the students' various choices for each sentence. Use discussion to build a logical and meaningful basis for selecting words to fill the blanks.
   d. After the class has chosen fill-in words and agreed that they are reasonable insertions, point out that they have proven the value of using context clues. Remind them that context clues consist of all graphics, sentences, and/or paragraphs useful for word pronunciation.
   e. From a 500-word selection, delete every seventh word. Duplicate the selection and give each student a copy. Lead students through the process of using graphic, sentence, and/or paragraph context clues to hypothesize and justify choices for the missing words.

3. *Generalization:*
   Through discussion, lead students to conclude that context clues are a valuable aid to pronunciation. You can record context clues on the evolving word-pronunciation strategy chart, or on the chalkboard for future reference, or direct students to record this step in their notebooks under the section reserved for this strategy. Point out that their strategy now has five steps.
   First: Look for a prefix.
   Second: Look for a suffix.
   Third: Locate the stem.
   Fourth: Divide into syllables using the CVC/CVC, CV/CV, or CVC/V pattern.
   Fifth: Try it in context.

Word-Pronunciation Lesson 7—Glossary, Dictionary, and Knowledgeable Reader

1. *Purpose:*
   This lesson is merely a set of necessary comments to make to your students. They will want to know what to do when the strategy does not work; this lesson will answer that question.
2. *Instruction:*
   a. Explain that the five-step word-pronunciation strategy will not help them identify every word they do not recognize in day-to-day

reading. The strategy may not lead to correct pronunciation of an unknown word if the word is not in their listening vocabulary or if they do not have sufficient word-pronunciation knowledge to pronounce the word.

b. Tell students that for a nearly infallible strategy, they need two additional steps. Number 6 is the use of a glossary or dictionary; number 7 is merely to ask someone who knows the word how to pronounce it.

c. Be sure students know how to use the glossary and dictionary to pronounce words. Module 6, "Helping Students Use Study Skills and Strategies," explains how to teach skills for using the glossary and dictionary. Resist the temptation to tell students to "look it up" before you know whether they have the necessary study skills to do so.

d. Caution students against skipping the last two steps; they are as important as the first five. Words they leave unpronounced return to produce the same frustration on following pages, and the frustration becomes greater as still more new, unrecognized words appear.

3. *Generalization:*

Record the following generalizations on a chart or chalkboard, or have students record them in their notebooks.

First: Look for a prefix.

Second: Look for a suffix.

Third: Locate the stem.

Fourth: Divide into syllables using CVC/CVC, CV/CV, or CVC/V pattern.

Fifth: Try it in context.

Sixth: Look it up in the glossary or dictionary.

Seventh: Ask someone.

PRACTICUM EXERCISE 6

You have now completed the seven lesson plans. List and describe each step in the three-step organization for every lesson plan.

1.

2.

3.

Answers to Practicum Exercise 6

1. The first step is *purpose*, containing the information teachers need to establish a purpose for the instruction. At this step you tell the student what he will be able to do as a result of acquiring this new learning.
2. The second step is *instruction*, containing the necessary directions and information to teach the specific skills.
3. The third step is *generalization*, with the information and procedures for incorporating the new skill into the larger word-pronunciation strategy. This step shows the relationship of the individual skill to the overall strategy.

FINAL COMMENT

Students who use the strategy will find it a valuable tool for pronouncing words. Ensuring that they apply the strategy is your responsibility. If you do not insist they use the strategy, students will soon forget it, and your instructional efforts will have been wasted. To reach the automatic application level, students need instruction, practice, and application opportunities under your direction.

If you have accomplished the three specific objectives in this module, you are ready for the Posttest. If not, complete them as directed. If you are having difficulty, return to appropriate Enabling Elements or see your instructor.

POSTTEST

Directions: Read each of the following statements and complete each Posttest item as directed.

1. You should now be completely familiar with teaching a word-pronunciation strategy. List, in order, the steps for helping students pronounce multisyllable words.
2. Did you prepare and use the Quick Test of Word Pronunciation (Forms A and B), Word-Pronunciation Strategy Test, and Class Record Form to determine students' word-pronunciation skill and strategy needs?
3. List and explain the three organizational steps in the word-pronunciation lesson plans.

Posttest Answers.

1. The word-recognition strategy in this module is listed in the order its skills should be used or taught.

   First: Look for a prefix.

   Second: Look for a suffix.

   Third: Locate the stem.

   Fourth: Divide the stem into syllables (CVC/CVC, CV/CV, CVC/V).

   Fifth: Try the word in context.

   Sixth: Look in the glossary or dictionary.

   Seventh: Ask someone who knows how to pronounce the word.

   Your answer need not be in exactly these words, nor do you need to have the same number of steps, but your answer should contain all the information presented in the strategy.

2. If you have *prepared* and *used* the Quick Test of Word Pronunciation (Forms A and B), Word-Pronunciation Strategy Test, and Class Record Form, you have satisfied this objective. If you have not completed all three, you must do so before you can consider yourself to have satisfied the second objective of this module.

3. The major organizational steps for lesson plans for teaching skills and strategy are:

   a. Establish a purpose for learning. Tell the student why she needs this instruction and what she will be able to do as a result of learning the skill.

   b. Provide instruction. This step contains the directions and information necessary to develop competency with a specific skill.

   c. Build a generalization. At this step, the student incorporates the new skill into a word-pronunciation strategy which she will use when attempting to pronounce multisyllable words.

REFERENCES

Burmeister, L. E. (1968). Selected word analysis generalizations for a group approach to corrective reading in the secondary school. *Reading Research Quarterly, 4*(1), 71–95.

Burmeister, L. E. (1975). *Words—From print to meaning*. Reading, MA: Addison-Wesley.

Cleary, D. M. (1976). Reading without vowels: Some implications. *Journal of Reading, 20*(1), 52–56.

Cheek, E. H., & Cheek, M. C. (1983). *Reading instruction through content teaching*. Columbus, OH: Merrill.

Cunningham, P. M., Cunningham, J. W., & Rystrom, C. (1981, March). A new syllabication strategy and reading achievement. *Reading World, 20*, 208–214.

Dawson, M. A. (Ed.). (1971). *Teaching word-recognition skills*. Newark, DE: International Reading Association.

Durkin, D. (1972). *Phonics, linguistics, and reading*. New York: Teachers College.

Fry, E. B., Fountoukidis, D. L., & Polk, J. K. (1985). *The new reading teacher's book of lists.* Englewood Cliffs, NJ: Prentice-Hall.

Elisiak, J. (1977, Summer). There is a need for word attack generalizations. *Reading Improvement, 14*(2), 100–103.

Hafner, L. E. (Ed.). (1974). *Improving reading in middle and secondary schools.* New York: Macmillan.

Heilman, A. W. (1985). *Phonics in proper perspective* (5th ed.). Columbus, OH: Merrill.

Ives, J. P., Bursuk, L. Z., & Ives, S. A. (1979). *Word identification techniques.* Chicago: Rand McNally.

Johnson, J. H., & Parades, E. (1975). The longest tome begins with a single phoneme. *Journal of Reading, 16*(5), 376–379.

Jones, D. R. (1980). The dictionary: A look at 'Look it up'. *Journal of Reading, 23*(4), 309–312.

Konopak, B. D. (1988). Using contextual information for word learning. *Journal of Reading, 31*(4), 334–338.

Kossack, S. (1987). Use the news: Context, Cloze, and consonants for poor readers. *Journal of Reading, 30*(5), 454–457.

Stauffer, R. G. (1942, February). A study of prefixes in the Thorndike list to establish a list of prefixes that should be taught in the elementary school. *Journal of Educational Research, 32,* 453–458.

Thomas, E. L., & Robinson, H. A. (1977). *Improving reading in every class: A sourcebook for teachers.* Boston: Allyn and Bacon.

Thorndike, E. L. (1941). *The teaching of English suffixes.* New York: Teachers College, Columbia University.

MODULE
EIGHT

Motivating
Reluctant Readers

CHAPTER OUTLINE

Overview
  Rationale
  Objectives
Enabling Element 1
  Motivation
Enabling Element 2
  Factors Influencing Motivation
Enabling Element 3
  A Motivation Strategy
Enabling Element 4
  Preparing Reading Assignments
Posttest
  Posttest Answers
References

210

OVERVIEW

Rationale

How often have you heard fellow teachers say, "How do I get Alfonso and Marian to read their assignments?" This is a question all teachers have about students at one time or another. Students like Alfonso and Marian, who have some reading ability but lack the motivation to complete reading assignments, are reluctant readers.

As teachers, we have a responsibility to motivate reluctant readers, that is, to manipulate variables in such a way as to entice students to read their assignments.

The ideas in this module will help you accomplish this task. The suggestions for motivation can be implemented as part of a daily routine in any content area course. They require minimal changes in teacher attitude or instructional technique, and they initiate considerable student motivation. Ultimately, they lead to completed reading assignments.

OBJECTIVES

General Objective

You will acquire and use the described strategy for motivating reluctant readers.

Specific Objectives

1. You will write a one-word synonym for *motivation* and list two sources of motivation.
2. You will list the eight major affective and cognitive factors that influence motivation.
3. You will list the core factors in a motivation strategy and prepare a mnemonic device for retaining the core factors.
4. You will incorporate a motivation strategy into a subject area reading assignment.

ENABLING ELEMENT 1
Motivation

Specific Objective 1

You will write a one-word synonym for *motivation* and list two sources of motivation.

Enabling Activities

1. Read Study Guide 1 to identify a one-word synonym for *motivation* and to discover two sources of motivation.
2. Using the Sources of Motivation form (at the end of Study Guide 1), see if you can separate the intrinsic from the extrinsic students in one of your classes. Ask yourself what factors influence student motivation in the extrinsic group. You may discover the very factors discussed in Enabling Element 2.
3. Discuss the extrinsically motivated students in your classes with other subject area teachers, and determine if they classify the students in the same way. Could some subject areas *spark* students more than others?
4. Interview five of the highest achieving students on your intrinsic list. Ask them to tell you what motivates them to achieve. Compare their answers to see if high achievers have similar motivation. Compare their answers with the factors listed in Enabling Element 2.
5. Distribute the Incomplete Sentences form at the end of Study Guide 1. Ask students to complete each sentence to show how they feel about reading assignments. Compile their answers. Do students' perceptions of reading assignments agree with yours?

STUDY GUIDE 1

Motivation often explains why Angela completes reading assignments but Ralph does not. Intelligence, language facility, cultural background, and other such factors may differ insignificantly for the two students; motivational differences may be the significant factor.

Motivation, at one level of understanding, may be considered a *need*. It is an individual need that causes a student to do something that will result in satisfaction. Need comes from within the learner's environment; thus, teachers manipulate factors in an attempt to create needs.

All of us have had students like Angela who complete their assignments seemingly regardless of what we do. No matter how casual we are in making an assignment or how unclear we are about the purpose of the assignment, Angela always gets the job done. Students like

Angela are motivated from within. Psychologists call them intrinsically motivated. These students have such a strong need to succeed academically that they always complete their assignments. Teachers need to change the environment very little for students like Angela.

Teachers also have students like Ralph, who occasionally complete their reading assignments. Ralph sometimes gets started, but often fails to reach completion. He often seems unconcerned about completing his reading assignment. Students like Ralph demonstrate low-level or nonexistent academic needs. They are not intrinsically motivated like Angela. Occasionally, however, Ralph does complete an assignment when he has a need to do so, although the need is created by someone other than himself. Students like Ralph are *extrinsically motivated*, motivated by something in their environment. For these students, teachers need to be aware of the factors that influence or bring about motivation. Awareness of the factors coupled with planned manipulation is likely to yield more completed reading assignments from reluctant students.

The Sources of Motivation form, which follows, will help you identify the extrinsically motivated students in your classes. Remember, these are students who are not self-starters and typically must be moved to complete their assignments by outside influences that create a need in them. The form contains definitions of intrinsic motivation and extrinsic motivation and two columns for students' names. Analyze each of your students in terms of the definitions of intrinsic and extrinsic motivation. Then enter each student's name in the appropriate column. After you have entered the names, examine each group to determine if you can identify specific intrinsic and extrinsic factors that motivate students to learn and complete tasks in school. What you learn will be helpful as you plan ways to motivate other students to complete assignments and learn subject area knowledge.

Use the Incomplete Sentences form to learn what your students believe and how they feel about the many reading assignments they get in school each week. The 20 sentence stems are to be completed by the students at their own pace. If you want the most candid answers, have the students complete the sentences anonymously. An analysis of the responses should provide additional clues to ways to motivate the more reluctant learners in your classes.

Feel free to modify the Incomplete Sentences form to suit your needs. Can you think of additional sentence stems that will elicit other important beliefs and feelings about the nature of your reading assignments?

You now have a definition of motivation and are aware of two sources of motivation. If you can list the motivational factors classroom teachers must manipulate to interest extrinsically motivated students, go to Enabling Element 3. If you are unsure of the factors, Enabling Element 2 identifies and discusses them.

Sources of Motivation

Intrinsic motivation: self-starter, started from within; moved to complete a task by innate need.

Extrinsic motivation: externally started; start comes from outside the learner; moved to complete a task by outside influences that create need.

Names	*Names*
1.	1.
2.	2.
3.	3.
4.	4.
5.	5.
6.	6.
7.	7.
8.	8.
9.	9.
10.	10.
11.	11.
12.	12.
13.	13.
14.	14.
15.	15.

Incomplete Sentences

Name _____

Class _____ Date _____

Directions: Complete each item to express how you feel about the many reading assignments you get in school each week. Make complete sentences.

1. I complete my reading assignment _____
2. Long reading assignments _____
3. Teachers who assign only page numbers for reading assignments

_____
4. What annoys me most about my reading assignments _____
5. Reading _____
6. Reading to find the answer to a question _____
7. People walking around the classroom when I am reading _____

_____
8. Reading at home _____
9. Hard books _____
10. Answering the teacher's questions correctly after completing my reading assignment _____
11. Reading about something that interests me _____
12. Reading textbooks _____

13. When I use the information from my reading, _____
14. Teachers make reading assignments _____
15. Easy books _____
16. When the teacher tells me I am wrong, _____
17. Being right _____
18. I would like to help my teacher _____
19. Reading newspapers and magazines _____
20. Reading is fun when _____

ENABLING ELEMENT 2
Factors Influencing Motivation

Specific Objective 2
You will list the eight major affective and cognitive factors that influence motivation.

Enabling Activities

1. Read Study Guide 2 and compile a list of factors that influence motivation.
2. In *one* of your classes, distribute the "What Motivates Me" form at the end of Study Guide 2. Ask students to complete the form and turn it in, or distribute the form and have students use it as a basis for a discussion of motivational factors and learning.
3. In another of your classes, discuss motivation individually with several high- and low-achieving students. Ask them to list factors that motivate them to achieve in your classes. Did you acquire any new insight into students' motives?
4. Write a one-paragraph description of one of your most reluctant readers using the motivation factors presented in Study Guide 2. This activity can reveal factors you can change or manipulate to increase the student's output.
5. Talk with other teachers who have the same student and compare your description. Are there differences in perceptions among the teachers? Might it be that some teachers have the *motivational keys* to some students, while others do not? Were any of the keys identified? You can learn a great deal about reluctant readers from talking with other teachers.
6. Want to learn something about yourself as a teacher? Distribute the "My Teacher" form found at the end of Study Guide 2. Ask students to complete the form and return it to you. No names are necessary. Tally and analyze the answers to see how your students perceive you.

STUDY GUIDE 2

The basic factors underlying motivation are well known and understood, but are often not applied. They can be divided into two categories: how students feel (affective factors) and how students think (cognitive factors). Affective factors include interest and attitudes; cognitive factors include purpose for reading, short-term goals, reading level, knowledge of results, success, and usefulness of knowledge. Although we will discuss these factors separately, together they operate to bring about a motivated student.

Affective Factors

The affective factors that influence motivation are *interest* and *attitudes*. These two factors interact to create a good or bad feeling in the learner.

Interest refers to curiosity or concern about something—in this case, subject area. For most students, interest in a subject area does not bloom overnight; rather, it develops after many exposures to intricacies that strike their curiosity. A social studies teacher who compares and contrasts marriage customs and ceremonies in different countries with junior- and senior-high-school students is appealing to their curiosity. Likewise, a mathematics teacher who deals with consumption and cost of gasoline to determine cost-per-mile of automobile operation is appealing to the curiosity of high-school students. Teachers develop interest in a subject area by continually relating course content to their students' curiosities. This requires not only knowledge of the content area, but knowledge of students' daily interests. The teacher who builds interest knows both content area and students, and can relate one to the other.

Attitude is a disposition or mental set toward something, and may be either positive or negative. Attitude, like interest, is a pervasive quality that develops only after a long period of pleasurable experiences. Parents and teachers have the greatest influence on students' attitudes toward education. Parents create the initial attitude; teachers refine the attitude toward school in general and their subject areas in particular. Teachers who think positively about their students generally create students who think positively about their teachers and the subjects they teach.

Cognitive Factors

The cognitive factors that influence motivation—purpose, short-term goal, adjustment for reading level, knowledge of results, success, and usefulness of knowledge—interact to stimulate the learner's cognitive, or thinking, processes.

Purpose. To be motivating, assignments must be given with a purpose. The purpose is a teacher's specific direction in an assignment. A teacher who tells students to read pages 27 through 54 for the next day provides a very unrealistic purpose for learning; the student perceives the purpose as getting to page 54, while the teacher perceives the purpose as being prepared to answer questions about the material. The student will not find out what the purposes are for reading until the teacher begins to ask questions on the following day. Suppose the student completes the assignment by reading pages 27 through 54, comes to class, and the teacher asks a few questions. Suppose also that the student is unable to answer the questions because she did not read the material for those purposes. The teacher will probably assume the student did not read the material, since she could not answer the questions. After a few such assignments, the student quits reading them. A better way to give a reading assignment is to write several questions on the chalkboard directed at the important points in the reading, and tell students to read whatever is necessary to answer the questions. They then have specific purposes for reading and are alerted to precisely what they need to obtain from the reading assignment.

Short-Term Goals.   When goals are short-range, students expect them to take very little time, and are less reluctant to do an assignment. When you give students questions for which to read, you are providing short-term goals. Each question becomes a goal in itself, and makes the assignment appear shorter.

Adjustment for Reading Level.   You must consider all students' reading levels when making assignments. Assigning the same material to students who read above, at, and below grade level makes the reading assignment nonmotivating for perhaps the above- and surely the below-average reader. One way to avoid this pitfall is to select a number of textual materials with a range of readability levels. Module 3 suggests ways to determine suitability of material for various students; Module 1 suggests ways to determine readability; and Module 2 provides ways to alter reading levels. Given enough time, a school or county librarian can locate many materials at various reading levels.

Knowledge of Results.   None of us achieves unless we know what we have done right and *specifically* what we have done wrong. A student who is told he used the right process to determine the latitude and longitude of Chicago on a globe assumes the same process will apply for finding the latitude and longitude of Orlando, Florida. Pointing out a specific error in a process and giving specific instructions to eliminate it help the student obtain the correct answer next time. Some teachers fail to tell students when they are correct, but consistently tell them when they are wrong. Knowing what is wrong tells us how *not* to respond the next time, but gives no clue as to *how* to respond next time. The best way to motivate students is to emphasize the positive and de-emphasize the negative. When you do provide feedback, *be specific*.

Success. Most people gravitate toward vocations and avocations in which they meet success. When we meet with repeated failure, we physically and mentally withdraw from the situation. Teachers who make reading assignments without providing a purpose probably ensure that students will meet with failure when the assignment is due. A student may easily read material for one purpose when the teacher has assigned it for another. A few recurrences of this experience creates a subject-area mental dropout; repeated experience across subject areas may produce a school dropout.

Usefulness of Knowledge. Knowledge acquired with no suggested application to daily problems or interests is fleeting knowledge indeed! Every teacher knows it is important to teach students the new vocabulary in a subject area, but if vocabulary is taught with no stress on application and use in the classroom, how long will students remember the vocabulary? And will they be interested in additional vocabulary study? Finding ways to relate content to life is not easy, but it is essential for motivation and retention.

There are other influential factors, including physical and cultural. The condition of the school plant and the home also influence motivation, although these factors often fall outside the realm of a classroom teacher. For the most part, a classroom teacher can only manipulate the affective and cognitive factors discussed in this Study Guide. Manipulating these factors will not bring success with every student, but will increase motivation for many.

The first form at the end of this Study Guide, "What Motivates Me," consists of questions about motivating factors to which students answer YES or NO, and takes about ten minutes to complete. Analyzing the answers will help you identify important motivational factors from the perception of your students. As an alternative, the statements on this form can be used as focuses for a class discussion of motivation.

The second form, "My Teacher," contains questions about you as a motivator of students and as a teacher. If you wish to learn something about yourself, reproduce copies of this form and distribute them to your students. The form takes about ten minutes for students to complete, and analysis of YES and NO responses will reveal the degree to which you consider motivation factors when you prepare reading assignments and lesson plans.

You are now familiar with a number of factors that affect motivation. If you can create a motivation strategy using the core factors identified in this Study Guide, you are ready for Enabling Element 4. If not, do Enabling Element 3.

What Motivates Me

Name _____

Class _____ Date _____

Directions: Read each of the following statements carefully and circle YES or NO for each one. Your answers will tell your teacher something about what motivates you to learn.

1. I read my assignments only when the teacher gives class time to do so. YES NO
2. I like to know what I am to learn from an assignment. YES NO
3. I prefer one long assignment to two short assignments. YES NO
4. The more I like a subject, the more likely I will complete my reading assignment. YES NO
5. I like to be told if my answers to questions are correct or incorrect. YES NO
6. When it is noisy in the classroom, it is difficult to complete my reading assignments. YES NO
7. I complete my reading assignments even if the material is difficult for me to understand. YES NO
8. I like to read about things I can make or use in my daily life. YES NO
9. Other people moving around or talking in the classroom make it hard for me to concentrate. YES NO
10. I like to be able to answer questions correctly. YES NO
11. When I do something right, someone should tell me so. YES NO
12. I like long reading assignments. YES NO
13. I like to receive a reward when I complete my reading assignment. YES NO
14. When I am right, the teacher can tell everyone; when I am wrong, the teacher should tell just me. YES NO
15. I like to help my teachers select my reading assignments. YES NO

My Teacher
Name _____
Class _____ Date _____

Directions: Your teacher would like to know more about himself as a teacher. Please read each of the following questions and then circle YES or NO after each question.

1. Does your teacher make fun of you when you are having difficulty reading? YES NO
2. Does your teacher often get you so interested in your reading assignment that you talk about the assignment outside of class? YES NO
3. When your teacher finishes telling you about your reading assignment, do you sometimes feel you want to go to the library to find out more about the assignment? YES NO
4. Does your teacher make material that looks hard to read seem easier to read? YES NO

5. Does your teacher tell you what you are to learn from your reading assignment before the assignment is due? YES NO
6. Does your teacher ask interesting questions about reading assignments? YES NO
7. Does your teacher help you find material you can read for your assignments? YES NO
8. Does your teacher give reading assignments from materials that are too difficult to understand? YES NO
9. Does your teacher explain or define the new words in reading assignments? YES NO
10. Does your teacher tell you when you did a good job on your reading assignment? YES NO
11. When you are reading, does your teacher try to keep down the noise level in the classroom? YES NO
12. Does your teacher give reading assignments that are too long? YES NO
13. Does your teacher help you see the value of reading assignments to your daily life or to daily events? YES NO
14. Does your teacher ever ask what you would like to read to complete an assignment? YES NO
15. Does your teacher ever let you decide how much reading you need to do to complete an assignment? YES NO
16. Does your teacher know what you are interested in reading? YES NO

ENABLING ELEMENT 3
A Motivation Strategy

Specific Objective 3
You will list the core factors in a motivation strategy and prepare a mnemonic device for retaining the core factors.

Enabling Activities

1. Read Study Guide 3 to identify the core components of a strategy to motivate reluctant readers.
2. Read Study Guide 3 to acquire a mnemonic device for remembering the strategy presented in this Study Guide.
3. Examine some of your subject area textbooks to see if they offer any motivation suggestions. If your subject area books are like many others, you will find few suggestions for motivation; however, your textbook may be one in which the authors provide not only suggestions, but also a motivational strategy such as that in this module.

If the textbook includes a motivational strategy, you might want to try both strategies to see which is more effective.
4. Discuss with colleagues the strategy in this module. Chances are they use the same strategy. You can learn a great deal from discussions of motivation.
5. There are many textbooks and popular paperbacks on the topic of motivation. You may find it beneficial to read one to further your understanding and ultimately enhance your techniques for handling students. Look at the references for suggestions.

STUDY GUIDE 3

Study Guide 2 identified a number of factors associated with motivation. All these factors contribute to a student's motivation and are therefore important, but it is probably unreasonable to expect most teachers to keep in mind the eight or more factors mentioned. Therefore, this module presents a brief but powerful four-step motivational strategy.

The four-step motivational strategy, which you can use when making reading assignments, employs a mnemonic device that makes the strategy easier to remember. The strategy was developed by identifying the many major factors that contribute to a student's motivation and reducing them to four core factors. Considering these core factors in lesson planning increases the probability of motivating students. To help you remember the motivation strategy, the first letter of the key word in each core factor has been used to form an acronym.

P *Purpose.*   Students acquire more meaning from what they read when they have a purpose for reading. Providing students with purposes for reading defines the specific information and understanding they are to look for as they read, and makes material more meaningful to the reader. Purposeful and meaningful assignments are motivating.

A *Attitude.*   Students must acquire a positive attitude toward reading. This quality develops through associations with teachers who have positive attitudes toward their students. Negative attitudes and reinforcement cause students to withdraw from teachers, their subject areas, and their assignments. Eternal optimism is essential to teachers who wish to motivate students and teach important skills.

R *Results.*   Students must be made aware of results by the teacher's stipulation of right and wrong responses. Providing students with knowledge of right and wrong is one way to teach them what they should and should not do the next time they face a similar situation.

S *Success.*   Students, like teachers, do not repeat experiences unless they meet with some success. Every student needs to find some success in every lesson you teach and in every assignment you make. Accumulation of successes increases motivation for future assignments.

Additional suggestions for implementing the core components appear at the end of this Study Guide.

The acronym formed by the first letter of each key word in the core factors is a familiar word. *Par* is what most golfers hope to score on every hole on the golf course; *pars* are what the golfer accumulates to signify satisfactory performance. Since satisfactory performance is every teacher's goal for every learner, PARS is a useful acronym and mnemonic device for remembering the four core factors in this motivational strategy.

You now have a strategy to apply when you make reading assignments to help motivate many of the reluctant readers in your classroom. To further help you implement the strategy, the following suggested activities are listed under the core component descriptors—Purpose, Attitude, Results, and Success.

Activities for Implementing the Motivation Strategy

Purpose provides direction for reading and gives meaning to what is read.

1. Prepare questions for setting a purpose for and guiding students' reading. Write the questions on the chalkboard, and leave them there for the duration of the assignment.
2. Prepare true and false questions over the assignment. Duplicate and distribute the questions and ask students to answer the true-false questions after they read the assignment.
3. Preview the reading assignment with the class. Ask students to create questions based on the preview that they can use to guide their reading. List the questions on the chalkboard or duplicate and distribute them before students read the assignment. Module 6 provides guidelines for creating questions by previewing.
4. Divide the class into small groups and have each group preview the reading assignment and prepare questions. Collect the questions, duplicate the best ones, and distribute them before students read the assignment.
5. Check the teacher's manual of your textbook to see which questions the authors think students should be able to answer at the end of a unit or assignment. After students preview the assignment and create their own questions, share the author's questions with them. Through discussion, agree upon a set of questions for guiding the students' reading. Assign questions of fact to the less able readers and inferential questions to the more able.
6. Have students preview the reading assignment individually and draw up their own purposes or questions for reading, then have them read the assignment to achieve their own purposes. Afterwards, conduct a class discussion of the assignment and determine agreement on reading purposes. Have students explain their

previewing techniques and their interest in the topic. Their interests will probably explain the different purposes.

Teachers have a responsibility to create positive *attitudes* toward school in general and to their subject matter areas specifically. Positive attitudes develop through teacher-pupil interactions.

1. Demonstrate to students that you are aware of what they know, as well as what they do not know, to show your concern for them as individuals.
2. Recognize the many excellent responses students make to build positive attitudes and motivation.
3. Avoid berating and degrading students. Berating students builds negative attitudes toward an individual teacher and ultimately toward education in general.
4. Avoid downgrading the school or your colleagues, which gives students negative associations. The negative associations ultimately turn into negative attitudes toward teachers and schools.
5. Speak positively about your subject area. It is difficult for students to become interested in a subject for which the teacher demonstrates no enthusiasm.

Immediate and frequent knowledge of *results* is instrumental to motivation.

1. Prepare answer sheets for students to check their own answers, so you can give immediate and frequent feedback.
2. Be sure the learning from one assignment adds to previous learning so students can see their overall growth in the subject area.
3. Do not overemphasize right or wrong responses. A student who is right too often is not likely to be challenged, and a student who is wrong too often is likely to become frustrated and give up the task. The teacher should emphasize rights more than wrongs, always keeping in mind that one way students learn is from their errors.
4. When emphasizing what a student has done wrong, be sure to follow up with instruction that tells the student specifically what to do to be right.
5. Students with poor attitudes toward a subject area need to have teachers recognize their correct responses in the presence of their classmates. Although teacher recognition is always important, peer approval means more.

Success breeds success; without it, there is no motivation.

1. Every day, find a task in your subject area that every student can accomplish successfully.

2. Display the successes of poorly motivated students in the classroom for others to see.
3. Contract with students for a certain grade and a certain quality of performance in a reading assignment.
4. Reach an agreement with students as to the purposes of assignments. If you and the student agree on purposes for reading, success for the student is much more likely.
5. Provide students with materials at their reading level.
6. Allow students to read an amount appropriate to their interest in a topic.
7. Pair a good reader with a reluctant reader to work cooperatively on an assignment.

You have now completed Study Guide 3 and are ready to apply the motivation strategy to a reading assignment. If you already know how to do this, go directly to the Posttest. If you are not sure how to incorporate the motivation strategy into daily reading assignments, go to Enabling Element 4.

ENABLING ELEMENT 4
Preparing Reading Assignments

Specific Objective 4
You will incorporate a motivation strategy into a subject area reading assignment.

Enabling Activities

1. Read Study Guide 4 to familiarize yourself with the procedure for incorporating a motivation strategy into your daily lesson plan.
2. Examine the subject area reading assignment example and incorporate the motivation strategy into this assignment to enhance its appeal.
3. Examine the reading assignments suggested by the authors of your textbook. Do these provide any material you can use as a component of the motivation strategy?
4. Authors sometimes provide discussion questions at the end of a unit. If your textbook has such questions, examine them to see if you can assign them as reading purposes.
5. Incorporate the strategy in this module into one of your reading assignments and evaluate the effectiveness of the lesson.

STUDY GUIDE 4

This Study Guide explains and demonstrates how the motivation strategy introduced in Study Guide 3 can enhance the appeal of reading assignments. An assignment is an important part of a lesson plan; if the student does not complete it, she will not have the necessary information for the subsequent discussion and will be unable to answer the teacher's questions. Assignments are often not completed because they are not planned and presented in a way that creates a need or motivates the reader.

Teachers' planning books often reveal this kind of reading assignment:

> Pages 127–152 for Tuesday. Continue discussion on WWII.

The teachers' manuals for textbooks more often give reading assignments this way:

> Pp. 127–152. This chapter describes the events leading up to the involvement of the United States in World War II. Important events, dates, places, and people are brought into perspective.

Neither example is likely to appeal to students. A few changes by the subject area teacher will make the assignment more motivating. Let us incorporate the motivation strategy (PARS) into this reading assignment.

Stating the Purposes

First we will read to establish a *general purpose* for reading the assignment. General purposes are most meaningful and directive when stated as questions, so turn the statements into questions. The general topic is the events leading to United States involvement in World War II; we can state our general purpose as the following question:

> *General Purpose for Reading*
> The United States generally does not want to fight others, and yet we were involved in a war. What major events led to the involvement of the United States in World War II?

This is a broad purpose that provides the student with direction for the reading assignment; without a broad purpose, students can become mired in details and lose sight of the overall organization of the assignment.

Second, *specific purposes* help students look for facts they can eventually compile into a list of major events leading to the involvement of the United States in World War II. Specific purposes are also most meaningful and directive when stated as questions. The questions serve as precise teacher directions for reading the textbook, and each question also serves as a short-range goal.

To get the reading assignment under way, all the teacher need do is assign the general and specific purposes along with a *beginning* page number and direct students to read to obtain the necessary information. Do not give a terminal page number. The following sample questions are arranged in the order they are discussed in the reading material and concern the *major events* asked for in the general-purpose question.

Specific Purposes for Reading

1. After World War I, the victorious Allies met in Paris, France, to arrange the terms of the peace treaty to be signed by the defeated Germans. Why were the German people unhappy with the terms of this peace treaty?
2. What was the economic and political situation in Germany following the signing of the peace treaty?
3. What conditions were present that allowed Hitler to come to power in Germany?
4. Why did Germany, Italy, and Japan join forces in World War II?
5. What was the reaction in the United States when Germany invaded Austria? Czechoslovakia? Poland?
6. What was the reaction in the United States when Germany invaded and conquered France and beat the British at Dunkirk?
7. Who were the candidates in the 1940 presidential election?
8. The winner of the 1940 presidential election interpreted his victory as a mandate from the American people to send aid to friendly, war-torn European countries. Why was this a significant event?
9. What did the Lend-Lease Act signal to the Germans, Italians, and Japanese?
10. What single event was responsible for the direct involvement of the United States in World War II?

Teacher Attitudes

The second component in the motivation strategy is *teacher attitudes.* Attitudes toward students and subject area appear in one's actions or disposition. Although attitudes and ensuing actions cannot, like purposes, be written into lesson plans, they are equally important. The teacher who differentiates reading assignments according to knowledge of students' reading levels and interests, emphasizes *right* responses, avoids ridicule and degradation, and demonstrates enthusiasm for the subject area, builds motivation and positive attitudes toward school and subject matter.

Knowledge of Results

The third component is *knowledge of results.* As mentioned earlier, immediate and frequent knowledge of results is instrumental to motivation, and is easy to incorporate into reading assignments or lesson plans. After agreeing on questions to define purpose for reading, tell students how they can check their answers. You may want to provide prepared answers to the questions used for setting purposes so students can read the answers immediately after they complete their assignment. If their answers differ, give them an opportunity to reread parts of the assignment to see where they were misled. An alternative procedure for immediate feedback is to pair students or have them form small groups to compare and discuss answers. You can also try individual conferences with students to discuss and clarify their answers; still another technique is the customary class discussion of answers. Reluctant readers should read part of their assignments in class and part outside class. Students who tend not to complete assignments often do so when they have an opportunity to start the assignment in class, especially if the teacher shows reluctant readers how much progress they have made with their assignments in class and assures them they are obtaining the desired information.

Success

The fourth component is *success*. If you have established purposes for reading, demonstrated your belief in the dignity of your students and the value of your subject area, and made arrangements for immediate feedback, you have done most of what is necessary to ensure that every reader will meet with some success. To further ensure success, you may want to include some motivating activities, such as a reading contract, or asking reluctant readers to read for fewer purposes, or assigning only one purpose per period of reading time and keeping the reading unit short. Pairing a good student with a reluctant reader is an additional way to ensure the success of the reluctant reader. Remember, success breeds success and enhances motivation, but the teacher must plan for success; it cannot be left to chance.

You now see how the motivation strategy enhances the appeal of a reading assignment. Often, changes in the nature of reading assignments and in our attitudes are necessary to motivate students.

Using Student Teams to Motivate Reluctant Readers

You may enjoy introducing reading assignments, then have students work on the assignments as teams. Three rather sophisticated plans for using student teams have been developed and field-tested at Johns Hopkins University by members of the Johns Hopkins Team Learning Project. The three plans are (1) Teams—Games—Tournaments (TGT); (2) Student Teams—Achievement Divisions (STAD), and (3) Jig-Saw.

The Teams—Games—Tournaments (TGT) approach, developed by David DeVries, divides students into four- or five-member learning teams. Each team has high achievers, average achievers, and low achievers. Students are encouraged to work together to help each other learn. When making reading assignments in the TGT program, the teacher gives each team a list of questions to answer. The team divides the questions among its members, the members answer the questions, and at the end of the week, they compete in games or tournaments against other teams. Each team's scores determine their standings. This form of team competition enables every student to have an opportunity to contribute a maximum number of points to the team, and students encourage each other to learn since the final product is a team score.

Research shows that teachers who use TGT in the classroom find the students are highly motivated to learn. Research also reveals that students in the TGT classes in grades three through nine learn significantly more in reading vocabulary than students in traditionally structured classes studying the same material. To divide students into teams, list their names in order from highest to lowest achiever, then divide them into teams as shown in Table 8–1. According to this method, each of the six teams would have five members. Team A would consist of members who rank Numbers 1, 12, 13, 24, and 25 and Team D, Numbers

Table 8–1
Assigning Students to Teams

	Rank Order	Team Name
High-Achieving Students	1	A
	2	B
	3	C
	4	D
	5	E
	6	F
Average-Achieving Students	7	F
	8	E
	9	D
	10	C
	11	B
	12	A
	13	A
	14	B
	15	C
	16	D
	17	E
	18	F
	19	F
	20	D
	21	B
	22	C
	23	B
	24	A
Low-Achieving Students	25	A
	26	B
	27	C
	28	D
	29	E
	30	F

4, 9, 16, 20, and 28. After you determine the teams according to achievement, make sure all team members are not of the same sex or race. Research indicates that mixing the teams promotes friendships among students of different races.

The Student Teams—Achievement Divisions (STAD) uses quizzes instead of games to check student achievement. Again, students are divided into teams as described previously, then work together to help each other learn. Students take quizzes to earn points for their team. Each student's score is compared to that of another student of similar past performance so that students of all ability levels have a good chance to earn points for their teams. The STAD approach was developed by Robert Slavin.

The final approach to using teams is Jig-Saw, developed by Elliott Arronson. In the Jig-Saw method, students are divided into six-member teams, and the academic material they are to read is broken down into as many parts as there are team members. Each student reads his part and shares the information with the other members. The students take a quiz over the information in the whole assignment, and can only do well on the quizzes by sharing information and paying close attention to what their peers have learned. Jig-Saw encourages students to show interest in each other's work.[1]

PRACTICUM EXERCISE

Now it is your turn to modify a reading assignment. To complete this section, all you need is a sheet of paper and a writing instrument. Answer each question in order, then compare your answers to ours.

Mr. Hernandez, an 11th grade biology teacher, is about to make a reading assignment to his students. The topic presently under discussion is the circulatory system of the human body. Pages 117–131 in the textbook discuss this topic. Mr. Hernandez has many reluctant readers in his class who consistently do not complete their reading assignments.

How would you advise Mr. Hernandez to prepare this reading assignment to enhance motivation?

Write your answers to the following questions, then compare them with the answers provided.

1. What are the key letters in the mnemonic device and key words in the motivation strategy that can be incorporated into this reading assignment?

---

[1]For more information on using team learning in the classroom, write to the Johns Hopkins University Center of Social Organization of Schools, 3505 North Charles Street, Baltimore, Maryland 21218.

2. The topic under study is the circulatory system, which includes the heart, blood, and blood vessels. What suggestions regarding *purpose* do you have for Mr. Hernandez?
3. What about the manner in which Mr. Hernandez makes the assignment? What are the important considerations about teacher attitude?
4. After Mr. Hernandez's students have completed the assignment, how can he provide for immediate feedback?
5. Mr. Hernandez has a reluctant reader for whom he wants to guarantee considerable success. What do you suggest?
6. Describe how Mr. Hernandez could use teams to complete reading assignments.

Answers to the Practicum Exercise

1. The basic mnemonic device is PARS. The key words are Purpose, Attitude, Results, and Success.
2. Mr. Hernandez needs to set one general reading purpose related to the broad topic—the circulatory system. Then he needs about three specific reading purposes, one for each major component of the circulatory system—heart, blood, blood vessels. Reading purposes are probably best stated in question form, which provides specific and clear direction for students.
3. If Mr. Hernandez takes into consideration his students' reading levels and interests, he demonstrates concern for them as individuals. If he is supportive of students' reading efforts (no matter how meager) and emphasizes their growth (no matter how small), he demonstrates his concern. By doing these things and showing enthusiasm for his subject area, he builds positive attitudes toward school, teachers, and subject area.
4. Knowledge of results can be provided immediately after students complete their reading assignments by (a) providing self-correction answer keys, (b) placing students in pairs or small groups to compare and discuss answers, or (c) holding teacher-pupil conferences. You may have thought of additional acceptable techniques for providing immediate feedback.
5. Success can be guaranteed through (a) writing a teacher-student work contract wherein the amount and quality of work is agreed upon in advance; (b) making a grade contract, which guarantees a certain grade for a specified quantity and/or quality of work; (c) pairing a reluctant reader with a good reader to work together to complete the assignment; (d) assigning material that is at or below the reading level of the reluctant reader and providing a single, short-range purpose for the assignment; (e) providing class time for reading the assignment.

6. Mr. Hernandez could use one of three approaches for having students work in teams. With the Teams—Games—Tournaments, he would divide students into four- or five-member learning teams with members who are achieving at different levels. He would encourage team members to work together to answer specific questions. They would study the answers to the questions, then compete in a game at the end of the week.

If your answers agree with the sample answers in content or intention—congratulations! You have reached the end of this Study Guide and should be ready for the Posttest.

One word of caution about motivation strategies before we close. Motivation strategies, like most other strategies, do not achieve their greatest effectiveness until they have been applied consistently over a long period, because motivation factors are not discrete entities, but interrelated factors. When manipulated by a teacher, each factor interacts with other factors. The ultimate cumulative effect is to create a need in some of even the most reluctant readers. This effect takes time to achieve, so do not be disappointed or give up if you do not see immediate results.

Final Comment

From this module, you have acquired a strategy to help motivate more students in your subject area. Applying this strategy is up to you, but we hope you will feel a professional and ethical responsibility to apply a motivational strategy. If you do, you will accomplish more of your instructional objectives, and many of your students will remember you as someone who cared.

POSTTEST

Directions: Read each of the following statements, and complete each Posttest item as directed.

1. Write a one-word synonym for *motivation*. List two sources of motivation.
2. List the eight major affective and cognitive factors influencing motivation.
3. List the core factors in the motivation strategy presented in this module and write its acronym.
4. List and explain the application of this strategy to enhance the appeal of this subject area reading assignment:

   Mr. Davis is a physical education teacher who wants to familiarize his classes with football theory. He is about to assign pages 22–31 from a basic textbook in sports. The topic under study is the Fundamentals of

Football, which consists of such subtopics as (a) time and periods of play, (b) kickoff, (c) scrimmage, (d) passing, (e) downs, and (f) scoring.

Posttest Answers

1. Appropriate synonyms for *motivation* are *need* and *desire*. Two sources of motivation are intrinsic (from within) and extrinsic (from without).
2. The major affective and cognitive factors are:

Affective	*Cognitive*
Interest	Purpose
Attitude	Short-term goals
	Adjustments for reading levels
	Success
	Usefulness of knowledge
	Knowledge of results

3. The core factors in the motivational strategy in this module are: Purpose, Attitude, Results, and Success and the mnemonic device to aid retention of the core factors is the acronym PARS.
4. The procedure for modifying the "Fundamentals of Football" reading assignment is to:
   a. Establish *purposes:* Prepare general and specific purposes in the form of questions for the reading assignment.
   b. Adjust your *attitude.* Consider the needs and interests of individual students, be supportive of individual efforts, and be enthusiastic about your subject area. Be positive!
   c. Provide *results.* Provide immediate knowledge of results through self-correction devices, small group discussions, or teacher-pupil conferences.
   d. Ensure *success.* See that every individual student succeeds on some part of the reading assignment.

If any of your answers and the sample answers disagree in content or intention, review the discussion of the specific components or the reading assignment on U.S. involvement in World War II. If you are still having difficulty, see your instructor.

REFERENCES

Ammann, R., & Mittelsteadt, S. (1987). Turning on turned off students: Using newspapers with senior high remedial readers. *Journal of Reading, 30*(8), 708–715.

Bank, S. (1986). Assessing reading interests of adolescent students. *Educational Research Quarterly, 10*(3), 8–13.

Briggs, L. D. (1987). A poor attitude: A deterrent to reading improvement. *Reading Horizons, 27*(3), 202–208.

Brophy J. (1987). Synthesis of research on strategies for motivating students to learn. *Educational Leadership.*

Estes, T. H. (1971). A scale to measure attitudes toward reading. *Journal of Reading, 15*(2), 135–138.

Guerra, C. L., & Payne, D. B. (1981). Using popular books and magazines to interest students in general science. *Journal of Reading, 24*(7), 583–586.

Haimowitz, B. (1977). Motivating reluctant readers in inner-city classes. *Journal of Reading, 21*(3), 227–230.

Heathington, B. S. (1979). What to do about reading motivation in the middle school. *Journal of Reading, 22*(8), 709–713.

Mason, G. E., & Mize, J. M. (1978). Twenty-two sets of methods and materials for stimulating teen-age reading. *Journal of Reading, 21*(8), 735–741.

Mueller, D. L. (1973). Teacher attitudes toward reading. *Journal of Reading, 17*(3), 202–205.

Nichols, J. N. (1983). Using predictions to increase content area interest and understanding. *Journal of Reading, 27*(3), 225–228.

Sanacore, J. (1988). Schoolwide independent reading: The principal can help. *Journal of Reading, 31*(4), 346–353.

Seaton, H. W., & Aaron, R. L. (1978, Summer). Modification of pupil attitude toward reading through positive reinforcement scheduling. *Reading Improvement, 15*(2), 96–100.

Shuman, R. B. (1982). Reading with a purpose: Strategies to interest reluctant readers. *Journal of Reading, 25*(8), 725–730.

Slavin, R. E. (1978). *Using student team learning.* Baltimore, MD: The Johns Hopkins University.

Smith, C. B., Smith, S. L., & Mikulecky, L. (1978). *Teaching reading and subject matter in the secondary school.* New York: Holt, Rinehart, and Winston.

Thelen, J. (1982). Preparing students for content reading assignments. *Journal of Reading, 25*(6), 544–549.

MODULE
NINE

Identifying and Helping Problem Readers

CHAPTER OUTLINE

OVERVIEW

Rationale

A constant frustration for content area teachers is having students who read far below grade level. These students often appear uninterested, rebellious, withdrawn, slow, or unmotivated. Usually, students who are poor readers do not complete assignments, often attempt to copy from other students, and fail to take part in class discussions. You may wonder why these students even come to school.

This module will (1) help you develop a better understanding of these students and (2) provide practical suggestions for identifying, helping, and referring students who have reading problems. Students with reading problems can survive—and learn—in content area classes. Their teachers must understand the symptoms and causes of reading problems, identify factors that may be interfering with students' responses to reading, be aware of sources of help, and have ideas for teaching students who cannot read the typical content materials. These competencies, along with the commitment to help students succeed, will enable students to perform better and learn more in your content area.

OBJECTIVES

General Objective

You will identify problem readers and factors that may be interfering with their responsiveness to reading tasks, and adapt instructional procedures to help problem readers succeed in your content area.

Specific Objectives

1. You will define the term problem reader, describe the characteristics of problem readers, and indicate three major responsibilities for helping problem readers succeed in your content area classes.
2. You will list and explain by categories those factors that may cause reading failure.
3. You will use nontesting devices to identify factors that may cause reading failure.

4. You will indicate appropriate referral sources for students who manifest certain symptoms, and state guidelines and techniques for adapting instruction to help problem readers succeed in content classes.

ENABLING ELEMENT 1
Characteristics of Problem Readers

SPECIFIC OBJECTIVE 1

You will define the term problem reader, describe the characteristics of problem readers, and indicate three major responsibilities for helping problem readers succeed in your content area classes.

Enabling Activities

1. Read Study Guide 1 to learn a definition of problem reader, the characteristics associated with problem readers, and your responsibilities for helping problem readers succeed in classes.
2. At a departmental faculty meeting or with the entire faculty in your school, discuss who is responsible for teaching basic reading skills to students who read below grade level. Will the English teachers assume this responsibility? Should special developmental reading classes be established? Is there a need for special remedial reading classes? Is there a sufficient number of reading classes to provide for the number of students who are problem readers?
3. List the names of ten students you have or have had who can be classified as problem readers. After each name, write two or three adjectives that describe them as students. Analyze your list to determine common characteristics among them. Think about the differences among the students, and list possible reasons for the differences. Why do some students learn to cope better with their problems?
4. Look at your students' achievement scores in reading, if they are available. You would expect one-third of the students to read *below* grade level, one-third of the students at grade level, and one-third *above* grade level. What percentage of your students read below grade level according to the results of a standardized achievement test in reading?
5. Imagine how problem readers feel in your class. How would it feel to be unable to complete the reading assignments and therefore unable to participate in class discussions? How would it feel to be given a test you could not read? How would it feel to be asked to read in front of your peers? Would you withdraw and say nothing, or try to save face by making fun of the situation or by creating a disturbance so as to avoid the unpleasant situation? Would you be inclined to cheat by looking at someone's else's work? Can you begin

to feel the frustrations of a problem reader? If so, are you committed to doing something to help them?

STUDY GUIDE 1

By the time students enter middle or secondary schools, they should be able to use an appropriate strategy for attacking unfamiliar words. They should be able to comprehend different types of written materials and have an extensive reading vocabulary. Students at this level should be able to use different study strategies and employ a flexible reading rate. They should be developing varied tastes and interests in reading and critically evaluating what they read. Students entering middle and secondary schools should also find reading an important source of pleasure and information.

Obviously, not all students exhibit these behaviors when they enter middle and secondary schools. Some students will be far behind in reading achievement. You will begin to identify some of the underachievers when you administer an Informal Suitability Survey. They will mispronounce many words or answer incorrectly many of the comprehension questions. Many students will be embarrassed to read aloud. Some may even refuse to read either aloud or silently because they are ashamed of their reading underachievement. As a content area teacher you should be concerned about these students' chances of success in your class, especially if there are frequent reading assignments.

Problem Reader Defined

From the point of view of a content area teacher, a problem reader is any student who is unable to read the materials commonly used for content area instruction. This usually means materials written at a level no more than two years below the student's grade level. For example, a student who is in ninth grade but who reads at the fifth grade level would be a problem reader because he would not be able to read many of the textual materials required to acquire the subject area knowledge. Another student in the same grade reading at the 7th grade level would not be classified as a problem reader because he would probably be able to read many of the textual materials to obtain subject area knowledge. Recall that subject area textual materials are not limited to the textbook. They include the vast array of print materials found in the library.

Problem readers typically need assistance to improve their reading skills beyond what you can provide as a subject area teacher. They frequently need the services of a specialist trained in remedial reading or learning disabilities. Usually this service is provided in special reading classes or at a private reading clinic.

One of your responsibilities is to identify problem readers and to refer them to someone who can help them. Another responsibility is to help these students so long as they remain in your classes. We will give you some suggestions for doing that later in this module.

Characteristics of Problem Readers

If you reflect for a moment on the modules you just completed, you may be able to identify the major characteristics of problem readers. The major characteristics are revealed by the titles of the last five modules. Write here what you believe the five major characteristics will be:

1.

2.

3.

4.

5.

    Let's see if you are right.

    The problem reader usually *has a limited vocabulary.* Problem readers know the meanings of some words in the content area, but most of their definitions could be classified at the specific level. They understand some words at the functional level of understanding, but rarely have conceptual definitions for your content area vocabulary. (Module 4)

    A problem reader will also exhibit a *low level of comprehension.* Problem readers have difficulty answering the higher level questions you ask to check comprehension. Frequently, they can answer recall or recognition questions, but fail to answer questions that involve translation, application, analysis, synthesis, or evaluation. A large part of the difficulty results from the lack of vocabulary, but even when they are given the meanings of words, problem readers still have trouble arriving at correct answers. (Module 5)

    You will also find that the problem reader *does not apply study skills or strategies.* When teachers make reading assignments, problem readers usually do not survey the materials or develop questions as purposes for reading. Problem readers rarely take time to recite, since they did not really have particular questions in mind, nor do they spend much time reviewing material they read. Besides having poor study strategies, the problem reader has not developed the study skills necessary for reading materials in your content area. (Module 6)

The problem reader *has inadequate word-pronunciation skills.* When you ask a problem reader to read orally during an Informal Suitability Survey, you will notice that the student fails to use context clues. Problem readers tend to skip hard words or guess at unfamiliar words, rather than analyze the word to see if there is a prefix, suffix, or stem. These students generally ask someone what the word is, rather than use a word-pronunciation strategy (described in Module 7).

A problem reader also often *appears uninterested or lazy.* Problem readers are *not motivated* during class, and frequently make you wonder why they are even in school. No matter how effectively you apply the PARS motivational strategy, the problem reader fails to read the assignment because he finds it too difficult. Some problem readers withdraw and try to "hide" when you ask questions as part of a class discussion; others make fun of the situation. Many problem readers have irregular attendance because they feel inadequate in classroom situations, and of course the irregular attendance continues to hinder their academic progress. (Module 8)

It will not take you long to recognize problem readers. You will identify them early if you use the Informal Suitability Survey described in Module 2. Surely you will notice the problem readers when you check on reading assignments or administer tests and quizzes.

The Content Area Teacher's Responsibility

As a content area teacher you cannot ignore the presence of a problem reader in your classroom. The most damaging thing you can do is to allow the student to sit quietly in the classroom and fall farther behind in reading achievement. Reading achievement is tied closely to literacy in our society and without literacy there is little chance for individual self-improvement.

You must accept your responsibilities to help all students including problem readers because a "mind is truly a terrible thing to waste." Your first task is to *identify problem readers* in your classes. As was pointed out, they are easily identified when you administer the Informal Suitability Survey or have discussions following reading assignments, quizzes, or tests. Potential problem readers can often be identified by examining test scores on standardized achievement tests administered yearly in most school districts.

Your second responsibility is to *identify those factors that may be causing reading failure.* Your students, if given a choice, do not want to be problem readers. They would like to be able to read the materials with ease! Rather than just classifying or describing these students as lazy, uninterested, or "turned-off" to schooling, you must try to identify the factors contributing to their lack of reading achievement. Behavior is *caused;* therefore, you must look for factors influencing a student's lack of response to reading instruction. (Study Guide 2 describes six factors that influence reading achievement and provides nontesting devices to help identify factors that are hindering a student's progress.) If you can identify the factors that are causing a reading problem, you may be able to find help to overcome the problem.

Your third responsibility is to *refer* problem readers to colleagues who can help them. The school nurse, guidance counselor, media specialist, administrators, school psychologist, and reading teachers may be able to help eliminate some of the factors causing a student's reading problems. Rather than give oversimplified answers to the student or the parent as to why a student has a reading problem, or say the student will "grow out of it," you must seek the help of colleagues with information or expertise beyond your own. Enabling Element 4 provides suggestions for referring problem readers.

When you refer problem readers, your responsibility is only beginning. The student will still come to your class to accomplish the objectives of the content area. Your fourth responsibility, then, is to *help* the problem reader achieve these objectives by adapting instructional techniques to help him succeed. You can use low-level reading materials, more audiovisual aids to convey information and ideas, administer oral tests, have students help each other, and/or make differentiated reading assignments. Students can achieve many of your objectives when they get information and ideas using techniques other than reading. Problem readers are especially skillful in getting information by listening to tapes, looking at pictures, participating in class discussions, and using audiovisual aids such as films, filmstrips, and overhead transparencies.

Your responsibility is to: (1) identify problem readers, (2) identify the factors that hinder their progress, (3) refer problem readers for specialized help, and (4) adapt instructional strategies to help them achieve content objectives. Now go to Enabling Element 2 to find out why some students are not able to read well enough to handle typical content area reading assignments.

ENABLING ELEMENT 2
Possible Causes of Reading Failure

Specific Objective 2
You will list and explain by categories factors that may cause reading failure.

Enabling Activities

1. Read Study Guide 2. Identify and be able to explain the six major factors that influence reading achievement.

2. Discuss how emotional problems can cause reading failure and how reading failure can influence emotional problems.
3. Elementary teachers are often blamed for reading failures. Explain why this is unjust.
4. Reading failure usually results from several interrelated factors. Describe some students who can be classified as problem readers, and indicate the various factors that may be working together to cause their problems.
5. Some reading specialists believe environment is the most important factor in reading achievement. Do you agree? Can parents of middle-school and secondary-school students help their children with reading? In what ways? How can these suggestions be communicated to parents?

STUDY GUIDE 2

Content teachers can offer valuable assistance if they know some of the reasons students fail to read at grade level. Using this information, they can help problem readers succeed. As you read about the possible causes of reading failure, think about ways to identify these factors in your students. Remember that problems often result from interrelated factors rather than one isolated factor.

Physical Condition
Several physical factors correlate with failure in reading. Disabilities in vision and hearing can produce reading problems. A student may have difficulty seeing the chalkboard or the textbook clearly. Reduced visual acuity, fusion difficulty, and weak eye muscles are a few of the visual disabilities that correlate with reading failure. Students with inadequate hearing or discrimination usually have problems in reading because they misunderstand oral directions and explanations.

The student's general health is also important in learning to read. Students who do not have a proper diet or sufficient rest may experience difficulty, because reading is an abstract task that requires a high degree of concentration. These students generally have poor attendance, and may have had many childhood illnesses that caused extended absences. Sometimes specific illnesses such as glandular disturbances or thyroid dysfunctions can hinder academic achievement, or students may take drugs or other substances that affect hearing, vision, and general health.

Language Development
The relationship between language development and reading success is obvious. Students who have a meager vocabulary, poorly developed sound-symbol relationships, and weak grasp of the language's grammar base have considerable difficulty with reading.

Not all students grow in height and weight at the same rate, nor do they all develop language facility at the same rate or have excellent language models. Students who mature slowly are likely to arrive at school too immature for the academic task of reading; likewise, students who have not heard standard English will experience difficulty when they encounter unfamiliar language patterns and words. Some students thus fall behind in reading—and remain behind—because of maturational factors and nonstandard language models.

Environment

Reading requires students to bring meaning to printed symbols. To find meaning is only possible, however, when students have had experiences that relate to what they are reading. Students who have not had many real or vicarious experiences are at a disadvantage; if a student is reading a selection about a country he has visited, he is likely to get more meaning from the material than the student who has never been out of the city in which he was born.

Parents are part of their children's environment and set an example for them. Parents who read and enjoy reading as a source of information and pleasure are likely to convey these attitudes to their children; students who come from homes where there are no reading materials may have difficulty learning to read because they have not learned to value this activity.

Aptitude

Among high-school students and adults there is a high positive correlation between reading achievement and intelligence because many of the factors measured by intelligence tests are the same factors required for success in reading. Most intelligence tests measure visual memory, auditory memory, the ability to make judgments, and general information and vocabulary, all of which are important in learning to read. A student who does not seem to have an aptitude for learning to read as well as other students usually falls behind; however, students with below average intelligence can still learn to read when instructional methods are adapted to their aptitudes.

Social-Emotional Problems

Social-emotional factors also influence reading achievement. Some students fail in reading because they are overwhelmed by personal problems brought on by unhappy relationships with parents, siblings, and peers. Symptoms associated with social and emotional problems, such as short attention span, preoccupation, and lack of desire to stay with a task, are the same behaviors associated with academic failure.

Educational Background

Schools have also caused many reading problems. Previous teachers may have used unsuitable materials or methods, or may have neglected students who attended irregularly or seemed unmotivated. In large classes teachers often find it impossible to provide for all the individual differences and cannot do as much as they would like or need to do to help each student. The result is that some students receive inappropriate and insufficient instruction.

PLEASE Remember the Factors
These factors work together to help or hinder reading progress, and teachers must consider all of them to determine why some students fail to learn to read as well as expected.

A mnemonic device to help you remember these factors is the acronym PLEASE. Each letter represents a major factor that influences reading achievement:

P—physical condition—health, hearing, vision, nutrition
L—language development—vocabulary, grammar, sentence structure
E—environment—home, attitudes toward reading, motivation
A—aptitude—visual memory, auditory memory, judgment, general information, vocabulary
S—social-emotional problems—relationships with parents, siblings, and peers
E—educational background—quality of teaching, appropriateness of materials, class size.

Perhaps you will remember this acronym because it is the plea made by problem readers—Please! Your task is to *PLEASE identify, PLEASE look for causes, PLEASE refer,* and *PLEASE help* problem readers. The other study guides in this module will help you perform these tasks.

ENABLING ELEMENT 3
Using Nontesting Devices to Identify Possible Causes of Reading Failure

Specific Objective 3
You will use nontesting devices to identify factors that may cause reading failure.

Enabling Activities

1. Read Study Guide 3. Compare the advantages and disadvantages of the different devices for identifying possible causes of reading failure.
2. Try the Observational Checklist with problem readers in your class. Can you identify some explanations for their reading failures? Remember, the more you use the checklist, the more automatic your

observations will become. Periodically reread the checklist to re-
fresh your memory.
3. Duplicate the Incomplete Sentences and Personal Inventory forms
and have students complete them. Think of ways to use this information for adapting instruction.
4. Talk with teachers in your building to determine who will use the
different devices. It is suggested that all teachers use the Observational Checklist as a guide to observing and talking with students,
and that others who have major responsibility for certain students
use the Personal Inventory and Incomplete Sentences. Adapt these
suggestions to your school.
5. Share results of the personal inventories with the school librarian.
Responses to items 7, 9, 13, and 20 can yield valuable information
for purchasing books, magazines, and other materials for the library
or media center.

STUDY GUIDE 3

If factors that seem to interfere with students' responsiveness to reading
can be identified, then students can be given appropriate help. Even
though content area teachers are not expected to provide remedial reading instruction, they can help identify factors that hinder progress. This
module includes four useful devices for identifying PLEASE factors.

Because students are different, teachers need to employ different
techniques for gathering information about problems. Some students
are eager to talk with teachers; others avoid talking about themselves,
so teachers must be able to observe or use paper and pencil inventories
to gather information. This Study Guide presents an Observational
Checklist, guidelines for interviewing students, and two paper and pencil inventories.

Using an Observational Checklist
The observational checklist in Table 9–1 provides guidelines for observing students who are experiencing reading difficulties. If you read the
the checklist periodically, you will keep these factors and specific
behaviors paramount in your mind as you observe. Remember the
mnemonic device in Study Guide 2—PLEASE; each of the letters in the
acronym should remind you of a number of reasons for reading failure: P-physical; L-language; E-environmental; A-aptitude; S-social-
emotional; E-educational. The checklist includes observable behaviors
for each factor.

You are not expected to complete the checklist for each student;
its purpose is to guide your observations as you try to identify possible
causes of reading failure. Your observations are often the key to identifying the causes of reading problems.

Table 9–1
Observational Checklist for Identifying Possible Causes of Reading Failure

Directions: Which areas seem to be interfering with a student's responsiveness to reading? Underline specific behaviors you observe; add comments as necessary.

Factor	*Comments*

_____ *Physical Factors*
When the student reads, does she
    Lose her place?
    Rub her eyes?
    Blink excessively?
    Tilt her head so as to use only one eye?
    Complain of blurred print, headaches, or watering eyes?
When you speak to the student, does she
    Tilt her head?
    Cup her ear?
    Appear inattentive?
    Ask you to repeat directions?
Does she appear well rested and generally healthy?
What is her attendance record?

_____ *Language Factors*
When she speaks, does she
    Have a meager vocabulary?
    Use poor sentence structure?
Does the student make frequent spelling errors that indicate lack of knowledge of sound-symbol relationships?
Does she have a past history of poor performance in language-related courses?
If you have had occasions to talk with parents and siblings, did you notice anything helpful for interpreting the student's language background?

_____ *Environment Factors*
Does the student talk about experiences, or places she has visited?
Does the student have books, magazines, or other reading materials of her own?
Do her parents seem interested in her and accept her?
Is education valued by the family?

_____ *Aptitude Factors*
Does the student ask questions?
Does she have a fairly good background of information?
Is she able to draw conclusions and make sound judgments based on facts?
Does she learn rapidly and remember what she has learned?
Is she able to see similarities and differences in concepts?

_____ *Social-Emotional Factors*
Is the student accepted by family and peers?

Is she able to get along with others?
Does she have a positive self-concept?
Is she able to control her emotions and concentrate long enough to complete a task?

_____ *Educational Factors*
Does the student have positive or negative attitudes toward school?
Does she have purposes for learning?
Has the student met with success or failure in most academic areas?
Has the student been enrolled in any remedial reading programs?
Are the appropriate materials available for the student?

Using a Personal Inventory

Consider using or adapting this Personal Inventory if you want to gather more information about your students. You can administer a personal Inventory to the students for whom you have the major responsibility. As you read the items, notice that they are geared toward the six major factors that influence reading achievement and general academic progress.

Notice that the directions tell the student to leave blank the items he or she does not wish to answer. You should make note of these items, then use observation to gather more information about them. As with all devices, remember that the responses indicate a student's feelings on a particular day. The answers must be combined with other samples of behavior before making any conclusions or judgments.

After administering the inventory, use the guidelines in Table 9–2 for interpreting the information. Keep in mind, however, that some responses may provide information about more than one factor.

Table 9–2
Guide to Interpreting Information from the Personal Inventory

Major Factor	Questions Designed to Provide Information
Physical Condition	2, 3, 4, 5, 6
Language Development	8, 17, 18, 25
Environment	12, 19, 24, 26
Aptitude	9, 10, 13, 20
Social-Emotional Problems	15, 21, 22, 23
Educational Background	1, 7, 11, 14, 16

Personal Inventory

Name _____ Date _____
Address _____ Age _____
Telephone _____

Directions: The following questions are designed to help me get to know you. Write your answers in the blanks. If you are not sure of an answer, or do not want to answer some question, leave it blank.

1. What other schools have you attended? _____
_____

2. Are you supposed to wear glasses? _____ If yes, when did you first get them? _____

3. Do your eyes bother you when you read or write?_____
In what way? _____

4. Is your hearing (circle one) excellent, good, fair, or poor?

5. Is your health (circle one) excellent, good, fair, or poor?

6. How many hours do you sleep each night? _____

7. Do you read for pleasure? _____ If yes, name some recent books or magazines you have read. _____
_____

8. Is your reading (circle one) excellent, good, fair, or poor?

9. What is the most interesting topic you like to study? _____
_____

10. What is the least interesting topic you must study? _____

11. How much time do you usually spend each day studying outside school? _____

12. List some of the places you have visited outside of (city) _____

13. What interests do you have outside of school? _____
_____

14. What school activities do you enjoy? _____
_____

15. How do you get along with your parents? _____
_____
_____

16. Circle the word that shows how most teachers think of you as a student: excellent, good, fair, or poor.

17. Is your vocabulary: excellent, good, fair or poor? (Circle one.)

18. Is your spelling: excellent, good, fair, or poor? (Circle one.)

19. Do you have a place to study at home? Please describe it. _____
_____

20. What kinds of responsibilities would you like to have as an adult?
_____
_____

21. How do you get along with the other students in this class? Do you know these students well? Who are your favorite students? _____
_____
_____

22. Why do some people like you? _____
_____

23. Are there some people who do not like you? _____

Why? _____

_____

24. What is your father's occupation? _____
    What is your mother's occupation? _____
25. What language is usually spoken in your home? _____
26. Do your parents talk with you about school? _____
    If so, what kinds of things do they ask? _____

_____

Incomplete Sentences

Some teachers like to use incomplete sentences like the following to gather information about students. The teacher who has the major responsibility for students should be the one to administer the incomplete sentences. When interpreting responses, remember that the student's responses represent feelings only on a particular day. Before making judgments, you should gather additional information from the guidance counselor, cumulative records, personal inventory, and other teachers.

Name _____ Date _____

Directions: Quickly complete the following sentences. Write down the first thing that enters your mind. There are no right or wrong answers.

 1. Reading is _____
 2. I like to _____
 3. My friends _____
 4. I feel _____
 5. The best magazine _____
 6. Elementary school was _____
 7. My eyes _____
 8. My ears _____
 9. My parents _____
10. Education is _____
11. I have been to _____
12. I wish I could _____
13. When I read to others _____
14. I am liked by _____
15. School is _____
16. My teachers _____
17. Books are _____
18. I sleep _____
19. When I finish school _____
20. My home _____
21. I need help in _____
22. My best subject is _____

23. Spelling is _____
24. Teachers usually _____

Although responses vary, you will find the guidelines in Table 9–3 useful for analyzing the responses. Certain responses will necessarily fit more than one classification; however, we have tried to make them as discrete as possible. For example, one student may complete item 4 with "I feel tired"; another student may say, "I feel lonely." In the first case, the response refers to a physical factor; the second response concerns social-emotional factors. You will need to adapt the guidelines to the students' responses.

Table 9–3
Guidelines for Analyzing the Incomplete Sentence Responses

Factor	Number of Sentence That May Provide Information
Physical	4, 7, 8, 18
Language	1, 13, 17, 23
Environment	5, 10, 11, 13, 20
Aptitude	12, 19, 21, 22
Social-Emotional	2, 3, 9, 14
Education	6, 15, 16, 24

Talking and Listening to Students

Some students are eager to share information with teachers if the teachers seem genuinely interested. Talking to and listening to students can be a useful technique to gather information about the six factors influencing reading achievement. All teachers have some responsibility to listen to students, because different students relate better to different teachers. If all the teachers on the staff are aware of the importance of listening to students and hold perceptive conversations with students, the staff will be better able to help students. A student may relate to the physical education teacher on the field, but not relate at all to the English teacher in the classroom; another student may relate better to the English teacher and avoid face-to-face encounters with the physical education teacher.

Many of the questions in the Personal Inventory form can be used in conversations with students. Of course, you will phrase the questions differently and ask them in a natural sequence as the conversation develops. A teacher who is aware of the six major categories, however, can organize student responses into meaningful categories for interpretation.

When talking to students, you must be sincere and concerned. Ask questions in such a way that students realize you are not "meddling," but are trying to help. You will want to help students accept themselves as they are, yet provide hope for improvement. Help students realize that reading and success in academic areas are important, but that there are other important things in life, too. Here are sample questions you can use during a *natural* conversation with the student.

- *Physical Condition:* Have you ever had any trouble seeing or hearing? What illnesses have you had? How many hours do you sleep in a day?
- *Language:* What language do your parents speak? Did they graduate from high school? College? Did you have any problems learning to spell, read, or write?
- *Environment:* What places have you visited on vacations? How do your parents feel about your school activities? Can you study at home?
- *Aptitude:* What things do you do best? Do you want to do better in school? Why? Do you think you can learn to read better?
- *Social-Emotional:* Who are your best friends? How well do you get along with your family? What kinds of things make you happy? Frustrated? Sad?
- *Education:* What kind of student were you in elementary school? Have you ever been in a special reading class? Do your teachers generally like you?

ENABLING ELEMENT 4
Referring and Helping Problem Readers

Specific Objective 4
You will indicate appropriate referral sources for students who manifest certain symptoms and state guidelines and techniques for adapting instruction to help problem readers succeed in content classes.

Enabling Activities

1. Read Study Guide 4 to identify possible resource persons to whom problem readers can be referred and note ways you can help such students in your classes.
2. Talk with the school nurse, psychologist, and guidance counselors to determine the specific services they offer and the procedures for initiating referral. Ask about professional services that are free to low-income families.
3. Talk with the reading specialist and developmental reading teachers to determine what reading services are offered in the school. What other types of reading instruction should be offered?
4. Discuss guidelines for referring students for special help. What are the school and county guidelines for referring problem readers? You should not refer students to specialists outside the school without the advice and consent of the appropriate person. Often the guidance counselor, assistant principal, school psychologist, or some

other resource person is able to use more elaborate screening devices to determine if referrals are necessary.

5. Talk with your colleagues about ways to involve parents in home-school tutoring programs for problem readers.
6. Read the Teacher's Daily Dozen Checklist. Note one item you would like to improve. Brainstorm with colleagues and review previous modules to determine specific ways to implement the behavior.

STUDY GUIDE 4

There are two additional ways content teachers can help problem readers. First, you need to refer students to the proper sources of help. You are not expected to teach beginning reading skills, diagnose or prescribe glasses or hearing aids, or act as a full-time guidance counselor. You need and must have the help of specialists. Second, even though you are not expected to teach primary-grade reading skills, you can make some adaptations in instructional strategies to help problem readers. You have some responsibility to help students reading two or more years below grade level to succeed in your content area while they try to overcome their reading deficiencies. Problem readers can succeed in content areas if you use the following suggestions.

Helping Students with Physical Problems

- Refer the student to the school nurse for further screening. Perhaps a visual, hearing, or health problem has been overlooked or has developed recently. If drug or substance abuse is evident, refer the student to the school counselor.
- Encourage the student to wear prescribed glasses or hearing aid. Help the student with self-acceptance by being honest about any physical limitations.
- Suggest short periods of work for close work such as reading and writing. Direct the student to set a time limit for studying.
- Have the student sit near the chalkboard, screen, or close to the action. Do not pay too much attention to her, because you do not want her to feel awkward and unusual.
- If necessary, contact the librarian to see if books with larger print are available. You might also see if cassettes are available or could be made for students who have a difficult time reading, yet are able to listen and comprehend.
- Remember not to turn your back on students when speaking or to put your hands in front of your face. Teachers are often not conscious of habits that interfere with their effectiveness. Evaluate yourself continuously to see if you are articulating clearly and maintaining good eye contact.

- It might be helpful to write key vocabulary words on the chalkboard and discuss the meanings and pronunciations of words using the suggestions in Modules 4 and 7.
- If the student is having health problems that hinder attendance, you might ask the visiting teacher to contact the parents. It may be necessary to adjust assignments and number of credits according to the student's capabilities.

Helping Students with Language Problems

- Refer the student to a remedial reading specialist or remedial English classes. Share with the specialist the information you have gathered about the student's reading skills and habits.
- If possible, give oral tests. You can often administer tests orally while other students are taking written exams. If this is not possible, see if a parent volunteer can help.
- Provide information on cassettes or have others read to students for whom suitable materials are not available. Students can often listen and understand what they are not able to read.
- Repeat the student's responses using correct grammar and sentence structure. Realize that you alone are not going to change the student's use of language overnight; however, if all teachers make conscientious efforts, and if the student wants to improve, it is possible to change language patterns.
- Use many visual materials to expand concepts. The old saying "a picture is worth a thousand words" may be trite, but it is true.
- Correct spelling errors by going over the frequently missed words. Point out sounds that may be confusing.
- To help students increase vocabularies at higher levels, use the ideas in Module 4. Many problem readers only have specific understandings of words.
- Suggest self-study books for improving spelling, reading, or writing. These books frequently include practical exercises and information.

Helping Students with Environmental Problems

- Use many visual and auditory aids to develop concepts. Students can develop many concepts through vicarious experiences when direct experiences are not possible.
- Refer the student to the guidance counselor if physical abuse is evident. Child abuse agencies rely on teachers for referrals; however, you should talk with the appropriate school authority before making referrals to outside agencies.
- Praise the student sincerely for ideas, suggestions, and so forth.
- Do not overdo praise so as to appear insincere.
- Be available to parents when they express concern.
- Have confidence in the student. Expect the best and show disappointment when you do not get her best efforts.

- Make students aware of the resources available at school and public libraries. If you use many reading materials in your classes, arrange visits to libraries to show students what materials are available and how to locate them. Provide opportunities for students to browse and use some of the materials that interest them.
- Help students realize the value of having a place for study and good study habits. Provide specific suggestions on how to study in your content area. Suggest places in the school or community where they can study and at the same time enjoy the company of other people.
- Read or tell stories about famous people who have become successful even though they came from disadvantaged environments. You cannot change attitudes in one day; however, if you take advantage of teaching opportunities on a daily basis, the change will occur.

Helping Students with Social-Emotional Problems

- Refer the student to the guidance counselor or school psychologist. Some students have problems that require special analysis and guidance. After the student has met with the guidance counselor and/or school psychologist, discuss their recommendations for helping the student in the classroom.
- Avoid antagonizing the student. Avoid behavior that tends to "set off" the student.
- Determine the student's strengths and praise her sincerely. At the same time, help the problem reader face her weaknesses and set goals for improvement.
- Be ready to listen to the student. Not all students are ready to talk, but when they want to, they are generally seeking advice even if they don't say so.
- Give responsibilities that interest the student. Differentiate assignments according to interests and abilities.
- Accept the student as she is. You may not like the behavior, but you can still like the person.
- Use discussion groups and group dynamic techniques to help students develop skill in working with and accepting others. Students often form stereotypes and cliques that hinder social development. It is important for teachers to help students appreciate differences among their classmates.
- Help students plan schedules that allow time for social activities as well as studying. Help students understand that most students enjoy socializing yet must spend some time studying if they are to succeed academically. Plan flexible schedules with the students.

Helping Students with Less Aptitude for Reading

- Refer the student to the school psychologist for an individual intelligence test to determine special aptitudes. An IQ score is not as meaningful as the scores for the intelligence factors the test measures.

Determine special areas in which the student might have better aptitude, such as visual or auditory memory, then capitalize on these strengths.

- Use many visual materials, first-hand experiences, and concrete objects. Remember that reading is a highly abstract task; it requires one to form mental images from printed symbols. Students who demonstrate low aptitude often have not had as many experiences as others.
- Adjust materials to capabilities according to results of the Informal Suitability Survey.
- Grade according to individual progress, if at all possible.
- Encourage students by creating pride in achievement. Help students realize the value of a job well done.
- Help students develop confidence in what they can do and be, rather than emphasizing what they cannot do or become. Remember, there are aptitudes for many different types of skills.
- Remember the importance of repetition and practice. Most students, especially those with low aptitude for reading, need many practice and reinforcement activities to learn new concepts or skills.
- Identify the most important concepts, attitudes, and skills for your content area and concentrate on these objectives.
- Divide students into teams to complete some assignments. Make sure each team has students of different achievement levels and aptitudes. You can have teams, rather than individuals, compete with one another to complete certain assignments.

Helping Students with Educationally Poor Backgrounds

- Make sure you provide materials the students are capable of reading. Apply some of your newly developed skills in administering and interpreting Informal Suitability Surveys.
- Use the different teaching strategies suggested for word meaning and word pronunciation skills. Since vocabulary is important to comprehension, identify the most important specialized words in your content area and emphasize these. Have students keep a record of new words as they learn them.
- If you need to use many materials that require reading, have one of the best readers put the most important sections of the materials on cassettes to keep in the library or classroom for use by poor readers. Use audiovisual aids to help students develop concepts without reading.
- Summarize the most important material on a handout written at a low reading level. Review Module 2 for specific suggestions on writing materials at specified reading levels.
- Ask the librarian or department chairman for books or other supplemental materials written at lower reading levels that contain the concepts and skills you are trying to teach. You can establish centers that focus on interesting topics or skills.

- Introduce assignments with a purpose so students can look for specific information. Discuss with them how the assignments will help them learn study strategies.
- Use involvement activities during class. Students can learn from each other while they do group research and have discussions. Simulation activities in which students actually apply newly acquired skills or concepts are especially appropriate for problem readers. Role playing and dramatization also make class sessions come alive.
- Use the textbook illustrations, pictures, and charts to explain content. Graphic aids, accompanied by your comments to questions, can convey the essential information in the text. Supplement this material by inviting resource people to your classroom.
- Outline, or teach students to outline, the most important information in the course. Comprehension is easier when thoughts are well organized, as is required when outlining. A skill group might help teach this skill or other important skills problem readers have not developed.

You are not expected to change problem readers into mature readers in the short time they are with you; however, a positive attitude toward problem readers, belief that they can succeed in your classes, and effective teaching techniques will enable problem readers to develop better concepts through success, and this, too, will help them grow in reading achievement.

Putting It All Together
A combination of factors usually influences reading achievement. A student may be plagued by social-emotional problems triggered by physical problems, which in turn result in educational problems. The following checklist will help "put it all together" as you try to help problem readers; it is not a series of steps to follow for helping problem readers. The emphasis is on *continual* effective teaching. Use the checklist to continually evaluate yourself to make sure you are not contributing to students' reading problems.

Teacher's Daily Dozen Checklist
1. Am I using materials the students are capable of handling? Do I use my department chairman and librarian as resources for getting such materials?   _____
2. Have I identified the most important concepts for my students? Am I teaching the concepts, skills, and attitudes that will make their lives better?   _____
3. Am I using a variety of activities in the classroom? Do I use activities such as simulation, role playing, resource people, discussions, and audiovisual aids?   _____

4. Do I differentiate assignments according to the needs of the students? After administering Informal Suitability Surveys, am I using the information to provide appropriate materials? Do I suggest to the students how to read the materials? _____

5. Do I accept my students as they are? Do I avoid labeling them? Have I determined their strengths, and do my instructional techniques maximize them? _____

6. Do I refer students who need specialized help? Do I know what support services are available in the school and community? _____

7. Do I identify and demonstrate enthusiasm for my content area? Am I stimulating students' interests and curiosity? _____

8. Am I continually observing students to determine factors that are helping or hindering their academic achievement? Have I used this information to help the students? _____

9. Do I take time for myself? Am I able to enjoy many experiences outside school that will make me a better teacher in the classroom? _____

10. Am I helping students increase their vocabularies and develop appropriate strategies for word pronunciation, comprehension, and study? _____

11. Am I aware of the reading skills required for the materials in my content area? Do I help students learn to read these specialized materials, or do I just assume that anyone can read them? Do I use skill groups and skill centers to provide for individual differences? _____

12. Am I implementing the PARS (Module 8) strategy for motivating reluctant readers? Will my attitude influence students to succeed in my classes? Do I have faith in students? _____

POSTTEST

Directions: The following questions are designed to measure your accomplishment of the objectives in this module. Read each item and respond as directed.

1. Define "problem readers," describe their characteristics, and list your three major responsibilities for helping problem readers succeed in content area classes.

2. List the six factors that influence reading achievement. After each

factor, give a specific example of how it can help or hinder reading achievement.

3. Read the following description of a fifteen-year-old problem reader and identify two factors that may be causing his reading failure, then indicate two possible referral sources and two ways you could help Tom in your class.

When Tom comes to your class, he seems to want to "goof off." He does not pay attention when you talk and never completes assignments. When you provide time for him to begin his textbook reading assignment in class, he doesn't even open the book. When you surveyed the suitability of the textbook for students, you found the major textbook was too difficult for him, yet when you read the textbook, he is able to understand with 100 percent accuracy.

According to Tom's cumulative record, he received a prescription for glasses when he was in the fourth grade, but you have never seen him wear them. As you think back, you have noticed that he squints when looking at the chalkboard.

Even though Tom fools around in class, once in awhile he does ask good questions. He is friendly and outgoing; however, you noticed he does not have many close friends in this class. He is always courteous when you talk with him individually.

When Tom's homeroom teacher administered the Incomplete Sentences (Study Guide 3) to the class, Tom was one of the first to complete the sentences. Read his responses to the Incomplete Sentences:

1. Reading is a ripoff.
2. I like to watch television.
3. My friends are OK.
4. I don't like these questions.
5. The best magazine is *Popular Mechanics*.
6. Elementary school was fun.
7. My eyes are OK.
8. My ears are on my head.
9. My parents work.
10. Education is a drag.
11. I have been to New York.
12. I wish I could find a job.
13. When I read to others I get nervous.
14. I am liked by my dog.
15. School is a drag.
16. My teachers are smart.
17. Books are hard.
18. I sleep in on Saturdays.
19. When I finish school I will make more money.
20. My home is near the expressway.
21. I need help in math.
22. My best subject is shop.
23. Spelling is OK.
24. Teachers usually like me.

Posttest Answers

1. A problem reader can be defined as a student who reads two or more years below grade level and is therefore unable to read common content area materials. Although the characteristics of problem readers vary, these behaviors are typical:
   a. Has limited vocabulary in speaking, writing, listening and reading.
   b. Experiences difficulty comprehending materials.
   c. Has not developed study strategy or specialized study skills necessary for success in content areas.
   d. Lacks systematic method for pronouncing unknown words.
   e. Is not motivated to achieve.
2. The six factors that influence reading achievement are:
   a. Physical Condition
   b. Language Development
   c. Environment
   d. Aptitude
   e. Social-Emotional Problems
   f. Educational Background
       Physical factors can help or hinder reading achievement in many ways. Excellent visual and auditory skills are prerequisites for the reading task, and good physical health enables a person to learn. If a student has visual, health, and/or auditory problems, chances for success in reading are limited.
       Language development can also influence reading achievement. Students who were generally slow in developing language skills, or who do not have adequate models to learn standard English, fall behind during the early school years. Concentrated efforts to improve language can help the student become a better reader.
       The environment is one of the most important factors in reading achievement. The student whose home does not have books or other reading material, or a place for him to study, is hindered. Reading progress is made more difficult by parents who do not support the schools or the student. Overprotective parents or those who put too much pressure on students can hinder achievement, too.
       Reading correlates highly with intelligence as measured by academic aptitude tests. A student who is below average in factors that influence reading—visual memory, auditory memory, and vocabulary—has difficulty learning to read.
       Social-emotional factors can help or hinder reading achievement. Reading requires a great deal of concentration and thinking, and a student plagued by social-emotional concerns will not be able to concentrate. A student who feels incapable of learning will also have a more difficult time learning to read.

Students with enthusiastic, dedicated teachers, who diagnose to determine appropriate objectives and activities, have a better chance for success in reading. Teachers who neglect the problem reader contribute further to the problem.

3. A visual defect may be influencing Tom's responsiveness to instruction. Glasses were prescribed when he was in the fourth grade, but he does not wear them. According to his response to item 7, he seems to avoid accepting this limitation. According to the description, Tom does not have friends in your class. Likewise, his responses to items 4 and 14 may indicate possible social-emotional problems. It could be he is "goofing off" to gain acceptance from peers. Also, he may not be wearing his glasses because he does not want to appear different from his peers. The interaction effects of poor vision and lack of appropriate peer relationships could be contributing to his lack of responsiveness to instruction.

At this time Tom should be referred to the school reading specialist to determine the extent of his reading disability and to suggest instructional materials that would be most beneficial for him. You might also refer Tom to his counselor, who might provide some insights into his "acting-out" behavior and negative self-concept. The school nurse could screen his vision again and talk with him about the visual defect. Try to give attention to Tom and motivate him by using the questions he asks in class. Involve him in activities that do not require reading. Perhaps you might have Tom listen to some tapes that include sections of the textbook you would like him to understand. If possible, relate some of your content area objectives to Tom's interest in cars, math, and industrial arts.

Final Comment

This module explains why certain students are problem readers and specifies techniques for adapting instruction for those students. These techniques will enable you to help problem readers acquire the skills and knowledge for your content area. Simply because a student is a problem reader does not mean he or she cannot succeed in school, but the student's success depends upon the most important factor in the educational process—you!

If you have correctly completed all Posttest items, you are finished with the module. If not, see your instructor for help, or go back through the Enabling Elements as necessary.

REFERENCES

Burrill, L. E. (1987). How well should a high school graduate read? *NASSP Bulletin, 71*(497), 61–64, 66–72.

Colwell, C. G. (1981). Humor as a motivational and remedial technique. *Journal of Reading, 24*(6). 484–486.

Darch, C., & Carnine, D. (1986). Teaching content area material to learning disabled students. *Exceptional Children, 53,* 240–246.

Davey B., & Porter, S. M. (1982). Comprehension-rating: A procedure to assist poor comprehenders. *Journal of Reading, 26*(3), 197–202.

DuBois, B., & McIntosh, M. (1986). Reading aloud to students in secondary history classes. *Social Studies, 77*(5), 210–213.

Early, M., & Sawyer, D. J. (1984). *Reading to learn in grades 5 to 12.* San Diego: Harcourt, Brace, Jovanovich.

Mercer, C. D. (1983). *Children and adolescents with learning disabilities* (2nd ed.). Columbus, OH: Merrill.

Meyers, M. J. (1987). LD students: Clarifications and recommendations. *Middle School Journal, 19*(1), 27–30.

Reis, R., & Leone, P. E. (1987). Teaching reading and study skills to mildly handicapped learners: Previewing and text summarization. *Pointer, 31*(2), 41–43.

Riley, J. D., & Shapiro, J. (1987). Providing effective instruction for problem readers. *Clearing House, 60,* 318–322.

Wilson, R. M. (1985). *Diagnostic and remedial reading for classroom and clinic* (5th ed.). Columbus, OH: Merrill.

INDEX

Readability formulas (continued)
Raygor's graph. *See* Raygor's
Graph for Estimating
Readability
SMOG grading system, 29–33
Spache formula, 9, 24
Reading problems. *See* Problem
readers
Reading questions. *See*
Classification Scheme for
Reading Questions
Reading scores, 43
Reading vocabulary, 90–91, 196
Recall or recognition questions,
119–20, 123
answering strategy, 133, 136
outlines for preparing, 126, 128
Recording for the Blind, Inc. (RFB),
82, 83
Robinson, Francis, 157–58, 175

Santos, Natividad, 119
Science. *See* Physical sciences;
Social sciences
Semantic feature analysis, 107–8
Semantic mapping, 106–7
Sentence length
and Fry's graph, 9, 10, 12–14
and Raygor's graph, 21–22
and SMOG grading system, 29
variability in text, effect of, 20–21
Sentences
counting, 11, 12–14
sentence sense, 184
Sherk, J. K., 96
Side headings in textual material, 5
Simple Measure of Gobbledygook
(SMOG) Grading System,
29–33
Simulation activities, 83, 105
Slavin, Robert, 229
SMOG Grading System to Estimate
Readability, 29–33
Social sciences
study strategy for, 157–63
word pronunciation quick test
form, 194
Spache, George, 163, 175
Spache Readability Formula, 9, 24
Speaking vocabulary, 90–91

Specific level of word meaning,
93–95, 102–3
SQ3R Study Strategy, 157–63
SQRQCQ Study Strategy, 168–75
STAD (Student Teams—
Achievement Divisions)
approach to motivation, 229
Stems of words, 183–84, 200–203
Strategies
question-answering, 129–36
study. *See* Study strategies
vocabulary building, 100–101
for word pronunciation, 183–85
Student Teams—Achievement
Divisions (STAD) approach to
motivation, 229
Study skills
defined, 150
general list of, 151–52
importance of, 149
indexes, use of, 154–56
of problem readers, 240–41
teaching of, 152–57
Study strategies
importance of, 149
PQRST, 163–68
of problem readers, 240–41
SQ3R, 157–63
SQRQCQ, 168–75
Suffixes, 183–85, 199–200
Syllables. *See also* Multisyllable
words; Vocabulary
in complex words, 183–84
counting, 8, 11–12, 14–15
defined, 11
variability in text, effect of, 20–21
Synonyms, 103, 104
Synthesis questions, 121, 123
answering strategy, 134, 136–37
outlines for preparing, 127, 128

Table of contents, 5, 6, 151, 153
Taylor, W. S., 60
Team competition for differentiated
reading assignments, 75–76
Teams—Games—Tournaments
(TGT) approach to
motivation, 227–29
Textbooks
design of, 39

ABOUT THE AUTHORS

Harry W. Forgan is currently a Professor of Education at the University of Miami, Coral Gables, Florida. He earned his Bachelor of Education, Master of Education, and Doctor of Philosophy at Kent State University. He has written nine books concerning reading methods and has coauthored four books. He has written a book for parents, *Help Your Child Learn to Read*, and several practical handbooks: *The Reading Corner, Phorgan's Phonics, Getting Ready To Read*, and *The Reading Skill Builders*. Dr. Forgan has been a classroom teacher and serves as a consultant to many school systems, teacher centers, and professional reading associations. He continues to work with students in elementary, junior high, and high schools in Dade County, Florida.

Charles T. Mangrum II is Professor of Education and Chairperson of the Graduate Program in Reading and Learning Disabilities at the University of Miami, Coral Gables, Florida. Dr. Mangrum did his advanced graduate work at Indiana University. He has taught in both elementary and secondary schools and served as a Reading Consultant. He served as Editor of the *Reading Aids Series* published by the International Reading Association and Editor of the *Florida Reading Quarterly* published by the Florida Reading Association. He is past President of the Florida Reading Association and coauthor of four textbooks and seven instructional programs. He continues to contribute to journals and present at conferences. He is also an author of the McGraw-Hill K–8 Reading Program.